Beneficial Ownership

Matthias Reinhard-DeRoo

Beneficial Ownership

Basic and Federal Indian Law Aspects of a Concept

Springer

Matthias Reinhard-DeRoo
Zurich
Switzerland

Inauguraldissertation zur Erlangung der Würde eines Doctor iuris der Rechtswissenschaftlichen Fakultät der Universität Bern. Die Fakultät hat diese Arbeit am 21. März 2013 auf Antrag der beiden Gutachter, Prof. Dr. Susan Emmenegger [Erstgutachterin] und Prof. Dr. Cyrill Rigamonti [Zweitgutachter] als Dissertation angenommen

ISBN 978-3-319-01685-6 ISBN 978-3-319-01686-3 (eBook)
DOI 10.1007/978-3-319-01686-3
Springer Cham Heidelberg New York Dordrecht London

Library of Congress Control Number: 2013950984

Printed on acid-free paper

Springer is part of Springer Science+Business Media (www.springer.com)

For my tribe

An intellect great enough to win the prize needs other food besides success.
The remoter and more general aspects of the law are those which give it universal interest.
It is through them that you not only become a great master in your calling, but connect your subject with the universe and catch an echo of the infinite, a glimpse of its unfathomable process, a hint of the universal law.

Oliver Wendell Holmes, The Path of the Law

Acknowledgments

It would be impossible to address each person whose encouragement and support accompanied me throughout the process of writing this thesis individually, but I appreciate the opportunity to specifically thank the following persons:

Prof. Dr. Susan Emmenegger, my doctor–mother, who guided and supported the development of my work with exemplary diligence and dedication in a manner that one could only wish for.

Prof. Dr. Cyrill Rigamonti, whose valued review inspired the direction taken in my thesis.

Prof. Dr. Stephen Berti, for his positive attitude and unique brand of sponsorship.

My wife, Diane Reinhard-DeRoo, for courageously defending her mother tongue against my barbarian attacks, but most importantly for believing in me for the past 24 years.

I also thank the following professionals, academics, and mentors for their time and encouragement:

Joerg Arnold, Nadine Balkanyi-Nordmann, Esq., Mary Donahue, Esq., Christopher Freeze, Esq., Larry Dickstein, Maja Dove, Esq., Thomas Plattner, Dr. Tom Fischer, Esq., Dr. Hanspeter Marti, Dr. Sigmund Tur, Dr. Klaus von Matt, and Matthias Wuersch.

I would also like to thank the Julius Library of New York University for graciously granting me access to their endlessly valuable resources, and to Anke Seyfried and the team from Springer Publishing for simplifying the daunting process of publication, and doing so in such a pleasant and humane manner.

The generous contributions of the Curt Rommel-Stiftung and the University of Berne deserve my sincere thanks.

I dedicate this publication to my parents, Hans and Yolanda Reinhard-Hess, and to the parents of my wife, John and Mary Virginia DeRoo-Morgan.

Matthias Reinhard-DeRoo
Zurich, Switzerland
October 2013

Abbreviations

A

admin.	Administrative
AK	Alaska
AL	Alabama
Ala.	Alabama
All ER	All England Law Reports (from 1936.
Am.	American
Am. Bus. L. J.	American Business Law Journal
Am. Hist. Rev.	American Historical Review
Am. J. Comp. L.	American Journal of Comparative Law
Am. J. Int'l. L.	American Journal of International Law
Am. J. Legal Hist.	American Journal of Legal History
Am. L. Rev.	American Law Review
Am. Rev. Soc.	American Review of Sociology
Am. U. L. Rev.	American University Law Review
App. Ct.	Appellate Court
approx.	Approximately
AR	Arkansas
Ariz. St. L. J.	Arizona State Law Journal
Art.	Article
asf.	And so forth
AZ	Arizona

B

B. U. L. Rev.	Boston University Law Review
BBl	Bundesblatt der Schweizerischen Eidgenossenschaft
BGB	German Civil Code
BGE	Decision of the Swiss Federal Court

Buff. Pub. Int. L. J.	Buffalo Public Interest Law Journal
Burr.	Burrow, English King's Bench Reports since Lord Mansfield

C

CA	California
Cal. L. Rev.	California Law Review
Can. J. L. Juris.	Canadian Journal of Law and Jurisprudence
C. App.	Court of Appeals (state)
Ch.	Chapter
Cir.	Circuit Court of Appeals (federal)
Civ.	Civil
CO	Colorado
Co.	Company
Colum. L. Rev.	Columbia Law Review
Comm.	Commissioner
Comp.	Comparative
Cornell L. Rev.	Cornell Law Review
Corp.	Corporation
Ct. Cl.	Court of Claims

D

DC	District of Columbia
DE	Delaware
Dep't	Department
Div.	Division

E

e.g.	Exempli gratia (for example)
Ed.	Edition
ER	English Reports
et al.	Et alteri (and others)
etc.	Et cetera
et seq.	Et sequitur
EWCA	England and Wales Court of Appeals (UK)
ex. rel.	Ex relatione

F

F 2d.	Federal Reporter, 2nd Series
F.	Federal (Reporter)
f.	Following
Fed. Supp.	Federal Supplement (Reporter)
Fed.	Federal, Federal Reporter
ff.	Following pages
FL	Florida
Fla. L. Rev.	Florida Law Review
Fla.	Florida

G

GA	Georgia
Ga. L. Rev.	Georgia Law Review
GB	Great Britain
Geo. Immigr. L. J.	Georgetown Immigration Law Journal

H

Harv. L. Rev.	Harvard Law Review
Hastings Int'l & Comp. L. Rev.	University of Hastings International & Comparative Law Review
Hen.	King Henry (Statute of)
HI	Hawaii

I

i.e.	*Id est*
IA	Iowa
ICC	Indian Claims Commission
ID	Idaho
id.	*Idem*
Idaho L. Rev.	Idaho Law Review
IL	Illinois
IN	Indiana
Inc.	Incorporated
Ind.	Indiana
Int'l & Comp. L. Q.	International Comparative Law Quarterly
Int'l	International
Int'l J. Ethics.	International Journal of Ethics

K

KS	Kansas
KY	Kentucky

L

L&E	Law & Economics
LA	Louisiana
Ltd.	Limited

M

MA	Massachusetts
MD	Maryland
ME	Maine
MI	Michigan
Minn. L. Rev.	Minnesota Law Review
Mich. L. Rev.	Michigan Law Review
Mich.	Michigan
MN	Minnesota
MO	Missouri
Mont.	Montana
MS	Mississippi
MT	Montana

N

n.	Footnote
N. M. L. Rev.	New Mexico Law Review
N.D.	Northern District
N.E.	North Eastern (Reporter)
N.W.	North Western
NC	North Carolina
ND	North Dakota
NE	Nebraska
NH	New Hampshire
NJ	New Jersey
NM	New Mexico
Notre Dame L. Rev.	Notre Dame Law Review
NV	Nevada
NY	New York

O

OAS	Organization of American States
OH	Ohio
OK	Oklahoma
OR	Oregon
OR	Swiss Code of Obligations

P

P.	Pacific Reporter
PA	Pennsylvania
Pa.	Pennsylvania
R.R.Co.	Railroad Company
Renaissance Q.	Renaissance Quarterly
Rep.	Report

R

Rev.	Review
RI	Rhode Island

S

S.C.	Supreme Court
S.D.	Southern District
S.W.	South Western
SC	South Carolina
SCO	Swiss Code of Obligations
SD	South Dakota
SEC	Securities and Exchange Commission
Sec.	Section
Sess.	Session
So.	Southern Reporter
SSRN	Social Science Research Network
St.	State
Stan. L. Rev.	Stanford Law Review
Stat.	Statute
Supp.	Supplement

T

Tex.	Texas
TN	Tennessee

trans.	Translated by
Tul. L. Rev.	Tulane Law Review
TX	Texas

U

U. Colo. L. Rev.	University of Colorado Law Review
U. Pa. L. Rev.	University of Pennsylvania Law Review
U.S.	United States (Supreme Court)
U.S.C.	United States Code
U.S.C.A.	United States Code Annotated
UCC	Uniform Commercial Code
UCC	Uniform Commercial Code (USA)
UCLA	University of California Los Angeles
UK	United Kingdom
UN	United Nations
UNCITRAL	United Nations Commission on International Trade Law
Unif.	Uniform
UNO	United Nations Organization
UT	Utah
UTC	Uniform Trust Code

V

VA	Virginia
Va. L. Rev.	Virginia Law Review
Va.	Virginia
Vict.	Queen Victoria (Statute of)
Vol.	Volume
v.	*Versus*
VT	Vermont

W

WA	Washington State
WI	Wisconsin
Wis.	Wisconsin
Wis. L. Rev.	Wisconsin Law Review
WV	West Virginia
WY	Wyoming

Y

Yale L. J.	Yale Law Journal

Z

ZGB	Swiss Civil Code

Contents

Table of Cases

D

E

F

G

H

Table of Statutes

Introduction

The old folk tales of the Gotthard mountain region in central Switzerland are filled with ghosts. Ghosts appeared everywhere and troubled the unfortunate farmers with storms, avalanches, fires, and sickness. It was believed that the only way to send a ghost back to where he came from was to force him to reveal his name. Supposedly, once that name was no longer secret, the ghost would instantly be dispelled. Deprived of the power to carry on with his evil business, the ghost would disappear and never come back. None of these old folk tales would tell us about a free-spirited man or woman who dared to ask *why* calling ghosts by their names would instantly dispel them. Believing in the method and its results was enough.

The majority of our civilization does not believe in ghosts anymore, but it certainly believes in disturbances. These disturbances are not caused by ghosts but by equally mean-spirited creatures like dictators, terrorists, money launderers, tax evaders, insiders and other criminals. Similar to the old farmers, it is believed that finding out the name of these villains will eventually neutralize them. Beneficial ownership has become a key element of the method to achieve this neutralization. Beneficial ownership is perceived as the sword that cuts through the Gordian knot that complex multi-party and multi jurisdiction business relationships currently resemble. The beneficial ownership concept has been welcomed by Swiss law so eagerly that its current implementation rules prove to be more rigid than their U.S. equivalent. This aspect alone is an invitation to analyze some fundamental aspects of beneficial ownership.

At the early stages of this thesis, the intention was to compare the Anglo-American beneficial ownership concept with civil law, and more specifically the Swiss law concept of beneficial ownership. However, deeper research revealed an abundance of source material in the former legal system while the latter was found to be wallowing in the early stage of development, a stage not unlike that of our folk tales phenomenon where solutions were simply accepted and not questioned. This did not prevent the inclusion of Swiss law and various civil law aspects wherever they would provide sufficient counterbalance.

Chapter "The Term Beneficial Ownership" opens with a discussion of the famous elephant metaphor and continues with an analysis of the term *beneficial*

M. Reinhard-DeRoo, *Beneficial Ownership*, DOI 10.1007/978-3-319-01686-3_1,

ownership. At the beginning of this chapter, elements of the analysis which are commonly not mentioned despite their great importance are introduced. The chapter closes with a comparison of the different language versions of the term *beneficial ownership* (English, German, French, and Italian).

Chapter "Beneficial Ownership as a Concept" approaches beneficial ownership conceptually. Is beneficial ownership a right? What does this right encompass? What is the value of this right compared to other rights? And if beneficial ownership *is not* a right, is it still a legally relevant relation? The basis for this analysis is HOHFELD's still highly influential *Fundamental Legal Conceptions as Applied in Judicial Reasoning*.

Chapter "Common Law, Equity, and Beneficial Ownership" is intended to locate beneficial ownership in the dual system of common law and equity by applying Pound's concept of Law, Anti-Law, and Non-Law.

Chapter "Beneficial Ownership Used in U.S. Supreme Court Decisions" is dedicated to the legal content that the U.S. Supreme Court has filled the beneficial ownership concept with for over a century. A review of twelve representative cases shall close with a distillate of typical beneficial ownership characteristics.

Chapter "Fundamental Aspects of Federal Indian Law" shall give an introduction to the relevant fundamental federal Indian law aspects. Along with the three foundational legal doctrines (doctrine of discovery, doctrine of dependent sovereign, doctrine of independence from the states), topic relevant foundational aspects of federal Indian law shall be discussed.

Chapter "The Beneficial Ownership Concept Applied in Federal Indian Law" continues the analysis by scrutinizing a typical federal Indian law aspect: the legal relevance of the concrete physical relation to an object. This will be followed by a review of the concrete instances where beneficial ownership is applied (expressly or impliedly) in federal Indian law. Such instances include theoretical concepts (communal and individual property), specific property concepts (aboriginal title), and federal Indian law trust concepts.

The Term Beneficial Ownership

1. About Elephants

a) "I Know Them When I See Them"

There is a popular statement of a former Bank of England official in 1987 regarding the definition of beneficial owners:

> They are like elephants; you know them when you see them.[1]

This reference to the now well-known *Elephant Test* is not uncommon in English Law.[2] Already 23 years before the English official, U.S. Supreme Court Justice POTTER STEWART said "I know it when I see it" in his concurring opinion in the decision *Jacobelli v. Ohio*.[3] A short excursion with significance to the entire thesis may be permitted here. Unlike their civil law colleagues, common law judges are not required to hide their personal opinion behind the decision of the majority. They are entitled to express their agreement (concurring opinion) or disagreement (dissenting opinion) with the decision. It is not uncommon that, over time, such opinions outweigh the significance of the original majority decision itself.[4] Probably the most famous example of such an opinion is Supreme Court Justice OLIVER WENDELL HOLMES'

---

[1] GEIGER, DER WIRTSCHAFTLICH BERECHTIGTE 1; Zulauf, Urs, Gläubigerschutz und Vertrauensschutz – zur Sorgfaltspflicht der Bank im öffentlichen Recht der Schweiz, ZSR 113, N 245, n. 70.

[2] Cadogan Estates Ltd v. Morris, EWCA Civ 1676 (1998).

[3] 378 U.S. 189 (1964).

[4] BELLEAU & JOHNSON, *I Beg to Differ: Interdisciplinary Questions about Law, Language and Dissent* 176; D'Amato, *Legal Uncertainty*, 71 CAL. L. REV. 9 (1983); an example in federal Indian law is the dissenting opinion in United States v. Alcea Band of Tillamooks (Tillamooks I), 329 U.S. 40 (1946) (propagating to differentiate between recognized and aboriginal Indian title in connection with compensation for taking) and Tee-Hit-Ton Indians v. United States, 248 U.S. 272 (1955) (applying such differentiation), see *infra* chapter "The Beneficial Ownership Concept Applied in Federal Indian Law", Sect. 3e).

M. Reinhard-DeRoo, *Beneficial Ownership*, DOI 10.1007/978-3-319-01686-3_2,

"still-echoing dissent"[5] in *Lochner v. New York.*[6] His quote "A constitution is not intended to embody a particular economic theory, whether of paternalism [...] or of laissez-faire"[7] is a powerful statement against the court allowing politics to interfere with the constitution. H.L.A. HART, in his famous article, *American Jurisprudence through English eyes*: *The Nightmare and the Noble Dream*, was convinced that Holmes would have many decisions with political motivation to protest against.[8]

Referring back to *Jacobelli v. Ohio*, the case was brought to the Supreme Court by the owner of a movie theater in Ohio who was heavily fined for showing the French movie *Les Amands* in his theater. It is stated that the movie

> involves a woman bored with her life and marriage who abandons her husband and family for a young archeologist with whom she has suddenly [...] fallen in love. There is an explicit love scene in the last reel of the film, and the State's objections are based almost entirely upon that scene.[9]

The question was whether the movie, particularly the love scene, was obscene and therefore not entitled to protection by the First and Fourteenth Amendments of the United States Constitution. Judge Stewart stated that

> [...] under the First and Fourteenth Amendments criminal laws in this area are constitutionally limited to hard-core pornography. I shall not today attempt further to define the kinds of material I understand to be embraced within that shorthand description; and perhaps I could never succeed in intelligibly doing so. But I know it when I see it, and the motion picture involved in this case is not that.[10]

This example shows the logical use of the *I know it when I see it* explanation in dealing with evidence in a legal case compared to our British bank official. It is clearly irresponsible to make beneficial ownership decisions in such a manner. To at least attempt a definition of such a term is necessary for the proper and fair operation of our legal systems.

---

[5] TAMANAHA, LAW AS A MEANS TO AN END: THREAT TO THE RULE OF LAW 73.

[6] 198 U.S. 45 (1905); Hand, *Due Process and the Eight-Hour Day*, 21 HARV. L. REV. 500 (1908) and for the aspect of *due process*: Cohen, *Transcendental Nonsense and the Functional Approach*, 35 COLUM. L. REV. 819f (1935); Grechenig & Gelter, *The Transatlantic Divergence in Legal Thought*, 31 HASTINGS INT'L & COMP. L. REV. 312 (2008); for the impact of *Lochner* on federal Indian law see: Lee, *Rediscovering the Constitutional Lineage of Federal Indian Law*, 27 N.M. L. REV. 286 ff. (1997).

[7] 198 U.S. 75; KATHERINE, *John R. Commons and the Origins of Legal Realism*; *Or*, *The Other Tragedy of Commons*, UCLA School of Law, Law and Economics Research Paper Series, Research Paper No. 08-19, 1-28 (2009).

[8] HART, *American Jurisprudence through English eyes*: *The Nightmare and the Noble Dream*, 5 GA. L. REV. 978 (1958).

[9] *Jacobelli*, 378 U.S. at 187.

[10] *Id.*

aa) The Problem with Metaphors

The official and the judge find themselves faced with the task of defining a *Ding an sich* (the thing in itself).[11] The *Ding an sich* is the concept of the German Philosopher IMMANUEL KANT.[12] FRIEDRICH NIETZSCHE (1844–1900) uses this idea to demonstrate human incapability to explain a concept without using metaphors. Concepts always consist of a multitude of elements. Because these elements are unique (no leaf is identical to another) metaphors oversimplify and never entirely capture every individual element of a concept. In line with NIETZSCHE, Supreme Court Justice BENJAMIN N. CARDOZO (1870–1938) said: "Metaphors in law are to be narrowly watched, for starting as devices to liberate thought they end often by enslaving it."[13] Before CARDOZO, LORD MANSFIELD warned: "Nothing in law is so apt to mislead as a metaphor."[14] However, for lack of better alternatives in bringing about a common understanding of a concept, metaphors remain a useful tool. In any event, to simply say *I know it when I see it* is not a solution, but rather a sign of premature intellectual resignation.

bb) Seeing Elephants v. Seeing Beneficial Owners

Quite contrary to a beneficial owner, an elephant is certainly not easy to overlook. Even little children can define elephants: big grey animals with a trunk and big ears and sometimes very long teeth. More importantly, elephants always fit that description. In other words, once you have seen an elephant, you can always recognize another one. A beneficial owner, on the other hand, can be a 70-year-old drug lord or a 3-year-old girl. As will be shown throughout this thesis, the forms of appearance of Beneficial Owners are so manifold that seeing *one* cannot set a precedent.[15] When I see *one*, I have done only that.

cc) Conclusion

The above sufficiently shows that using the elephant test to describe the nature of beneficial ownership might be amusing but of limited use. Saying *I know it when I see it* dodges a definition which does not depend on a concrete example. A different

---

[11] NIETZSCHE, *Über Wahrheit und Lüge im aussermoralischen Sinn* 309. English translation available on: http://www.e-scoala.ro/biblioteca/friedrich_nietzsche.html.

[12] KANT, PROLEGOMENA §13, Note II.

[13] Umbeck, *Might Makes Rights: A Theory of the Formation and Initial Distribution of Property Rights*, 19 ECON. INQUIRY, 39 (1981), 245 N.Y. 602 (1927); GROSSWALD CURRAN, *Comparative Law and Language* 9.

[14] Quoted in Hohfeld, *Fundamental Legal Conceptions as Applied in Judicial Reasoning*, 26 YALE L.J. 711 (1917) n. 4.

[15] Bederman, David J., *Beneficial Ownership of International Claims*, 38 INT'L & COMP. L. Q. 938 (1989).

approach is necessary. When discussing the approach, another story that deals with an elephant may be more useful, i.e., *The Blind Men and the Elephant*.

b) The Blind Men and the Elephant

aa) The Story

An ancient fable that is told in different versions in several civilizations also deals with an elephant. There is even a famous poem by JOHN GODFREY SAXE called *The Blind Men and the Elephant*. Here are the first two verses[16]:

It was six men of Hindustan
To learning much inclined,
Who went to see the Elephant
(Though all of them were blind),
That each by observation
Might satisfy his mind.

The *First* approached the Elephant,
And happening to fall
Against his broad and sturdy side,
At once began to bawl:
"God bless me!-but the Elephant
Is very like a wall!

The poem continues with the second man touching the tusk of the elephant, taking it for a spear, the third taking the trunk for a big snake, and so on. A heated debate arises amongst the six blind men which the poem does not resolve. There are different versions of the story where a *Deus Ex Machina* impersonated by a king or a wise man tells the blind men that each of them is right and wrong at the same time.

bb) Symbolism for Approaches

The blind men symbolize the different approaches to understanding the essence of an object. The blind men did not fail to understand the essence of an elephant because of their blindness, but because of their stubbornness. If only they accepted that what they discovered did not compete with what their brethren discovered, they would have combined their individual knowledge and a comprehensive understanding of the essence of an elephant would be within their reach!

Everyone who has spent just a few moments pondering about the essence of beneficial ownership will agree that what applies to the elephant also applies here. As will be shown throughout this thesis, beneficial ownership is a very colorful concept that cannot be adequately described with classical legal analysis. Legal

[16] By JOHN GODFREY SAXE (1816–1887) available at: http://www.suite101.com/content/theadventure-of-culture-writing-a7944.

analysis is just one element albeit prominent. But, so much being told already at this point, beneficial ownership is a concept to be located at the border between legal and non-legal issues. Non-legal issues are given more importance than usual.[17]

2. Elements of the Analysis

The previous section discussed the apparent reluctance to define beneficial ownership beyond the acknowledgement of its mere existence. One of the reasons behind this reluctance is the fact that the beneficial ownership concept despite its ubiquitous use cannot be easily captured in classic legal terminology and conception. If classical legal analysis does not seem to provide the necessary instruments to better capture the beneficial ownership concept, other methods of analysis need to be reviewed. These elements will provide support for the discussion of the location and concrete perusal of the beneficial ownership concept in the second part of this thesis. Several elements (several fields of thought) have been selected to prepare such foundation.

"Once we see the need to study law in an international context, things really get messy."[18] The first element of analysis involves this *messiness* in the different perceptions of lawyers from different jurisdictions. The second element focuses on the functionality and realism each sustainable legal solution must contain. The third element discusses history, which is particularly important if common law is involved. The fourth element is often overestimated by practitioners and underestimated by academics: experience. The fifth element is language, which in many ways can be seen as the central element around which all the other elements revolve. This chapter will close with a discussion of the Law & Economics movement and its potential influence on the development of the beneficial ownership concept.

a) Perceptions

aa) What Are Perceptions?

One of the main pitfalls of legal analysis can be found in its different underlying perceptions. Perceptions are to be understood in this context as the learned and experienced, sometimes expressed and sometimes implied, understanding of a legal system and its concepts. Perceptions are often the fertile ground in which legal thought is planted. Perceptions build part of the collective unconscious of legal thought: they resemble the mentality of the members of a legal system. Quite similar to the mentality of people of any given country, perceptions are not always easily accessible to rational thought, nor are they commonly documented. Legal fields like federal Indian law,

---

[17] For the interpretation of non-legal, illegal, and anti-legal see *infra* chapter "Common Law, Equity, and Beneficial Ownership".

[18] Macauly, *The New versus the Old Legal Realism*, 2 Wis. L. Rev. 401 (2005).

as will be shown below, are filled with different perceptions. Not paying attention to perceptions can render court decisions incomprehensible.[19] The fairly generic yet typical example below shall demonstrate the importance of respecting perceptions.

bb) Some Perceptions of Property

Article 544 of the French civil code, with its most celebrated definition of property worldwide states[20]:

> La proprieté est le droit de jouir et desposer des choses de la manière la plus absolue, pourvu qu'on n'en fasse pas un usage prohibité par les lois ou par les règlements (Property is the right to use and control things in the most absolute manner provided this use and control are not prohibited by the law.).[21]

This Article shall now be compared with its less famous but, at its introduction, not less celebrated Article 641 of the Swiss Civil Code[22]:

> Le propriétaire d'une chose a le droit d'en disposer librement, dans les limites de la loi. (The owner of an object is free to dispose of it as he or she sees fit within the limits of the law.).[23]

A certain similarity in the method applied to these two articles exists. Both work along the lines of a general rule followed by an exception. However, when looking at the composition of these articles, important differences surface. The French article uses property itself as the subject while the Swiss article uses a person, the owner. This is not a simple matter of preference but representative of the programmatic French style versus the more practical Swiss style of legislation.[24] At the root of the differences of these styles are the French perception with the emphasis on the right of property and the Swiss' perception with its emphasis on the responsibility of the owner.

The French version still echoes the French Revolution. The revolutionary claim for redistribution by abolishing feudal property had, at least ideologically, the purpose to entitle every French citizen to private property. The right to dispose of property in *the most absolute manner* (*de la manière la plus absolue*) has a

[19] Bowers & Carpenter, *Challenging the Narrative of Conquest*: *The Story of* Lyng v. Northwest Indian Cemetery Protective Association 492 ff. (explaining the cultural significance of a certain area of land which was largely ignored by the Supreme Court); see *infra* chapter "Fundamental Aspects of Federal Indian Law" Sect. 3b).

[20] Mattei, Basic Principles Of Property Law 19, 74.

[21] About the general application of this notion of limited absolute ownership in modern civil law codes see Parisi, *Entropy in Property*, 50 Am. J. Comp. L., 605, 609 (2002) with references to § 903 of the German BGB and the Italian Codice Civile.

[22] Zweigert & Koetz, An Introduction To Comparative Law 171 (3rd ed. 1998) ("With the coming into force of the Swiss Civil Code the concert of European private law codes was enriched with a powerful new voice representing the particular style of Swiss legal thinking").

[23] Official translation by the Swiss Government available at: http://www.admin.ch/ch/e/rs/c210.html.

[24] Zweigert & Koetz, *id.* at 172.

conceptual significance, but also a political ideological connotation.[25] The protection of every citizen's right to freely dispose of his own property had not been codified as explicitly before the Code Civil. Until then, property had been understood as a negative right to prohibit other individuals or the government from unwanted interference.[26] Despite the obvious difficulties to implement such a generous rule which ended up in countless bureaucratic restrictions, the French Revolution demanded a bold commitment to the law.

The right to dispose of property *in the most absolute manner* does not appear in the Swiss version. The Swiss Civil Code entered into force in 1907, a little more than 100 years after the French Civil Code. The revolutionary passion had faded in the meantime and France had already had other kings and even an emperor. The Swiss Code Civil shifted its focus from the idea of property as a freedom to grant to the simple owner with his rights and obligations, leaving the more programmatic aspect to the Swiss Federal Constitution.[27]

cc) Conclusion

The example above gives a first impression of the significance of perceptions. Laws, decisions, and commentaries have the purpose to prescribe and explain rules of an individual nation. National laws only have to make sense to their subjects; they do not have to make sense to persons or nations who are not affected by them. Nevertheless, the moment a need arises to explain why one national law is different from another, perceptions can help clarification.

Further, the mere semantic comparison of the wording of regulations from different nations would be too superficial because "*foreign legal data* are not comparative law."[28] Such a method of comparison resembles the hopeless attempt to literally translate a funny story or, even more difficult, a joke, into a foreign language: Unfortunately the punch line usually gets lost in translation. The purpose of understanding perceptions is to prevent exactly that from happening.

The perceptions that nourish concepts like beneficial ownership vary. They depend on the individual case and legal topic at hand. For instance, the role of beneficial ownership in federal Indian law is nourished by the current perception that the redistribution of land resources that followed the colonization of the New World was unfair. It is further perceived that this unfairness can only be remedied by granting Native Americans the freedom to own their land legally and not just physically. The federal Indian law discussed in this thesis will have to take these perceptions into account because the mere physical relationship to a resource is

---

[25] Kent, Michael B., *From 'Preferred Position' to 'Poor Relation'*, 39 N.M. L. Rev. 8 (2009).

[26] Claeys, *Jefferson meets Coase, Land-use Torts, Law and Economics, and Property Rights*, Notre Dame L. Rev. 154 (2010).

[27] Guarantee of ownership: Art. 26 of the Swiss Federal Constitution.

[28] Zweigert & Siehr, *Jhering's Influence on the Development of Comparative Legal Method*, 19 Am. J. Comp. L., 220 (1971).

often referred to as *beneficial ownership*.[29] An actual discussion of these perceptions would prove to be futile since perceptions are not a result of intellectual debate but rather a matter of awareness.

b) Functionality

According to ZWEIGERT and SIEHR, the best legal method consists mainly of the analysis of solutions to legal issues and their functionality. "The basic methodological principle of all law is functionality."[30] The so-called *functional approach* to law is a key element of Legal Realism,[31] a highly influential movement lead by American legal scholars such as OLIVER WENDELL HOLMES (1809–1894), KARL LLEWELLYN (1893–1962), FELIX S. COHEN (1907–1953),[32] and ROSCOE POUND (1870–1964) who were strongly influenced by the German scholar RUDOLF VON JHERING (1818–1892).

> For him [VON JHERING] law came to mean law only if it was effectively applied, while the aims and objects of law became the legally protected interests.[33]

Legal Realists insisted "that law must be seen as it actually functions, not as an abstract body of rules, concepts and principles."[34] ARTHUR LEFF, a more skeptical mind, summarized the role of Legal Realism as follows:

> [. . .] out of the hills, came the Realists. What their messianic message was has never been totally clear. But it is generally accepted that, at least in comparison to the picture of their predecessors which they drew for themselves, there were much more interests in the way law actually functioned in society.[35]

What are these *other interests* that LEFF mentions here? ZWEIGERT and KOETZ refer to these interests as the *needs of social life* which require a search in the domains of other social sciences, such as economics, sociology[36] or political science.

---

[29] *See infra* chapter "The Beneficial Ownership Concept Applied in Federal Indian Law", Sect. 1.

[30] ZWEIGERT & KOETZ, COMPARATIVE LAW 46 (3rd ed. 1998).

[31] For the German equivalent *Freirecht* movement see Grechenig & Gelter, *The Transatlantic Divergence in Legal Thought*, 31 HASTINGS INT'L & COMP. L. REV. 348 ff. (2007).

[32] Cohen, *Transcendental Nonsense*, 35 COLUM. L. REV. 821 (1935), with a passionate plea for functionalism as a defense against meaningless concepts.

[33] Zweigert & Siehr, *Jhering's Influence*, 19 AM. J. COMP. L., 217 (1971); see also MATTEI, BASIC PRINCIPLES OF PROPERTY LAW 22; Grechenig & Gelter, *The Transatlantic Divergence in Legal Thought*, 31 HASTINGS INT'L & COMP. L. REV. 347 (2007).

[34] TAMANAHA, LAW AS A MEANS TO AN END 103; COHEN, *supra* n. 32.

[35] Leff, *Some Realism about Nominalism*, 60 VA. L. REV. 453 (1974); Macauly, *The New versus the Old Legal Realism*, 2 WIS. L. REV. 369 (2005); Grechenig & Gelter, *id.* at 359 (2007).

[36] Leff, *id* at. 473; GEORGAKOPOULOS, PRINCIPLES AND METHODS OF LAW AND ECONOMICS 57; for the United States, see ZWEIGERT & KOETZ, COMPARATIVE LAW 44, 247 (3rd ed. 1998).

What is compelling about the functional method is the notion to invite legal thinking to fill in where legal data is missing.[37] To assume an intention behind every silence of the legislator or legal scholar is only one possibility of many. One of the intentions behind this thesis is to show that beneficial ownership is a concept that has been familiar to common law countries for at least two centuries. This long history might reveal some functional elements which can help establish a better understanding of the beneficial ownership concept.

Without subscribing to Legal Realism in its entirety, the functional approach will not be honored here as a matter of principle, but rather as an intelligible approach for dealing with a concept of a nature that cannot be clearly considered as a *legal* concept. As will be shown throughout this thesis, beneficial ownership is such a concept.

c) *History*

The development of concepts has a history. Concepts have a history. The history of a concept may go much further back in one legal system than in another. Regarding the history of beneficial ownership, the American concept is much older than the European concept.[38] This alone would not be enough to reflect on the role of history in this thesis. Of course, there is the importance of history as an element of any academic research in general and of legal research in particular. Law is created by people and the conception of law finds its roots in history. By creating law, a minority or a majority of people decide which individual or collective human interests need protection. To study history means to understand the environment in which laws have been created. History can explain the cultural, political, and socio-economic circumstances a law was born into.

> History must be a part of the study, because without it we cannot know the precise scope of the rules which it is our business to know.[39]

However, a *caveat* must be placed here. The historical analysis of the law must not be exaggerated. Holmes warns:

> We must beware of the pitfall of antiquarianism, and must remember that for our purposes our only interest in the past is for the light it throws upon the present.

With regard to that light of the past, Goethe's *Mephisto* makes an important observation in this regard:

---

[37] Hart, *American Jurisprudence through English eyes*, 5 Ga. L. Rev. 987 (1958) (giving a valid account of the cultural differences between US- and English Law using this problem as an example).

[38] *See infra* chapter "Beneficial Ownership Used in U.S. Supreme Court Decisions".

[39] Holmes, *The Path of the Law*, 10 Harv. L. Rev.

> Weh Dir, dass Du ein Enkel bist! Vom Rechte, das mit uns geboren ist, von dem ist leider! nie die Frage (Woe unto thee, that thou'rt a grandson born! As for the law born with us, unexpressed; That law, alas, none careth to discern).[40]

That lack of synchronicity between a generation's needs and the law is important to bear in mind when analyzing phenomena like the concept of beneficial ownership. This is particularly true in the case of Swiss law importing Anglo-American legal concepts instead of creating legal concepts which are rooted in Swiss law. If the light of the past is switched off, the light of the present is darkened with incomprehensiveness.

Special weight will be put in this thesis on the historical analysis. The intention is to look beyond an ordinary account of historical facts and dates in order to identify historical circumstances which facilitated the concept of beneficial ownership. For this purpose, traditional legal institutions and concepts need to be scrutinized and checked for their potential to foster an idea that combines factual, economical, and legal elements in the same way as the beneficial ownership concept.

d) Experience

aa) As a Method

At the beginning of this thesis,[41] the expression *I know it when I see it* has been analyzed. In the given context, the half-sentence could be added: *once I have experienced seeing it* without changing the content of the sentence. To resort to experience if the law does not seem to provide a satisfactory answer is not an uncommon method.[42] An example can be found in the suggestion that the Swiss legislator *intentionally* avoided a definition of beneficial ownership to avoid prematurely narrowing down the amount of beneficial ownership cases.[43] In other words, the legislator decided to wait and see what could qualify as beneficial ownership and perhaps then decide on a definition. Not only is such a decision in clear contrast to the wisdom that good legislation should be based on matured and established facts, but to entirely omit a definition of a key term or concept would be the work of a legal *cascadeur*. Officials would thereby be vested with the power to decide what in their experience qualifies as beneficial ownership. Such an approach is very similar to the *I-know-it-when-I-see-it* approach and thus equally unacceptable.

---

[40] GOETHE, FAUST, DER TRAGÖDIE ERSTER TEIL 57; English translation from E-text released in 2002 and prepared by David Reed from Project Gutenberg: www.gutenberg.com; VON KLEIST wrote an amusing *anecdote* about a soldier who demands to be executed for the violation of an antiquated code which the legislator had simply forgotten to abrogate; VON KLEIST, SÄMTLICHE ANEKDOTEN UND ANDERE PROSA 59.

[41] *See supra* Sect. 1 of this chapter.

[42] *See id.*

[43] GEIGER, DER WIRTSCHAFTLICH BERECHTIGTE (VSB) 1 f.

COHEN states that:

> In every field of law we should find peculiar concepts which are not defined [. . .], and thus bar the way to intelligent investigation of social fact and social policy. *Corporate entity*, *property rights* [. . .] are such concepts [. . .] and all the rest of the magic 'solving words' of traditional jurisprudence.[44]

The premises of this sentence could be changed by speaking of *the law* instead of *social fact and policy* and of *current* instead of *traditional* jurisprudence. This would not change the underlying appeal to intelligent investigation when defining a concept. If no heed is paid to this appeal, concepts like beneficial ownership fall in that unwanted category of *magic solution words*. This is particularly true for Swiss law.

bb) Some Theoretical Aspects of Experience

Experience is not often expressly stated in codes (except occasionally as a personal requirement for a certain group of persons such as professionals, government officials, or investors). In legal theory and even more so in philosophy, experience has been studied so extensively that it is not possible to provide a satisfactory short summary here.[45]

HOLMES introduced the famous dichotomy between the law as logic and the law as experience which has become a stereotype in American legal thought: "The life of the law has not been logic: it has been experience."[46] According to H.L.A. HART this is "perhaps the most misused quotation from any American jurist",[47] because HOLMES had no intention to make an anti-intellectual statement, but rather to protest against the notion of his contemporaries, in particular the first dean of Harvard Law School, CHRISTOPHER COLUMBUS LANGDELL (1826–1906), the famous inventor of the case method which is still applied at U.S. law schools today[48] and the so-called *classical legal thought*.[49] LANGDELL was convinced that the common law in its early days contained an imminent logic well worthy to be preserved to the present day.[50] HOLMES called him the "greatest living legal theologian."[51] To HOLMES it was clear

---

[44] Cohen, *Transcendental Nonsense*, 35 COLUM. L. REV. 812, 820 (1935).

[45] MAUTHNER, WÖRTERBUCH DER PHILOSOPHIE 290 ff., gives a concentrated overview of the history of the term and meaning of experience reaching from XENOPHON (with "εμπειρια μεθοδικα" as the expression word that, according to him was poorly translated but still provides the root for the term "empirical") to KANT.

[46] HOLMES, The Common Law 30; See also ZWEIGERT & KOETZ, COMPARATIVE LAW 246 f. (3rd ed. 1998).

[47] HART, *American Jurisprudence through English eyes*, 5 GA. L. REV. 975 (1958).

[48] ZWEIGERT & KOETZ, *supra* n. 48 at 244.

[49] Grechenig & Gelter, *The Transatlantic Divergence in Legal Thought*, 31 HASTINGS INT'L & COMP. L. REV. 311 (2007).

[50] Wetlaufer, *Systems of Belief in Modern American Law: A View from Century's End*, 49 AM. U. L. REV. 2 (1999).

[51] TAMANAHA, LAW AS A MEANS TO AN END note 23; Grechenig & Gelter, *id.* at 309.

that, without logic, law would not persist. As one of his famous brethren in the U.S. Supreme Court, Justice BENJAMIN CARDOZO (1870–1938) said: "[. . .] HOLMES did not tell us that logic is to be ignored when experience is silent."[52] HOLMES did not advocate the abrogation of logic. With his monumental statement he did not answer an *either/or* question but rather a *what-comes-first* question.

As opposed to logic, experience cannot be deduced as easily from premises that withstand the test of true or false.[53] Experience is the result of past engagement in a certain unknown situation. Experience depends on hindsight and not on logic. Experience is the result of experiments and "every new case is an experiment."[54]

In mathematical terms, each new experiment could be defined as a value infinitely moving towards the value $\sum_s p$ (representing the sum of all similar elements (s) of a precedent case (p)[55]) without ever reaching that value. The sum of elements that are *not* part of the precedent distinguish the precedent from the new case. In other words, each new case consists of elements that are not covered by a precedent. If these elements cannot be tied to another precedent, their influence on the outcome of the case cannot be easily predicted. The fact that all cases contain such free floating elements lead HOLMES to the conclusion that: "The primary rights and duties with which jurisprudence busies itself [. . .] are nothing but prophecies."[56]

If prophecies were based on logic they would not be called *prophecies*. They would be called *conclusions*. Prophecies are based on experience and when analyzing the relationship between legal experience and legal theory, there is no better area to explore than the border between legal study and legal experience or, for that matter, practice. However, over 12 years of practice in fields of law which regularly deal with the beneficial ownership concept have left the author of this thesis unsatisfied with the current theoretical conception of beneficial ownership.

In practice, the identification and documentation of the beneficial owner is the overarching topic. In most cases this identification is not depending on the application of a comprehensive conception on the individual case but rather on simple (self-) declarations of the beneficial owner. Simply put: in practice, beneficial ownership is a topic of administration rather than of legal conception. To respond to this dissatisfactory realization is one of the motivations of this thesis.

---

[52] CARDOZO, THE NATURE OF THE JUDICIAL PROCESS 31.

[53] Singer, *Property and Coercion in Federal Indian Law*, 63 S. CAL. L. REV. 1823 (1990).

[54] *See id.*

[55] GEORGAKOPOULOS, PRINCIPLES AND METHODS OF LAW AND ECONOMICS 132 f.

[56] Holmes, *The Path of the Law*, 10 HARV. L. REV. 457 (1879); Llewellyn, *A Realistic Jurisprudence – The Next Step*, 30 COLUM. L.J., 448 (1930); Ostas, *Postmodern Economic Analysis of Law*, 36 AM. BUS. L.J., 195 (1998), with a comprehensive summary of the central characteristics of LANGDELL's view on the law; Cohen, *Transcendental Nonsense*, 35 COLUM. L. REV. 835 (1935).

cc) Conclusions

Experience is nothing more than something that has happened in the life of a particular person. The educational value of experience has to be determined by the person who makes the experience. People quite often refuse or are unable to learn any lesson from experience. On the other hand, it can be said in general that negative experiences are to be avoided and positive ones are to be found. On that level, experience used wisely can be a guide to avoid a bad and find a good situation. Experience invites the search for lessons to be learned for new situations. These new situations, however, will never be identical to the original experience. Without an intellectual effort, experience just tells us what was but never what *ought to be*.[57] As the famous German sociologist MAX WEBER points out:

> When legal practice and teaching are purely empirical, legal thinking always moves from the particular to the particular and never tries to rise from the particular case to the general principles from which the decision in the particular case can then be deduced.[58]

One of the ambitions of this thesis is to locate the beneficial ownership concept between these two extremes.

e) Language

> The language of law is bound to the inner grammar of legal systems, cultures and mentalities, which in turn impede communication in words that are borrowed from another legal system, culture and mentality.[59]

Every person who has practiced law long enough will agree that at the root of many legal conflicts are the various interpretations of language. Anthropologists teach us that "language is primarily a pre-rational function."[60] This may be the reason for most conflicts along with psychological reasons. Such reasons are articulated precisely in the expression *not coming to terms*. Reasons that can be found on the surface of a legal conflict are varied: the lack of precision in the wording of a contract, misleading statements of a party, different premises of the parties, purposely hidden information, or even the unintentional omission of essential wording. All these reasons are closely tied to incorrect use of a language.

Law students in the first semester have to learn to discipline their language and often re-learn the meaning of many terms and expressions. This exemplifies the crucial role of the correct use of language in general. If additional languages come

[57] MAUTHNER, WÖRTERBUCH DER PHILOSOPHIE 294.

[58] Quote in ZWEIGERT & KOETZ, COMPARATIVE LAW 193 (3rd ed. 1998).

[59] GROSSWALD CURRAN, *Comparative Law and Language* 1.

[60] Cohen, *Transcendental Nonsense*, 35 COLUM. L. REV. 812 (1935) with further references to anthropologists.

into play, it becomes even more apparent that language aspects are a key element of law. The term *law* itself can serve as a perfect example:

> [. . .] the well-known ambiguity of the Latin *jus*, the German *Recht*, the Italian *diritto*, and the French *droit*, terms used to indicate both "law" as such and "a right" considered as a concrete relation created by law [. . .].[61]

aa) Roman Law and Old Common Law

Before the institution of the English Court of Chancery was established,[62] pre-classic Roman law and common law gave the precise (if not to say pedantic) use of language an importance that appears strange to our modern day understanding. A Roman's claim had to be articulated in one of the precise formulas that were originally held in storage by the *pontifex*, a religious leader.[63] Rules of these days "were thought of almost exclusively as rules of remedies."[64] The nervously awaited and softly spoken "I do" in modern weddings, or the *Hippocratic Oath* pledged by medical school graduates are remnants of the ancient days that POUND calls the "esoteric phase"[65] of the law of republican Rome, when a formula outweighed meaning.

> The strict law takes no account of will and intention as such. The words operate quite independent of the thought behind them.[66]

Very similar to this strict law of the Romans is the old English Common Law system of *writs* which, as will be shown, was replaced by systems which would require from judges not just to ensure the correct use of formulas but rather require them to read between the lines in order to achieve more equitable results.[67] However, the rule of *stare decisis* which requires courts to observe precedents would eventually lead to new formalisms. But Supreme Court Judge CARDOZO's *dictum* in the famous *Wood v. Lucy, Lady Duff-Gordon* case still holds true:

> The law has outgrown its primitive stage of formalism when the precise word was the sovereign talisman and every slip was fatal.[68]

---

[61] Hohfeld, *Fundamental Legal Conceptions*, 26 YALE L.J., 715 (1917).

[62] ZWEIGERT & KOETZ, COMPARATIVE LAW 187 (3rd ed. 1998).

[63] KASER, RÖMISCHE RECHTSGESCHICHTE 61f, 160 (15th ed. 1986).

[64] Llewellyn, *A Realistic Jurisprudence*, 30 COLUM. L.J., 436 (1910).

[65] Pound, *The Maxims of Equity*, 34 HARV. L. REV. 811 (1921).

[66] Pound, *id.* at 813.

[67] ZWEIGERT & KOETZ, COMPARATIVE LAW 186, refer to PETER, ACTIO UND WRIT, EINE VERGLEICHENDE DARSTELLUNG RÖMISCHER UND ENGLISCHER RECHTSBEHELFE, Eine vergleichende Darstellung römischer und englischer Rechtsbehelfe, Tübingen (1957); a concrete example is the *ejectment action* which played an important role in the proceeding at the outset of Johnson v. M'Intosh, 21 U.S. 543 (1823), one of the most important leading cases of federal Indian law, see Robertson, *The Judicial Conquest of America* 31 ff.

[68] Wood v. Lucy, Lady Duff-Gordon, 222 N.Y. 88, 118 N.E. 214 (1917).

CARDOZO's great influence on U.S. law is in many ways due to his strong command of language.[69] This same talent gained the ancient Roman CICERO the reputation of being an outstanding litigator. CICERO's pleadings are famous for their rhetorical finesse rather than their legal craftsmanship.

The distinction between law and language are a recurring issue in this thesis. As will be shown, the term beneficial ownership describes a phenomenon which cannot be easily captured as a legal term. Neither is the term used consistently. And yet, the term is very frequently used in the context of legal issues. This disparity between lack of comprehensive legal content and frequent use in the language of courts and legislators will remain a constant topic throughout this thesis.

bb) Legal Interest in Nineteenth Century Germany

In nineteenth century Germany, the greatly influential theory of *Interessen-jurisprudenz* which echoes to our day was led by the German jurist RUDOLF VON JHERING (1818–1892). In his very amusing essay *Im juristischen Begriffshimmel* (The Heaven of Legal Concepts), VON JHERING dreams that he finds himself at the gate of that heaven.[70] Before being granted access, he has to pass several tests including the successful operation of the hair splitting machine, the interpretation press, the eliminator, and the drill of dialectics. He is also told by the 'Psychophoros' (the "soul carrier"), a companion similar to Dante's Virgil in the *Divina Commedia*, that there is no sunshine in the Heaven of Concepts, which makes it almost predictable that the hero will wake up from his nightmare at the end of the story.

Though this essay may appear to be a harmless amusing piece of literature, more meaning lies behind the words then might be expected. VON JHERING's essay can be looked at as an old testimony of people's reservations towards what laymen call *Legalese*, *Law-French*,[71] *or Juristenlatein.*[72] These terms are used to describe an indigestible compilation of clauses with exceptions, caveats, definitions, and warranties and, like taxi cabs; they're never there when you need one. The frustration with legal terms has a long tradition, but frustration is not what bothers VON JHERING. He is more concerned that formalistic legal reasoning is detached from reality.

A jurist's focus should be more on content than on form, and content, for VON JHERING, is the parties' interests. What do the parties need? How can the law find a

---

[69] Powell, *"Cardozo's Foot": The Chancellor's Conscience and Constructive Trusts*, 56 LAW AND CONTEMP. PROBS. 16 (1993) (showing that *Cardozo*'s influence on the development of the constructive trust concept in U.S. law "lies not in the holdings of the court for which he [CARDOZO] spoke, but in the language he used."); see generally Radin, *The Chancellor's Foot*, 49 HARV. L. REV. 44 ff. (1935) (referring to the origin of the metaphor).

[70] Von Jhering, *Im juristischen Begriffshimmel* 4 ff.; Zweigert & Siehr, *Jhering's Influence*, 19 AM. J. COMP. L., 219 (1971); Cohen, *Transcendental Nonsense*, COLUM. L. REV. 809 (1935) (using VON JHERING's essay as an introduction to his criticism of the all too abstract legal thought of his days).

[71] *See infra* chapter "Common Law, Equity, and Beneficial Ownership".

[72] Literally translated from German: *Lawyer's Latin.*

balance, mend the disagreements, help or refuse a claimant, serve the interest of government that wants more safety for its citizens and so forth?

Law should focus on realities, and realities are found in people's interests. By focusing on these interests, VON JHERING invites other disciplines of thought, such as economy and early forms of sociology, to help understand people's interests and their protection. This realistic approach to the law invites concepts that are not the result of legal reasoning but nevertheless complete the picture. It is argued in this thesis that beneficial ownership is such a complementary non-legal concept. The fact that the term *beneficial ownership* had already been used before VON JHERING's philosophy is not relevant here.[73] VON JHERING had not discovered the approach to consider economic and other realities in a legal context, he simply pleaded for this approach to deserve higher estimation.

cc) Conclusions

Language is the main vehicle of law. No legal rule or regulation reaches its addressees without first being formulated in a language, written or spoken.[74]

It cannot be established that the German *Interessenjurisprudenz* movement stood at the cradle of the beneficial ownership concept. The focus of this movement on *interests* rather than conceptions is representative of a legal approach that is more holistic than rigid. From this perspective it may be rather comprehensible that beneficial ownership is often referred to as beneficial *interest.*

f) Law and Economics

Law and Economics (L&E) is unquestionably the most prominent school of legal thought of the twentieth century. It was one of HOLMES' stupendous prophecies regarding the future relationship between law and economics when he anticipated in 1897, that

---

[73] The first U.S. court decision found is Leadman v. Harris, 14 N.C. 144 (1831). The case deals with a claim for the payment of a security ("deed") which according to defendant Harris was fraudulently issued. The debt has been issued by the heavily indebted Mr. Levin Kirkman, Jr., himself not a party to the dispute who, as the defendant claims, fraudulently issued the security to the plaintiff. The term *beneficial ownership* comes into play in connection with the judge's statement regarding the evidence of fraud: "[. . .] in every case, where it is made manifestly to appear, that notwithstanding the deed, the debtor is to have the real use, as it were, the beneficial ownership of the property, it is a presumption of law, to be delivered to the jury, the deed is fraudulent." The judge seems to have a clear understanding of what beneficial ownership is. He uses the term to point at the discrepancy between the contractual agreement (the deed) on the one hand, and the reality, i.e. the fact that the use remains with the debtor on the other hand. This suggests an early conceptual understanding of beneficial ownership as a factual ownership to be discerned clearly from legal ownership.

[74] HOLMES, COMMON LAW 278.

> [...] for the rational study of the law the blackletter [sic] man may be the man of the present, but the man of the future is the man of statistics and the master of economics.[75]

At an early stage of research for this thesis it became clear that beneficial ownership was not a classical legal concept, but rather consisted of a combination of legal and economic aspects. This lead to the seemingly logical assumption that beneficial ownership was a concept based upon, or at least inspired by, the L&E movement. After further research, this initial supposition became untenable. There is no point in walking the reader through this erroneous path step by step.[76] It will suffice to summarize the most important reasons as follows:

- The origins of the beneficial ownership concept date further back in history than the L&E movement[77];
- As will be shown, traditional common law and equity principles,[78] legal theory,[79] case law,[80] and historical elements[81] are the main ingredients of beneficial ownership;
- L&E stands for an economic approach to the law. L&E thus operates with the tools of a young academic discipline to render the law more efficient. The methods to achieve this do not depend on concepts such as beneficial ownership to fulfill their purpose;
- The economic elements of beneficial ownership are of a rather simple fact-based nature: The beneficial owner just enjoys the economic benefits of a thing;
- Technical mechanisms of L&E, such as cost, output, resources, and value, may play a role in a concrete case that involves beneficial ownership. However, in such cases beneficial ownership comes into play at a point before L&E would even begin;

---

[75] Holmes, *The Path of the Law*, 10 HARV. L. REV. 464 (1879); see also Grechenig & Gelter, *The Transatlantic Divergence in Legal Thought*, 31 HASTINGS INT'L & COMP. L. REV. 317 (2007).

[76] The finding is mainly based on the works of a group of representative authors of the Law and Economics movement. The sources can be found in the bibliography of this thesis. The most important names are *Posner*, CALABRESI, BEBCHUK, CARRUTHERS, SUNSTEIN, CLAEYS, MATTEI, PARISI, STRHILEVITZ, SUNSTEIN, WRIGHT. Special mentioning deserves GEORGAKOPOULOS for his very comprehensive introduction of Law and Economics by using the famous Meinhard v. Solomon case, 249 N.Y. 458 (1928), as a recurring example. The author also provides a very comprehensive overview of the major contributors and their contributions to L&C, GEORGAKOPOULOS, PRINCIPLES AND METHODS OF LAW AND ECONOMICS 7.

[77] The oldest source that could be found dates back to the 1830s (Leadman v. Harris, 14 N.C. 144 (1831), while Law and Economics dates back to the 1960s or even later (POSNER's chef d'oeuvre *Economic Analysis of Law* was originally published in 1973).

[78] *See infra* chapter "Common Law, Equity, and Beneficial Ownership".

[79] *See infra* chapter "Beneficial Ownership as a Concept".

[80] *See infra* chapters "Beneficial Ownership used in U.S. Supreme Court Decisions" and "The Beneficial Ownership Concept Applied in Federal Indian Law".

[81] *See infra* chapter "Fundamental Aspects of Federal Indian Law".

- L&E analyses the economic impact the administration of legal system has in a society while beneficial ownership is merely a concept that describes a semi-legal position within that legal system;
- Although it cannot be denied that all legal concepts once applied have economic consequences, such consequences are not necessarily helpful for the understanding of these concepts. The egg does not define the chicken.

3. The Term Beneficial Ownership in the Crosshairs

The following analysis will scrutinize the term *beneficial ownership* and its translation into German, Italian, and French. Do the translations fit the original English version or are there ambiguities of the kind HOHFELD[82] perfectly exemplifies with the term *right?* As opposed to the Latin *ius*, the German *Recht*, the French *droit*, and the Italian *diritto*, the English term *right* does not indicate both *law* and a *right*.

a) English Version

aa) Beneficial

Standing alone, both terms *beneficial* and *ownership* are very common in the English language. As a general term, the word *beneficial* stems from *beneficium* (late Latin for favorable, advantageous, resulting in good[83]) and can be traced back to Middle English. As a legal term, the word *beneficial* is used in relation to rights other than legal title. The differentiation will have to be elaborated on throughout this thesis. This discussion will not focus on the linguistics, but rather the legal theory aspects of the relationship.[84] GREEN may go a little too far by stating that "the influence of the philosophy of language on the philosophy of law has been largely negative."[85] He focuses too much on the relationship between mind and language instead of the relationship between the law and language.

bb) Ownership

The term *ownership* has its origin in the Old English adjective and pronoun *ãgen* (owned, possessed). The indiscriminate use of 'own' and 'possess' might be a sin

[82] Hohfeld, *Fundamental Legal Conceptions*, 26 YALE L.J., 715 (1917) with further references.

[83] NEW OXFORD AMERICAN DICTIONARY (2nd ed. 2008).

[84] Green, *Dworkin's Fallacy*, 89 VA. L. REV. 1946 (2003).

[85] *Id.*

for a lawyer but obviously not for a linguist.[86] Etymologically, the German pronoun *eigen* (proper) hints to the common Germanic roots of the English and German word.[87] Despite common linguistic roots, the meaning of the English and the German version seem to have developed in different directions over time. While the English word *ownership* remained faithful to its Old English meaning, the German word *Eigentum* appears to have relied on its Latin equivalent.

The German language equivalent of the English word *property* is the word *Eigentum* and not its etymologically related word *Ownership*. The word *Ownership* cannot be translated as easily into German. The term *Ownership* is closer related to the Latin *Dominium*[88] which has a comparable meaning to the old-fashioned German word *Herrschaft* (*rule*, as in *the rule of law* but also *the rule of King Henry VIII*). This brings us closer to the notion of ownership as a right[89]: The right of a person to dispose of an object in a certain way.

But what is the difference between ownership and property? To answer this question, one can resort to the comparison between the property articles of the French and the Swiss Civil Code above.[90] Both articles cover the same topic but from a different perspective. The French version focuses on property; the Swiss version focuses on the owner.[91] Property describes the legal principle while ownership describes the legal relation. On this abstract level, property is the absolute while ownership is the relative aspect of the same thing.

cc) The Combination of Beneficial and Ownership

In the U.S. legal world, the term *beneficial ownership* has been very common for very long. As already pointed out, the oldest decision mentioning beneficial ownership dates back to the early nineteenth century.[92] The term *beneficial ownership* can be found in a multitude of legal fields ranging from tax law to federal Indian law. An entire separate chapter would be necessary merely to give an idea of the pervasiveness of the beneficial ownership concept in U.S. law.

---

[86] Heinsohn & Steiger, Eigentum, Zins Und Geld 89 ff. (4th ed. 2006); New Oxford American Dictionary (2nd ed. 2008).

[87] According to Mauthner, Wörterbuch Der Philosophie 228 ff., the term property was originally reserved for individual as opposed to common property.

[88] Mattei, Basic Principles Of Property Law 73.

[89] *See infra* chapter "Beneficial Ownership as a Concept", Sect. 2b).

[90] *See supra* Sect. 2a) of this chapter.

[91] The term *proprietor* is used here as a synonym of *owner*. This may be contradictory to the etymology of this term. But it is not unusual that namely a Latin or Greek term, depending on the purpose and time of entry into another language reach a different meaning than the original one. The Greek term for private person is *ιδιωτησ* (*idiotes*), a term etymologically related to *ιδιαζουσα* (*idiazousa*), the Greek term for property. Who would have guessed the *ιδιωτησ* would become the idiot?

[92] Leadman v. Harris, 14 N.C. 144 (1831); see *supra* note 75.

b) German Version

aa) Wirtschaftlich

Similar to the word *beneficial* in English, the word '*wirtschaftlich*' is very commonly used in German. Much can be said about the similarities. *Wirtschaftlich* does not translate into *beneficial*. *Wirtschaftlich* translates into *economic*,[93] a term that, as has been shown above,[94] has gained a specific significance in U.S. Law ever since RICHARD POSNER, judge on the United States Court of Appeals for the Seventh Circuit in Chicago, professor at the University of Chicago Law School, and one of the most quoted legal scholars of our day, published his book on *Economic Analysis of Law* in 1973. No evidence can be found that RICHARD POSNER or any other promoter of Law and Economics stood at the cradle of the beneficial ownership concept or even its translation into German or any other language. Posner is a "hedgehog who knows one big thing",[95] but that one big thing does not include the beneficial ownership concept. The German term *wirtschaftlich* is used here in a rather generic manner simply describing the economically relevant aspects of a resource.

bb) Berechtigung

The term *Berechtigung* translates into *entitlement*. The word *entitlement* that has been most prominently used in the Law and Economics movement. ARBEN GUIDO CALABRESI, former Dean of Yale law school, articulated a system of entitlements differentiating between property rules, liability rules and inalienability which has become a standard element of U.S. Law[96]:

- ***Property rules*** refer to entitlements which are protected in a way that whoever wants to remove them has to buy them.
- ***Liability rules*** entitle a person to compensation for damaged property.
- ***Inalienability*** refers to the limitations on transferability of property.

While the word entitlement has been categorized in U.S. legal science, the word *Berechtigung* remains on a less refined level in Swiss Law. It simply means entitlement without further specifications.

Translating *ownership* to German with the word *Berechtigung* poses another problem. *Berechtigung* contains the word *Recht*, and *Recht* means *right* or *law*.

---

[93] *Wirtschaftlich* can also be translated into *frugal or economical*. But this has obviously no further bearing to the subject matter presented here.

[94] *See supra* Sect. 2f) of this chapter.

[95] Cunningham, *Traditional Versus Economic Analysis: Evidence from Cardozo and Posner Torts Opinions*, 62 Fla. L. REV. 5 (2010), who, with further references, compares POSNER with CARDOZO, the "fox who knows many things".

[96] Calabresi & Melamed, *Property Rules, Liability Rules, and Inalienability*, 85 HARV. L. REV. 1089 ff. (1972).

In English, *beneficial* ownership is used as a correlative to *legal* ownership. This reveals the difference between de jure and de facto ownership. The beneficial owner does not necessarily have legal title. By using the term *Berechtigung*, it is insinuated that there is a legal relationship between the beneficial owner and the object, and that is misleading.

A better translation for *owner* would be *Inhaber*. Beneficial owner could then be translated into *faktischer* or *materieller Inhaber* and legal owner could then be translated into *rechtlicher* or *formellrechtlicher Inhaber*. The *Aurbach v. Gallina* case[97] provides a visual example. The case deals with a car accident caused by an 18 year old girl. The title to the car was not registered with her, but with her mother. The question was whether the parents could thus be held jointly liable for the damages caused by their daughter. The case explicitly calls the daughter *beneficial* and the parent(s) *legal* owner(s). This approach is not foreign to Swiss law: In Article 58 of the Swiss Road Traffic Code (*Strassenverkehrsgesetz, SVG*), Swiss law too differentiates between the liability of the legal owner and the factual owner (the so-called *Halter*) of a vehicle. The separation between factual and legal ownership can also be observed in other areas than traffic law. Another example would be Article 56 of the Swiss Code of Obligations which differentiates between the legal owner and the factual owner of an animal when deciding on the liability for damages caused by the animal.

In using a non-specific legal term—just like *Berechtigung*—it is important to point out that even the term *Eigentümer* (owner) would be less confusing. Instead of *wirtschaftlich Berechigter* (economically entitled person), one could speak of the *faktische Eigentümer* (*factual owner*) and so forth. Unfortunately, to further elaborate on these alternatives would be a futile effort. Once a term is established in the legal world: to replace it would be harder than to push toothpaste back in the tube.

cc) The Combination of Wirtschaftlich and Berechtigung

The term *wirtschaftliche Berechtigung* has a younger origin. According to Geiger, it can be traced back to the pre WWII era.[98] It can also be found in documents of the Swiss Federal authorities. These documents mention "true" or "real" ownership as opposed to legal title. The English term *beneficial ownership* used in a Swiss Law context can be found in a 1954 Article for the British Institute of Comparative Law. The author, Hermine Herta Meyer in 1954 writes about Trusts and Swiss Law and states that

[97] 753 So. 2d 60 (Fla. 2000).

[98] Geiger, Der Wirtschaftlich Berechtigte Im Sinne Der Vereinbarung Über Die Standesregeln Zur Sorgfaltspflicht Der Banken (VSB) 53.

> Swiss Law does not recognize a separation of legal and beneficial ownership. [...] Switzerland adheres to that rule with great consistency.[99]

With this statement, Meyer provides one great reason for civil law academia's struggle with a conceptual integration of beneficial ownership into its legal system. Legal ownership and beneficial ownership are opposites unfamiliar to civil law. In civil law understanding, the term *ownership* is a legal term. Ownership always means *legal* ownership. Mindful of the risk to introducing a tautology, the originators of the German term for *beneficial ownership* chose not to literally translate the term *ownership* to the German *Eigentum*. Instead, the more abstract term *Berechtigung* was used. Although the idea to avoid a literal translation is laudable for the reasons mentioned above, its execution is a jump from the frying pan into the fire for the two reasons explored below.

First, it does not take a linguist to confirm that in both languages the terms *ownership* and *Eigentum* belong into a different category than *privilege* and *Berechtigung*. While the former clearly belong to the category of well-established legal terms, the latter belong to a more abstract category, e.g., there is a right to property but there is no right to a privilege because the term *privilege* in itself already contains a legally relevant entitlement.

Second, the term *privilege* plays an eminent role in the American conception of rights which was developed by Wesley Newcomb Hohfeld. A detailed introduction and analysis of Hohfeld's conception will be made further below. For this section, it will suffice to state that privilege, right, power, and immunity, the so-called *Hohfeldian Incidents* have been the cornerstones of conceptual legal thinking in the United States since the early twentieth century.

It cannot be said that, without understanding Hohfeld's fundamental conceptions there is no understanding of the beneficial ownership concept. After all, the concept of beneficial ownership pre-dates Hohfeld.[100] by at least five decades. It is not exaggerated to state that Hohfeld's conception may well best explain some of the most fundamental characteristics of U.S. legal thought: characteristics which have an impact on the understanding of concepts such as beneficial ownership.

c) *Italian and French*

aa) L'ayant droit/l'avente diritto

L'ayant and *l'avente* are present participles of the French verb *avoir* and the Italian verb *avere* (both mean 'to have'). *Droit* and *diritto* translate into *right*. The literal translation of *l'ayant droit*, resp. *l'avente diritto*, is *the one having a right*. So combined, the French and the Italian translation of *beneficial ownership* can be translated to *one having an economic right*. What the French and the Italian

[99] Meyer, *Trusts and Swiss Law*, 1 Int'l Comp. L. Q., 378 (1954).

[100] *See infra* chapter "Beneficial Ownership Used in U.S. Supreme Court Decisions".

versions have in common with the German version is that they combine the word 'right' or, in the case of German, a relative of that word, with the word *economic*.

bb) Economique/Economico

The French *économic* and the Italian *economico* can be seen as equivalents to the German *wirtschaftlich*. With regard to the English *economic*, one may recall what has been said above. Ever since great scholars like POSNER, COASE,[101] and CALABRESI[102] decided to analyze and interpret law from an economics perspective, the term *economic* points towards the Chicago School. In the given context, that hint is misleading. There is no equally strong movement in Europe which prefers the economist's view on the law to the extent that the Law and Economics movement does. As already pointed out, the history of the term *beneficial ownership* reaches further back in Anglo-American history than in the legal history of the other two systems. The term *economic* only *appears* to be identical in English and French when in fact it is charged in each language with a different meaning. This also applies *mutatis mutandis* to the Italian version.

cc) L'ayant droit économique and l'avente diritto economico

Since the development of Swiss law does not originate in one specific national language, one can safely conclude that the first appearance of the French and the Italian version of *beneficial ownership* coincide with the German version.

d) Observations and Conclusions

The findings from above can be put in the following equations. The letters stand for the first letter of the respective language (E = English, F = French, G = German, and I = Italian):

[101] RONALD HARRY COASE (1910), Nobel Prize carrier, famous for his Theorem (COASE Theorem) dealing with economic externalities. His major works are *The Nature of the Firm* (*1937*) and *The Problem of Social Cost* (*1960*); GEORGAKOPOULOS, PRINCIPLES AND METHODS OF LAW AND ECONOMICS 95 ff.

[102] GUIDO CALABRESI (*1932), Legal Scholar (former Dean of Yale Law School, senior judge on the United States Court of Appeals to the Second Circuit, his most quoted work (with DOUGLAS MELAMED) is: *Property Rules, Liability Rules, and Inalienability*: *One View of the Cathedral*, 85 HARV. L. REV. 1089–1128 (1972).

aa) Regarding Beneficial, Economic, Economico, Wirtschaftlich

$$
\begin{array}{l}
E \neq F \\
E \neq I \\
E \neq G \\
F = I \\
\left.\begin{array}{l} F \sim G \\ G \sim I \end{array}\right\} \quad \textit{slight}\text{ match}
\end{array}
$$

In relation to English, the other three translations match neither the literal nor the intrinsic meaning of the word *beneficial* while the French and Italian form a pair which can be more or less matched with their German equivalent. It can be concluded that at least with regard to the translation of *beneficial*, some consistency exists.

bb) Regarding Ownership, Droit, Diritto, Berechtigung

$$
\begin{array}{l}
E \neq F \\
E \neq I \\
E \neq G \\
F = I \\
\left.\begin{array}{l} F \neq G \\ I \neq G \end{array}\right\} \quad \text{No match!}
\end{array}
$$

With regard to the English word *ownership*, equations are identical to the ones regarding the term *beneficial*. Also, French and Italian form a pair again which, remarkably this time, does not match the German version in a sense that the former emphasizes the absolute (*droit*) while the later emphasizes the relative aspect of the same thing (*Berechtigung*). As has already been shown above,[103] the correct equivalent to *droit* and *diritto* would be *Recht*.

cc) Degree of Abstraction

An analysis of the degree of abstraction follows. As mentioned previously, precision and clarity are essential. Legal terms have to address concrete questions. There is no room for *l'art pour l'art*. "When we study law we are not studying a mystery but a well-known profession."[104] In order to prevent vague and biased results, "the judge

[103] *See supra* Sect. 3b).

[104] Holmes, *The Path of the Law*, 10 Harv. L. Rev. 457 (1879).

[. . .] decides in view of particular cases, and with reference to problems absolutely concrete."[105] Once the eagle has spotted the rabbit there is no more circling up in the air. If a ranking were to be made as to the degree of abstraction of the different terms under scrutiny in this thesis, the following results could be reached:

Among *Beneficial*

Rank #	Word
1	Ayant Droit
1	Avente Diritto
2	Berechtigter
2	Beneficial

Among *Ownership*

Rank #	Word
1	Ayant Droit
1	Avente Diritto
2	Berechtigter
3	Ownership

As with the equations above, there is disparity also here albeit not along the same lines. While French and Italian would be the clear winners of the Puchta Award for Abstraction,[106] the least abstract expression here would be the original English term *ownership*.

The equations that have been made and the abstraction ranking make it clear that, from a language perspective, the term *beneficial ownership* is lost in translation. The focus of the translation has clearly not been on accuracy and precision. What is particularly disturbing is the fact that this is also the case among the different Swiss versions.

After this analysis of beneficial ownership as a stand-alone term, the following chapter is intended to approach beneficial ownership from a conceptual point of view. Can beneficial ownership be identified and categorized in the context of legal theory? The immediately following chapter tries to answer this question by fitting beneficial ownership into HOHFELD's fundamental legal conceptions.

[105] CARDOZO, THE NATURE OF THE JUDICIAL PROCESS, 87; Von Jhering, *Im juristischen Begriffshimmel* 4 ff.

[106] GEORG FRIEDRICH PUCHTA (1798–1846), most famous representative of the *Begriffsjurisprudenz*, a movement villanized by the followers of *von Jhering's Interessenjurisprudenz*, Zweigert & Siehr, *Jhering's Influence*, 19 AM. J. COMP. L., 217 (1971).

Beneficial Ownership as a Concept

1. About Concepts in General

A concept is not a legal tool. According to LLEWELLYN

> It is a thinking tool. It is to make your data more manageable in doing something, in getting somewhere with them.[107]

Having its roots in the sixteenth century stemming from the Latin word *conceptum* (something conceived), the word *concept* stands for an abstract idea, a general notion, a plan, or an intention.[108] Lawyers borrowed the method of conceptual thinking from another ancient academic discipline: Philosophy. From ARISTOTLE to NIETZSCHE, concepts (or conceptions[109]) have played and still play an eminent role in philosophic thinking. To show and analyze the various views and interpretations of philosophical concepts could easily transform this thesis from a legal into a philosophical one which is clearly not its purpose. Instead, with the modesty appropriate to an academic of another discipline, a conceptual analysis of beneficial ownership shall be attempted. This analysis will be mainly inspired by the unequaled *Legal Conceptions* of WESLEY NEWCOMB HOHFELD.

While thinking in theoretical concepts is a characteristic method of the civil lawyer, the same cannot be said about the common lawyer:

> [The lawyer from Continental Europe] scans the English legal scene in vain for [...] an integrated structure of legal concepts rationally ordered. He finds that legal technique, instead of being directed primarily to interpreting statutory texts or analyzing concrete problems so as to 'fit them into the system' conceptually, is principally interested in precedents and types of case; it is devoted to the careful and realistic discussion of live

[107] Llewellyn, *A Realistic Jurisprudence*, 30 COLUM. L.J., 431 (1930); *see also* MILL, System of Logic Chapter II *in totum* (8th ed. 1882).

[108] NEW OXFORD AMERICAN DICTIONARY (2nd ed. 2008).

[109] *Synonym*.

M. Reinhard-DeRoo, *Beneficial Ownership*, DOI 10.1007/978-3-319-01686-3_3,

> problems and readier to deal in concrete and historical terms than think systematically or in the abstract.[110]

While being quite commonly used in constitutional law and sometimes also in contract law,[111] the development or understanding of concepts are neither systematically taught nor used in the legal profession *per se*. This applies to common and to civil law countries. Legal scholars, who strive to detect the law's innermost force which binds the world, and guides its course,[112] usually resort to philosophy which, before being demonized by Legal Realism and other movements, has always been an important source for legal thought.

An example of that traditional interaction between law and philosophy is HEGEL's concept that collective interest is different from the sum of individual interests, and hence private property is not considered to be promoting progress but rather the expression of free will.[113] This concept had significant influence on the Enlightenment Era scholars such as BLACKSTONE, BECCARIA,[114] and the founding generation of the United States.[115] To give just one example: If the U.S. Supreme Court in the case *Lynch v. Household Financial Corporation* states that: "In fact, a fundamental interdependence exists between the personal right to liberty and the personal right to property,"[116] HEGEL's concept still shines through. And LLEWELLYN's call remains true:

> Concepts are not to be eliminated; it cannot be done. Behavior is too heterogeneous to be dealt with except after some artificial ordering.[117]

LLEWELLYN's call is also a warning. A warning against random definitions which are merely based on the experience of the occasional encounter with the phenomenon that ought to be defined. The expression *we cross the bridge when we come to it* only makes sense if we know what and where a bridge is. "[. . .] legal or non-legal, chameleon-hued words are a peril both to clear thought and to lucid expression.[118]" HOHFELD's highly influential concept of legal rights in the United States, will be introduced below and afterwards applied to beneficial ownership in order to remove chameleon hues and reveal the true color of this concept.

---

[110] ZWEIGERT & KOETZ, COMPARATIVE LAW 181 (3rd ed. 1998).

[111] One may think of the concept of good faith in Article 2 of the Swiss Civil Code. This fundamental legal principle of Swiss Law and can be also found the American UNIFORM COMMERCIAL CODE – General Provisions, art. 1, §§ 201, 304.

[112] "[. . .] was die Welt im Innersten zusammenhält", GOETHE, FAUST, DER TRAGÖDIE ERSTER TEIL 7.

[113] MATTEI, BASIC PRINCIPLES OF PROPERTY LAW 21; HOLMES, Common Law, 226; Parisi, *Entropy in Property*, 50 AM. J. COMP. L., 601 (2002).

[114] TAMANAHA, LAW AS A MEANS TO AN END 42.

[115] TAMANAHA, *id.* at 30; Grechenig & Gelter, *The Transatlantic Divergence in Legal Thought*, 31 HASTINGS INT'L & COMP. L. REV. 320 (2007).

[116] 405 U.S. 538, 552 (1972).

[117] Llewellyn, *A Realistic Jurisprudence*, 30 COLUM. L.J., 453 (1910); NIETZSCHE, *Über Wahrheit und Lüge im aussermoralischen Sinn* 309.

[118] Hohfeld, *Some Fundamental Legal Conceptions as Applied in Judicial Reasoning*, 23 YALE L. J., 29 (1913).

2. HOHFELD's Fundamental Legal Conceptions

a) Significance of the Conceptions

HOHFELD's *Fundamental Conceptions of Legal Reasoning*[119] have shaped the American understanding of rights in a way that "has become part of the vernacular of constitutional documents and common law dicta."[120] HOHFELD's concern was quite practical:

> One of the great hindrances to the clear understanding, the incisive statement, and the true solution of legal problems frequently arises from the express or tacit assumption that all legal relations may be reduced to "rights" and "duties".[121]

With his *Conceptions*, HOHFELD "offered a logical basis for the redefinition of every legal concept in empirical terms, i.e. in terms of judicial decisions."[122]

HOHFELD was not only highly regarded in his times.[123] The sustainable significance of HOHFELD's conceptions can be demonstrated by the 1988 *Detroit Edison Company v. Michigan Air Pollution Control Commission* case[124] in which the owner of an industrial plant claimed that the legal protection of his property included a right to cause pollution. Almost a 100 years after HOHFELD first issued his *Conceptions*, the court reasoned:

> To constitute a protectable right, a person must have more than an abstract need, desire or unilateral expectation of the right. Rather, there must be a legitimate claim of entitlement to it. It has been recognized that there exists no right to pollute. Since no such right exists, a polluter has not been deprived of any protected property or liberty interest when the state halts the pollution.[125]

The underlined terms *right, claim, no right, and liberty* build a part of the molecular model of rights that will be introduced later in this text. With this model, HOHFELD encourages discipline of legal thought and expression. HOHFELD's

---

119 HOHFELD's *Conceptions* have been published in two separate law journal articles (Hohfeld, *id.*, *idem, Fundamental Legal Conceptions*, 26 YALE L.J. 758 (1917)). The first article, published in 1913 discusses the individual legal relations of right/privilege/power/immunity. The second article, published in 1917 predominantly analyses the differences between rights *in personam* (in *HOHFELD's* terminology *paucital* rights) and rights *in rem* (*multital* rights). The following analysis is predominantly based on the first article.

120 CASS, Property Right System, 3; see also: Pound, *Legal Rights*, 26 INT'L J. Ethics, 97 (1915); MATTEI, BASIC PRINCIPLES OF PROPERTY LAW 22; Halpin, *Fundamental Legal Conceptions Reconsidered*, Can. J. L. JURIS., 41; Cohen, *Transcendental Nonsense*, 35 COLUM. L. REV. 828 (1935).

121 Hohfeld, *Some Fundamental Legal Conceptions*, 23 YALE L.J. 28 (1913).

122 Cohen, *Transcendental Nonsense*, 35 COLUM. L. REV. 828 (1935).

123 Pound, *Legal Rights*, 26 INT'L J. Ethics, 100 (1915).

124 167 Mich. 661 (C. App. 1988).

125 *Id.*, emphasis added.

conceptions enable clear, logical, conclusive, and comprehensive understanding of the very complex matter.

In order to find answers to the conceptual nature of beneficial ownership, HOHFELD is certainly a very important source. In the following, the *Conceptions* will be introduced and their relevance with regard to the beneficial ownership concept will be analyzed.

b) The Conceptions

aa) The Four Hohfeldian Incidents

Based on an extensive analysis of case material and legal theories, HOHFELD refined and expanded the classical right/duty scheme by introducing four *strictly fundamental relations*, also called incidents:

Right (Claim[126]**):** "A right is one's affirmative claim against another."[127] E.g., the employee's claim to salary payment.

Privilege (Liberty[128]**):** "A privilege is the opposite of a duty.[129]" "A privilege is one's freedom from the right or claim of another."[130] E.g., the privilege to enter another person's house (thus having no duty to stay out like a stranger).

Power: The ability[131] to assume control over or change the legal status of another person, e.g., the power of a police officer to order a person to step out of the car (control) or to arrest a person (change the person's legal status) who does not follow the order.

Immunity: The absence of a person's responsibility towards (the power) of another person, e.g., the immunity of a person from paying a certain tax.

bb) First and Second Order Incidents

The four incidents can be divided into two different orders. This division is based on HOHFELD's introduction of two major categories of facts: *operative* (constitutive, causal) facts and *evidential* facts which are subsidiary to the operative facts. HOHFELD uses a signed piece of paper as an example for an evidential fact, which, "along with other evidential facts [only] tend to prove the actual operative facts"[132]

[126] Hohfeld, *Some Fundamental Legal Conceptions*, 23 YALE L.J. 32 (1913).
[127] *Id.* at 55.
[128] *Id.* at 36.
[129] *Id.* at 32.
[130] *Id.* at 55.
[131] *Id.* at 45.
[132] *Id.* at 26.

Fig. 1 First order relation

that every case needs in order to "suffice to change [or confirm] a legal relation."[133] In federal Indian law, an operative fact would be tribal membership while the respective membership card would be an evidential fact. Simply put, evidential facts prove operative facts.[134]

The ***first order*** *incidents* are related to the evidential facts as they are directly related to the object of interest (e.g., the right to keep my book untouched by any other person or the privilege of entering a piece of land).

- **Right (Claim)**
- **Privilege**

These incidents can be visualized as follows (Fig. 1):

The ***second order*** *incidents* are related to the operational facts as they change a legal relation to another person (Fig. 2):

- **Power**
- **Immunity (Exemption)**

These incidents do not affect an object directly but another person's legal position (e.g., the power of one person to accept an offer of another person, resulting in a liability of that other person to enter into a contractual agreement, or the tax immunity of a person which disables the authorities from collecting taxes from that person).

The division of the four Incidents into two orders is very helpful for the understanding of the author's entire approach. This will become specifically clear once the correlatives and opposites of the four incidents have been reviewed below. What can already be pointed out at this point is that each first and second order incidents consist of an incident with an affirmative effect (right and power) and an incident with a protective aspect (privilege and immunity).[135]

---

[133] *Id.* at 25.

[134] Santa Clara Pueblo v. Martinez, 436 U.S. 49 (1978); see generally COHEN'S HANDBOOK OF FEDERAL INDIAN LAW (2005 ed.) § 3.03 [1,2]; Valencia-Weber, *Three Stories in One*: *The Story of Santa Clara Pueblo v. Martinez* 453.

[135] The Stanford Encyclopedia of Philosophy, http://plato.stanford.edu/entries/rights, 7. also discusses the active and passive right aspect of the incident. Such discussion creates different pairs: Privilege and power are active rights, since they regulate the holder's behavior. Right and immunity are passive rights, as they regulate another person's behavior. This is not very convincing because each incident has an active and a passive side and the holder should not be the one in focus.

Fig. 2 Second order relation

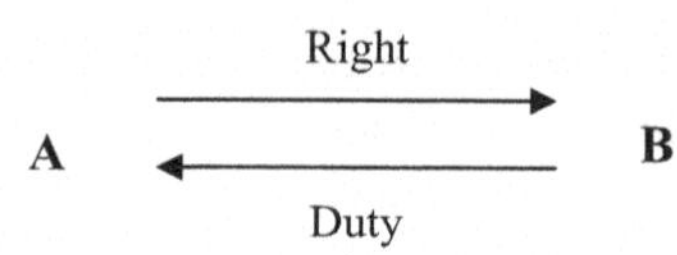

Fig. 3 Classical claim/duty Correlation

cc) Correlatives

Correlatives are very common in normative thought. They are a necessity. Already in Law School, students are familiarized with correlations between the parties involved in a case: government and citizen, buyer and seller, assignor and assignee, creditor and debtor to name a few. Students have to identify and analyze the rights and duties between the parties. The classic correlatives which have already been established long before HOHFELD are certainly *right and duty*:

Already before HOHFELD, the description of legal relations was based on the following claim/duty incident[136] (Fig. 3):

HOHFELD presents a correlative to each incident (Table 1):

What may appear unusual is the term *no-right* (which HOHFELD chose for lack of another term to express this conception[137]). But once juxtaposed next to the familiar right/duty correlation in a concrete example,[138] the inherent logic of this no-right reveals itself (Table 2).

The *privilege* example above demonstrates its previously mentioned denying effect. Any person is denied from interfering with the holder of a privilege, unless, needless to say, additional legal circumstances allow it (e.g., the person who granted the privilege now withdraws it). A similar denying effect can be observed in the *immunity* incident: Any person with a specific *power* is denied from exercising its power against a person with an *immunity*. Privilege and immunity both fence off infringements of other parties by invalidating the attacks. The difference is in the way the defense operates in the two cases. In the privilege incident the *counterparty's right* is *ab initio* inexistent while in the immunity incident the *counterparty itself* is *ab initio* disabled. What has been stated here about the relationship between the privilege and the immunity incident can be stated *mutatis mutandis* about the relationship the right and the power incident. Here too, the focus is on the right (or claim) or respectively the power (ability) of a person.

---

[136] HOHFELD uses the term *right* but suggests himself for ease of reference to use the term *claim* instead. This will be done consistently from here on.

[137] Hohfeld, *Some Fundamental Legal Conceptions*, 23 YALE L.J., 33 (1913).

[138] *Id.*

Table 1 Concepts and correlatives

Concept/incident	Correlative
Right, claim$^{(1st)}$	Duty
Privilege, liberty$^{(1st)}$	No right
Power$^{(2nd)}$	Liability
Immunity$^{(2nd)}$	Disability

Table 2 Content of correlatives

Correlatives	Correlative of A	Correlative of B
Right/duty	A has a **right** that B shall not enter her land	B has a **duty** not to enter on A's land
Privilege/no-right	(but if) A has a **privilege** to enter B's land	B has a **no-right** that A shall not enter

dd) Opposites

HOHFELD's *conception* also contains *opposites*. Opposites describe what an incident *is not* or *lacks*. The idea to include such negative conceptions shows HOHFELD's true genius.

In the first footnote of his first essay on the *fundamental legal conceptions*,[139] HOHFELD cites Lord FRANCIS BACON's (1561–1626) opinion on the concept of so-called uses:

> The nature of an [sic] use is best discerned by considering what it is not, and then what it is.[140]

This citation from 1602 may have been his main inspiration to elaborate on opposites. Although this cannot be proven, the method to first consider what something *is not*, before considering what it *is*, essentially contributes to the comprehensiveness of HOHFELD's conception. The workings of opposites can be visualized as follows (Fig. 4):

As with the *correlatives*, HOHFELD also presents one opposite for each incident. The table below shows the opposites together with the previously discussed correlatives (Table 3):

What immediately stands out is that the *opposites* consist of the same terms as the correlatives (duty, no-right, liability, disability) only this time they are re-shuffled: The *no-right* is now the *opposite* of a *right*; duty is the *opposite* of a *privilege*; disability is the *opposite* of a *power*; and *liability* is the *opposite* of *immunity*.

How so? Comparing Figs. 1 and 2 above, they are based on the same premise of a legal relationship involving a party A. Figure 1 visualizes the correlation between that party A and a party B and Fig. 2 visualizes the incident A is tied resp. not tied

[139] Hohfeld, *Some Fundamental Legal Conceptions*, 23 YALE L.J., 16 (1913).

[140] *Id.*

Fig. 4 Hohfeld's *Opposite*

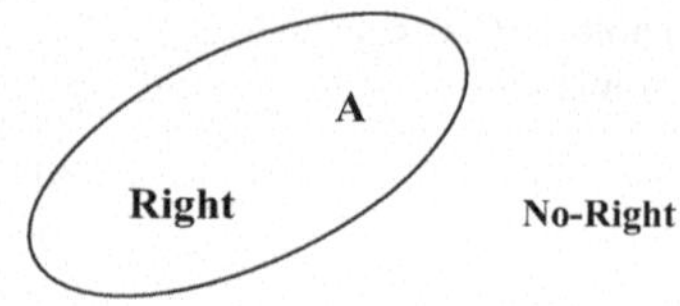

Table 3 Opposites and correlatives

Concept	**Correlative**	**Opposite**
Right, Claim	Duty	No right
Privilege, Liberty	No right	Duty
Power	Liability	Disability
Immunity	Disability	Liability

Table 4 Content of Opposites

Correla-tives	Correlative of A	Correlative of B	**Opposite of A**	**(Opposite of B)***
Right/Duty	A has a **right** that B shall not enter her land	B has a **duty** not to enter on A's land	A has a **no-right** that B shall enter her land	(B has a **no-duty** not to enter on A's land)
Privi-lege/no-right	(but if) A has a **privilege** to enter B's land	B has a **no-right** that A shall not enter	A has a **duty** not to enter B's land	(B has a **right** that A shall not enter)

*B's opposite incidents are only listed here to demonstrate the continuous logic of HOHFELD's conception.

to. To use the examples of Table 2 above, one could simply add columns containing the opposites and spell these out (Table 4):

ee) Conceptual Definition of Beneficial Ownership

The above conception of legal relations can now be applied to the beneficial ownership concept in order to gain a better conceptual understanding of its theoretical foundation.

Following Francis Bacon's method quoted above, it will first be established what beneficial ownership is *not* and then what it is.

Beneficial ownership is not a right. The relation between a party who beneficially owns an object and the counterparty who grants the beneficial ownership cannot be accurately described as a right/duty relationship. The beneficial owner may be allowed to use and enjoy the proceeds etc. of the counterparty's property but he has no means to claim this enjoyment. For example: B is the owner of a banana tree and allows A to eat as many bananas from that tree as she wishes. If B decides to cut down the banana tree, A has no right or claim to stop B from doing so. In turn, B has no duty to A to not cut the tree down.[141]

Beneficial ownership is not a power. The exercise of beneficial ownership has no impact on the legal status of any other person. The beneficial ownership has neither control nor the ability to change the legal status of another person. Logically, the beneficial owner is not able to cause a *liability* in a counterparty.

Beneficial ownership is not an immunity. The legal status of the beneficial ownership does not disable the power of a counterparty. To stay with the example of a banana tree: If the tree is planted in a public zoo and a zoo keeper orders A to leave the bananas to the elephants, A must obey that order. The situation would be different if the Zoo officially allowed all children up to 12 years old to eat as many bananas as they like. If A was 7 years old, she would be immune to the zoo keeper's order based on his *power* to prohibit banana eating to people above the age of 12.

Beneficial ownership is best categorized as a *privilege*. The beneficial ownership's enjoyment of the proceeds of property that she does not own herself results in third parties having *no right* that the beneficial owner shall not enjoy. As has been shown above, *duty* is the opposite of *privilege*. The beneficial owner thus has *no duty* to abstain from enjoying the proceeds.[142]

3. Conclusion

The plea to a conceptual analysis of a term in order to come to better understanding of a term has proven worthwhile. Thanks to the application of HOHFELD's refined legal conceptions, a clearer understanding of the beneficial ownership concept could be gained. HOHFELD's differentiation between *rights* and *privileges* enables us to define the beneficial ownership concept as follows:

- Beneficial Ownership is not a *right*
- Beneficial Ownership is a *privilege*
- Beneficial Ownership is correlated to a third person's lack of right ("*no-right*") to interfere with the Beneficial Owners privilege
- The Beneficial owner has no *duty* to abstain from exercising his *privilege*

[141] It may be worth noting at this point that, in a legal relationship, one person can assume more than one legal position at the same time. In a trust relationship, e.g., the trustee can also be the beneficial owner of an object. Such person may have rights, but these rights never accrue from the beneficial ownership position.

[142] For a vivid example see United States v. Algoma Lumber Co., 305 U.S. 415 (1939), *infra* chapter "Beneficial Ownership Used in U.S. Supreme Court Decisions", Sect. 3.

- The person granting beneficial ownership has the power to withdraw the *privilege* from the Beneficial Owner

After this conceptual analysis, the location of beneficial ownership in the dual Anglo-American system of common law and equity shall be attempted in the following chapter.

Common Law, Equity, and Beneficial Ownership

The discussion of the relationship between equity and law requires an understanding of what HOLMES calls the "remoter and more general aspects of the law [...] which give it universal interest." This shall be attained by combining a review of the more general theoretical aspects of equity and law with the specific findings regarding Anglo-American law and equity concept.

1. Law, Anti-Law, ...

In a general sense, equity can be described as a set of rules and standards which have the purpose to ensure justice but which is not an integral part of law.[143] Equity in this general sense is closely related to the principle of equity in civil law countries; the Swiss Civil Code in its Article 4 speaks of equity (*équité*, *equità*, *Billigkeit*) as a measure of discretion of the judiciary where the law remains silent. The Anglo-American system of equity has provided the basis for an additional set of rules and standards: This specific type of equity represents one side of the idiosyncratic Anglo-American *dual system*.[144] Civil law systems have never developed an entire court and case-law system that complements and competes with the traditional law and that is based on the principle of equity. This is one of the fundamental differences between common law and civil law systems.

POUND has summarized the phenomenon of sets of rules and standards competing with the law as follows:

---

[143] *See generally* ZWEIGERT & KOETZ, COMPARATIVE LAW 180 ff. (3rd ed. 1998); BLACKSTONE, COMMENTARY ON THE LAWS OF ENGLAND 65 ff.; Tate, Joshua C., *Ownership and Possession in Early Common Law*, 48 AM. J. L. H., 285 ff. (2006); Fortier, *Equity and Ideas: Coke, Ellesmere, and James I*, 51 RENAISSANCE Q., 1255 ff., (1998); Corwin, *The "Higher Law" Background of American Constitutional Law*, 42 HARV. L. REV. 151 (1928); HUDSON, EQUITY AND TRUSTS 10 ff.; Powell, *"Cardozo's Foot"*, 56 LAW AND CONTEMP. PROBS., 7 ff. (1993).

[144] Hohfeld, *The Relations between Equity and Law*, 11 MICH. L. REV. 546 (1913).

M. Reinhard-DeRoo, *Beneficial Ownership*, DOI 10.1007/978-3-319-01686-3_4,

Fig. 1 Law v. Anti-Law

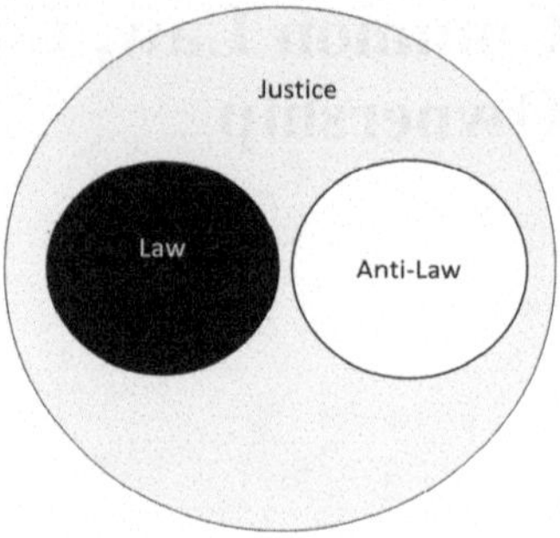

> Before the law, we have justice without law; and after law and during the evolution of law we still have it under the name of discretion, or natural justice, or equity and good conscience, as an anti-legal element.[145]

POSNER defines a system that ensures justice without law as anti-law and equity is an element of anti-law.[146] Equity follows its own rules and standards. The law thus cannot describe what is *anti-legal*.[147] *Anti-law* is not a part of the law. The term *anti-legal* belongs to a sphere that the law does not reach (yet). *Anti-legal* elements can create justice without the help of the law. Anti-legal elements operate within the realm of justice but outside the realm of the law. As such, equity is an independent system of rules and standards that ensure justice. From a set theory perspective, legal and anti-legal elements can be described as sub-sets of justice (Fig. 1).

These general observations on law and equity allow the following specific observations of the Anglo-American system of law and equity.

LANGDELL's biting comment on equity was:

> As equity wields only physical power, it seems to be impossible that it should actually create anything.[148]

The first half-sentence of LANGDELL's remark ("equity wields only physical power") points to the most characteristic aspect of equity. The second half-sentence ("it seems to be impossible that it should actually create anything") could be fully subscribed to had he added the term *legal* at the end ("...create anything *legal*").

[145] Pound, *The Decadence of Equity*, 5 COLUM. L. Rev, 20 (1905).

[146] Equity is not the only element of anti-law. Other examples are customs, etiquette, manners, morals, taboos, conventions, and habits.

[147] For the interpretation of the law itself we concur with Cohen, *Transcendental Nonsense*, 35 COLUM. L. REV., 814 (1948), n.4 quoting ROGUIN: "Nothing is more fallacious than to believe that one may give an account of the law by means of the law itself." This thought is in line with GOEDEL's mathematical theorem which, very roughly explained, proves the inability of any system to justify its own truth by solely using its own axioms; ENZENSBERGER, DIE ELIXIERE DER WISSENSCHAFT 9.

[148] This is the only quote that HOHFELD uses in both his articles about fundamental legal conceptions, Hohfeld, *Fundamental Legal Conceptions*, 26 YALE L.J. 758 (1917) and Hohfeld, *Some Fundamental Legal Conceptions*, 23 YALE L.J. (1913), n.3.

When LANGDELL speaks of *wielding physical power*, he implies that equity does not have the same "real" (and here again) *legal* effect as the common law. To call equity claims inexistent simply because such claims were not heard in the common law courts[149] can only be the statement of a purist common law *afficinado* like LANGDELL. For the claimant who applies for an injunction based on an imminent breach of trust, the outcome of her claim, whether granted or not, seems real enough.[150] But whether one subscribes to LANGDELL's denial of the *legal* reality of equity or not, it certainly proves one thing: if one can contend that the other one does not exist,[151] there *must* be fundamental differences. However, such a statement is only valid from a competitor's perspective. From a general perspective, law and equity may compete but also complement each other.

A representative scenario for the complementary function of equity could be found at the very beginning of equity justice. This scenario includes a landowner who went to fight in the crusades[152] and entrusted his property to another person until his return.[153] If, upon his return, the trusted person refused to give the land back, the original owner was given only financial remedies such as damages or restitutions. The law would not help him to re-install his title. Equity, i.e. the Lord Chancellor came to help.[154]

Based on the *maxims that equity will not suffer a wrong to be without a remedy* and that *equity looks to the intent rather than to the form*,[155] the crusader became the *beneficiary* and the trusted person became his *trustee*. The trustee was given the responsibility to operate in the interest of the beneficiary or else be sued for breach of trust. By giving the crusader the status of a beneficiary and the caretaker the status of trustee along with all the responsibilities pertaining thereto, the Court of

---

[149] *Id.*

[150] For a detailed comparison of common law and equity claims and remedies see HUDSON, EQUITY AND TRUSTS 13.

[151] LANGDELL is even more explicit when he states: "[. . .] as in contemplation of equity such [equitable] rights do exist, equity must reason upon them and deal with them as if they had an actual existence [underline added]", HOHFELD, *id.*

[152] Gaudiosi, *The Influence of the Islamic Law of Waqf on the Development of the Trust in England*, 136 U. PA. L. REV. 1241 (1988).

[153] The example used in ZWEIGERT & KOETZ, COMPARATIVE LAW 188 (3rd ed. 1998), refers to a specific pre-trust instrument of tax avoidance named *Use* which was prohibited in 1535 by KING HENRY VIII with the Statute of Uses, (27 Hen.8 c.10).

[154] The example has not been chosen coincidentally or for entertainment purposes. Recent historical research traces the trust back to the Islamic *waqf*. Gaudiosi, *The Influence of the Islamic Law of Waqf on the Development of the Trust in England*, 136 U. PA. L. REV. 1250 (1988) even suggests that the statutes of one of the oldest English law colleges (written in 1264), the Merton College of Oxford, had a striking resemblance to typical *waqf* deeds; see generally HUDSON, EQUITY AND TRUSTS, 13f.

[155] *See generally* Pound, *The Maxims of Equity*, 34 HARV. L. REV. 833 (1921) (providing further background information on the maxims); Hohfeld, *The Relations between Equity and Law*, 11 MICH. L. REV. 550, (1913).

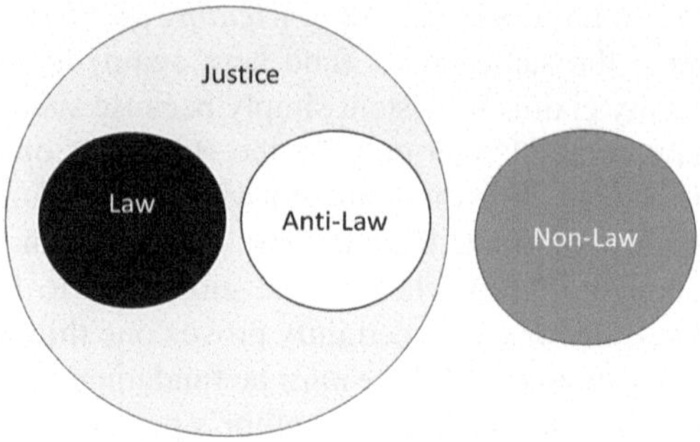

Fig. 2 Law and Anti-law v. Non-Law

Chancery was able to prevent an injustice that the common law had no means to cure.

This example shows the inner workings of the relationship between common law and equity. Equity functioned as a corrective of the common law and was eventually merged with the latter.[156]

2. . . .and Non-Law (Fig. 2)

The introduction of the non-legal element does not directly contribute to the description of the relationship between law and equity. It is however necessary for the conclusions that will be drawn further below regarding beneficial ownership. The term *non-legal* must not be confused with the term *anti-legal*: The term *non-legal* describes "mental and physical facts that call [. . .] [plain] relations into being."[157] Non-legal and legal incidents get confused quite often. A good example is the term *property*, a term which (unfortunately) can describe a legal as well as a non-legal incident:

> In strict legal sense, land is not 'property', but the subject of property. The term 'property', although in common [non-legal] parlance frequently applied to a tract of land or a chattel, in its legal signification [. . .] denotes a right over a determinate thing.[158]

Non-legal elements can be given legal relevance. Proving possession is an old example. The old Roman law rule: *in pari delicto melior est conditio possidentis* (in a case of equal or mutual fault the condition of the party in possession is the better one)[159] says nothing more in this context than: In a dispute over property which obvious, factual situation shall decide. Whoever holds the purse in his hands

[156] England had issued a new Judicature Act in 1873 which officially abolished the separate court system. This institutional reform was, however, not followed by an instant reform of the minds, *United Scientific Holdings Ltd. vs. Burnley Borough counsel*, 2 All ER 62 (1977).

[157] Hohfeld, *Fundamental Legal Conceptions*, 26 Yale L.J., 20 (1913).

[158] *Id.* at 22 with further notes.

[159] Liebs, Lateinische Rechtsregeln Und Rechtssprichwörter 95 (4th ed.).

shall win the dispute over possession. Therefore "in ninety-nine cases out of a hundred, it is about as easy and cheap to prove at least a *prima facie* title as it is to prove possession."[160] Possession in this context is the physical manifestation of the will to own an object, recognized by law.

Possession and beneficial ownership have in common the physical relation to an object. The difference between possession and beneficial ownership is their legal significance resp. lack thereof. While the position of the possessor is well protected by law, the beneficial owner's position is a mere physical manifestation of "ownership" without inherent recognition by law. This lack of recognition does not imply that beneficial ownership is legally irrelevant. Beneficial ownership may even play an eminent role in a legal case.[161] But this role is never an active role. Like the famous *smoking gun*, beneficial ownership only contributes to the factual circumstances on which any legal case is based upon.

3. Conclusions

The relationship between equity and law in a general sense can be described as the relationship between law and anti-law as two separate subsets within the set of justice. Equity also exists in civil law systems as a principle applicable to judicial discretion. But in this civil law version, equity has never developed into an entire court and case system.

Equity and common law, in a narrower sense, were the idiosyncratic counterparts of the Anglo-American dual system until they were merged into a single system of law. Although this merger was institutionalized in 1873, the dual-system mindset of Anglo-American law has survived.

The relationship between equity and common law can be characterized as competitive yet complementary. The institutionalization of trusts is representative for this relationship. The crusader example demonstrated the capability of English law to respond to legal issues that could not be solved with traditional rules. Thus the equity courts were granted the power to solve legal issues which were beyond the reach of traditional common law concepts.

The beneficial ownership is neither a product of equity nor of law. The concept rather belongs to a category which Pound calls *non-law*:

	Law	Anti-Law	Non-Law
Rule set	Common law	Equity	Nature
Institutions	Legal ownership	Equitable ownership	Factual ownership
Person	Legal owner	Beneficiary	*Beneficial Owner*

[160] Holmes, Common Law 227.

[161] *See infra* chapters "Beneficial Ownership Used in U.S. Supreme Court Decisions" and "The Beneficial Ownership Concept Applied in Federal Indian Law".

It has to be noted that the above table does not take into account the transformability of non-legal elements. Furthermore, the items listed under institutions and persons are merely examples. These *caveats* do not interfere with the main purpose of this table: To explain why beneficiary and beneficial owner must not be confused, the beneficiary correlates with the common law owner while the beneficial owner belongs to a category outside of the dual system.

Beneficial Ownership in U.S. Supreme Court Decisions

The two previous chapters discussed the beneficial ownership concept in legal theory. This chapter shall discuss the concept in legal practice. For this purpose, a careful selection of twelve United States Supreme Court decisions from different fields of law shall be scrutinized. The way these cases deal with the beneficial ownership concept allows for representative conclusions which will be summarized at the end of this chapter.

1. Hellenic Lines, Ltd. v. Rhoditis[162]

Mr. Rhoditis, a Greek seaman with a Greek employment contract, suffered an accident on a Greek vessel. The vessel was owned by Hellenic Lines, Ltd., a Greek corporation with its largest office in New York and another office in New Orleans, the latter being the place of the accident. The manager and 95 % shareholder of Hellenic Lines, Ltd., Mr. Callimanopoulos, was a Greek national and lawful resident alien living in Connecticut. The sailor filed suit under Section 688 of the Jones Act[163] which provides that:

> Any seaman who shall suffer personal injury in the course of his employment may, at his election, maintain an action for damages at law, with the right to trial by jury, [. . .].

The question at hand was whether the employer of the sailor was subject to the Act despite the case's many non-U.S. nexus. The Supreme Court said yes, arguing that the owner's residential status, the place of the accident, the forum chosen, and the base of the owner's business operations were all in the United States. The court also discussed the previously established seven criteria for the applicability of the

---

[162] 398 U.S. 306 (1970).

[163] 46 U.S.C. § 688 (1920).

M. Reinhard-DeRoo, *Beneficial Ownership*, DOI 10.1007/978-3-319-01686-3_5,

Jones Act, the so-called *Lauritzen* test.[164] The court held that "the Lauritzen test, however, is not a mechanical one."[165] The list of criteria mentioned in the test thus should not be considered as exhaustive. Other factors may come into play, in particular the place of the operations of the employer:

> [...] the facade of the operation must be considered as minor, compared with the real nature of the operation and a cold objective look at the actual operational contacts that this ship and this owner have with the United States.[166]

The Court's reliance on the *real nature and a cold objective look at the actual operational contacts* is based on a notion that can be found in many beneficial ownership cases.[167] The separation between the legal situation, the *façade* (employer is a Greek corporation (95 %-owned by a Greek national, Greek-flag vessel, employment contract governed by Greek law), from the factual situation (operations carried out regularly in or with the United States). As in other precedents, the court decides to let reality, the real nature of the operation prevail over the legal situation. Not unanimously though: Three of the 9 Supreme Court Justices dissented.[168]

Reference to the term *beneficial ownership* is only made in their dissenting opinion. This reference is based on another decision, *McCulloch v. Sociedad Nacional*, in which the Supreme Court declined to override the well-established international flag principle which holds that, absent expressed contrary Congress intention, the law of the flag a ship flies shall apply.[169]

In *McCulloch*, the term *beneficial ownership* was used to describe a factual element of the case (a vessel was "beneficially owned" by a U.S. corporation). The question was whether beneficial ownership on a ship together with other factual elements would provide sufficient reason to override the well settled international law principle which holds that the flag a ship flies determines the applicable law.[170] The court "declined to rely on the beneficial ownership of the vessel and other "substantial United States contacts," [...].[171] It thus voted in favor of the flag

---

[164] Lauritzen v. Larsen, 345 U.S. 571 (1953) (defining seven criteria to determine whether an employer shall be held liable under the Jones Act: 1. Place of the wrongful act; 2. The law of the flag; 3. The allegiance or domicile of the injured seaman; 4. Allegiance of the defendant ship owner; 5. The place where the contract of employment was made; 6. the inaccessibility of the foreign forum; and 7. the law of the forum).

[165] *Hellenic Lines*, 398 U.S. at 308.

[166] *Id.* at 310; *See* also Belton v. Buesing, 240 Or 399, 402 P2d 98 (1965).

[167] *See e.g.*: Bollinger v. Commissioner, 807 F.2d 65 (6th Cir.1986) Whittaker v. Whittaker Corp., 639 F.2d 516 (9th Cir.1981); Lafkowitz v. Jackson, 13 F.2d 370 (8th Cir.1926); Waddil v. Weaver, 53 Ala. 58; (1875); Haker v. McKissok, 12 N.J. 310 (1953); Gebhard v. West Allis, 89 Wis. 2d 557 (1974); State *ex rel.* Mitchell Aero, Inc. v Board of Review, 74 Wis. 2d 268 (1976).

[168] Burger (Chief Justice), Harlan (Associate), and Stewart (Associate).

[169] 372 U.S. 10, 12 (1963).

[170] In United States v. Kun Yun Jho,, 534 F.3d 398, the Court of Appeal defines and recognizes the flag principle, but holds that the principle does not apply if the "[mis-] conduct occurred [...] entirely within the ports of the United States".

[171] *Hellenic Lines*, 398 U.S. 312.

principle, against the factual elements. The dissenters in *Hellenic Lines* maintained that the *McCulloch* decision should also apply *mutatis mutandis* to *Hellenic Lines*. In their opinion, factual elements alone should not outweigh a well-established principle of international law. There may be room for a different valuation of the factual situation if the law was only concerning a national legal issue. But with regard to the Jones Act, this was not the case:

> While some legislation in its purpose obviously requires extension beyond our borders to achieve national policy, this is not so, in my opinion with an Act concerned with prescribing particular remedies, rather than one regulating commerce or creating a standard of conduct [i.e. the Jones Act].[172]

SUMMARY: The term *beneficial ownership* in the *Hellenic Lines* case is only used in the dissenting opinion. In it, the dissenting judges discuss whether *beneficial ownership* together with other factual elements of the case contributes to the legal outcome of the case. Their conclusion is that it should not. Thus, *Hellenic Lines* only discusses *what role* beneficial ownership may play, but it does not discuss what beneficial ownership *is*. The Court, however, disregards the 95 % foreign legal ownership of the shipping company in favor of the factual operational activity of that company. Although *beneficial ownership* does not directly compete with legal ownership in the present case, it is certainly categorized as a factual element that together with other factual elements, *can* overrule legal ownership.

2. Tooahnippah (Goombi) v. Hickel[173]

In his will, George Chahsenah, a Comanche Indian, left his estate which consisted of three allotments to his niece, Viola Atewooftakewa Tate, and her three children.[174] In the document, Chahsenah stated that he decided to leave nothing to his heirs in law for they had shown no interest in him. As a consequence, Chahsenah's illegitimate daughter, Dorita High Horse, was left out of the will. High Horse and certain nephews and nieces of the testator challenged the will, contending that Chahsenah was incompetent due to his alcoholism and poor health condition.

An important aspect has to be mentioned before further analyzing the role of beneficial ownership in the present case. Federal Indian law limits the Indian's liberty to dispose of allotments. *In casu*, based on the Act of 1910 and its amendment of 1913[175] a testament of a Native American disposing of allotments needs approval of the Secretary of Interior. The Secretary's representative, the Examiner of Inheritance,[176] approved the will. "He concluded [...] that the evidence presented by

---

[172] *Id.* at 313.

[173] 397 U.S. 598 (1970).

[174] For the significance of allotments in federal Indian policy, see *infra* chapter "The Beneficial Ownership Concept Applied in Federal Indian Law", Sect. 2a).

[175] 36 Stat. 856 Sec. 2 (1910) and 37 Stat. 678 (1913).

[176] Office of the Solicitor, Department of the Interior.

the contestant [Dorita High Horse] was not sufficient to outweigh the presumption of correctness attaching to a properly executed will [. . .].[177]" High Horse appealed to the regional solicitor who disapproved the will on the ground that the Examiner did not reasonably exercise his discretionary responsibility. The regional solicitor further ordered the whole estate to be distributed to High Horse as the sole heir at law. The conflict was brought to the U.S. District Court who remanded the case with the directions to approve the will.[178] This decision was reversed by the Court of Appeals, holding that the Regional Secretary's action was unreviewable by the lower court.

The core questions in this case whether the Secretary of the Interior was subject to judicial review and, if so, whether the Secretary's decision on the validity of Chasenah's will was still within the scope of the Secretary's authority.[179] Regarding the first question based on the 1910 Act,[180] the Supreme Court held that it could not find any section that "contains language cloaking the Secretary's actions with immunity from judicial review."[181] Regarding the second question, the Supreme Court held that "[. . .] under 25 U.S.C. § 373, we perceive nothing in the stature or its history or purpose that vests in a government official the power to revoke or rewrite a will [. . .]. The regional solicitor's action was based on nothing more that we can discern than his concept of equity [. . .]."[182]

What is particularly interesting with regard to beneficial ownership is the Supreme Court's dictum regarding the legal nature of Indian allotment:

> [. . .] here we deal with a special kind of property right under allotment form the Government.[183] The right is not absolute; the allottee is the beneficial owner while the Government is trustee. [. . .]. The Indian's right to make *inter vivos* dispositions is limited, and requires approval of the Secretary. The legislative history reflects the concern of the Government to protect Indians from improvident acts or exploitation by others.[184]

The term *beneficial ownership* is used as a synonym for the term (trust) *beneficiary*. The Supreme Court mentions beneficial ownership on another occasion but without providing further explanations.[185] This leads to the question whether these fragments are sufficient to allow further conclusions to be drawn regarding the nature of beneficial ownership. It is believed that they are.

SUMMARY: As opposed to the previously discussed *Hellenic Lines v. Rhoditis* case, the Supreme Court does not use the term *beneficial ownership* in connection with the separation between factual and legal elements. The term is used here to

177 *Tooahnippah*, 397 U.S. at 601.

178 *Id.* at 605.

179 Based on 25 U.S.C. § 373.

180 25 U.S.C. § 408.

181 *Tooahnippah*, 397 U.S. at 607.

182 *Tooahnippah*, 397 U.S. at 610.

183 Emphasis added.

184 *Tooahnippah*, 397 U.S, at 609.

185 *Id.* at 607, 612, (mentioning the Indian's *beneficial interest* in connection with the trustee role of the government but without any further explanations).

describe a special kind of property that has been created with the governmental purpose to protect the Indians from themselves and from others. That purpose will have to be revisited in the *United States v. Algoma Lumber Co.* case below.

3. United States v. Algoma Lumber Co. et al.[186]

The Supreme Court had to decide in this case whether the Court of Claims, a court specialized for monetary claims against the federal government,[187] had jurisdiction over a dispute between a group of lumber companies (Algoma et al., respondents) and the U.S. government (petitioner). The former claim against the government was based on the argument that a sale was executed through an agent of the U.S. government,[188] the Superintendent of the Klamath Indian School, representing the Secretary of the Interior. Another government official, the Indian Commissioner, had fixed the price of the timber. Thus, the respondents argued that, regardless of the role as an agent of the Indians, the United States acting as guardian or trustee of the Indians became their contracting party.[189] The Supreme Court disagreed, arguing that the U.S. government official may well have been given the responsibility by treaty to supervise the sales contracts between the Indians and the purchasers of lumber,[190] but this role as a protector of Indian interests did not allow the assumption of an obligation of the United States. The contract of sale was, even on its face, concluded between the Indians and the purchasers of the lumber, and the Superintendent according to the terms of the contract (who was explicitly acting for and on behalf of the Klamath Indians).

In this decision, the Supreme Court mentioned beneficial ownership in several passages, some of which deserve further scrutiny. In one passage the court stated that:

> The United States acquired no beneficial ownership in their [the Klamath's] tribal lands or their proceeds.[191]

The court does not specify what kind of ownership the United States acquired instead ("[. . .] however we may *define* the nature of the legal interest acquired by the government"[192]).

---

[186] 305 U.S. 415 (1939).

[187] Replaced in 1982 with the U.S. Court of Federal Claims with newly established U.S. Court of Appeals for the Federal Circuit as appellate instance. It has the same responsibility as its preceding court (28 U.S.C. §1491).

[188] For the differences between the agency concepts of common law and civil law see ZWEIGERT & KOETZ, COMPARATIVE LAW 431 ff. (3rd ed. 1998).

[189] For the characterization of the U.S. as guardians and the Indians as wards, see Worcester v. Georgia, 31 U.S. 48 (1832); see also below 4.3 d).

[190] According to the Supreme Court this was agreed upon based on the Treaty of February 17th, 44 Stat. 560 (1870) between the United States and the Klamath, *Algoma*, 305 U.S. at 420.

[191] *Algoma*, 305 U.S. at 421.

[192] *Id.*

The court focused its reasoning on an analysis of the role of the government in the disputed transaction. It concluded that the U.S. government was merely an agent vested "with plenary power to take appropriate measures to safeguard the disposal of property of which the Indians are substantial owners."[193] That role of the government as an agent did not include a responsibility for the pricing of the lumber.

The court further did not agree with the respondents (*Algoma*) that the United States was "acting as guardian or trustee of the Indians through the Secretary and Superintendent."[194] It qualified the involvement of the government instead as a matter of implementation of public policy rather than a contractual engagement:

> The action of Congress in authorizing the sale of timber [. . .] are to be viewed as the means chosen for the exercise of the power of the government to protect the rights and beneficial ownership of the Indians.[195]

The most interesting element of this quote is not the qualification of the government's action but the *en passant* juxtaposition of *rights and beneficial ownership*. This is a good example to show that HOHFELD's legal thinking is fully integrated in the United States. In a Hohfeldian sense, beneficial ownership is not a right (claim) but a privilege. As explained above, a privilege entitles its holder to the use of an object. The objects in the present case are "[. . .] the land and the timber standing upon it and the proceeds of their [the Klamath's] sale [. . .]."[196] The privilege to use these objects was granted by the U.S. government who had the respective power to do so. The explicit inclusion of the timber sale into that beneficial ownership privilege protected the government from potential Klamath claims. Privileges do not construe claims but a correlative non-right *in casu* of the government to interfere with its enjoyment. A claim could only have been construed if the government would have been considered a trustee of the Klamaths. However, the Supreme Court rejected a respective suggestion of the claimants.

As has been shown, the dispute here is between private lumber companies and the U.S. government: The Klamath Indians were not directly involved. Nevertheless, it is worth noting that the qualification of the government as trustee and the Indians as beneficiaries has become standard in recent cases. The most famous case representing this change is the *Cobell* litigation in which the government is sued for billions of dollars for mismanagement of individual Indian assets.[197]

SUMMARY: Beneficial ownership is a privilege, not a right.

---

[193] *Id.* (using the term *substantial* instead of *beneficial* twice on this page without further explanation).

[194] *Id.* at 422; see *infra* chapter "The Beneficial Ownership Concept Applied in Federal Indian Law", Sect. 4b).

[195] *Id.* at 421.

[196] *Id.* at 420.

[197] *See infra* chapter "The Beneficial Ownership Concept Applied in Federal Indian Law", Sect. 4b); Riley, *The Apex of Congress' Plenary Power over Indian Affairs: The Story of Lone Wolf v. Hitchcock* 225.

4. United States v. Shoshone Tribe of Indians[198]

On July 2nd, 1863, the United States entered into a treaty with the Shoshone Indian tribe which granted the tribe some 44 million acres of land in Colorado, Utah, Idaho, and Wyoming to build a reservation.[199] In another treaty, concluded between the same parties 5 years later on July 3rd, 1868, the Shoshones ceded that reservation to the United States. The Court did not provide any background information on that cession. However, in the latter treaty, the United States agreed that some 3 million acres "shall be [...] set apart for the absolute and undisturbed use and occupation of the Shoshone Indians."[200] In 1878, the United States allowed, without consent of the Shoshones, a band of Arapahoe Indians to reside on the Shoshone reservation. It was not disputed by the United States that this constituted a taking and that the Shoshones were entitled to compensation. What was in dispute though was the amount of compensation; respectively, if the taking also included the value of the timber and minerals on the Shoshone reservation.

In this discussion of the content of the taking, beneficial ownership played a key role. The Supreme Court clearly allocated the beneficial ownership on the land to the Shoshones:

> The words of the grant [treaty], coupled with the government's agreement to exclude strangers, negative the idea that the United States retained beneficial ownership. The grant of right to members of the tribe, severally to select and hold tracts on which to establish homes for themselves and families, and the restraint upon cession of land held in common or individually,[201] suggest beneficial ownership in the tribe.[202]

At the same time, the Supreme Court established that the United States always had legal title in the Shoshone land and power to manage the affairs of the Indians but that the legal title did not give the United States the power to exploit the land without rendering just compensation "for that would be not the exercise of guardianship or management, but confiscation."[203] The Indians had the right of occupancy with all its beneficial incidents and that right was "as sacred as the fee [title]."[204]

---

[198] 304 U.S. 111 (1938).

[199] The original meaning of the term *reservation* changed its meaning the course of time. Originally the term was used in treaties of the 17th century to describe the part of land the Indians would reserve for themselves and not convey to the United States, Singer, *Erasing Indian Country: The Story of Tee-Hit-Ton Indians v. United States* 242.

[200] *Shoshone*, 304 U.S. at 113.

[201] *See generally infra* Chapter "The Beneficial Ownership Concept Applied in Federal Indian Law", Sect. 2.

[202] *Shoshone*, 304 U.S. at 115.

[203] Worcester v. Georgia, 31 U.S. 48 (characterizing the U.S. as guardians and the Indians as wards); see also *infra* chapter "The Beneficial Ownership Concept Applied in Federal Indian Law", Sect. 6e).

[204] *Shoshone*, 304 U.S. at 117.

As in the *Algoma Lumber* case, the Supreme Court qualified the land ownership of an Indian tribe as *beneficial ownership* thereby avoiding a legal qualification that could serve as a basis for a property claim. To call the right of occupancy, the most fundamental element of Native American possession *sacred as the fee title* is not unusual. According to COHEN:

> [...] cases might perhaps be classified according to whether they refer to the Indian right of occupancy as a "mere" right of occupancy or as a "sacred" right of occupancy: All the cases, however, agree in saying that the aboriginal Indian title involves an exclusive right to occupancy and does not involve an ultimate fee.[205]

In other words, the sanctification of the right of occupancy at best constituted a moral obligation towards the Indians. As opposed to the Algoma case, the Supreme Court did consider the government as a guardian of the Shoshone tribe and called on the government's duty not to fulfill its duties as such. This leads to the conclusion that certain elements of beneficial ownership (*in casu* on timber and minerals) may quite well enjoy protection if based on treaty.[206] To derive from this a general duty of the government to protect the beneficial interests of the Indians as in the *Algoma Lumber* case does, however, not exist automatically.

SUMMARY: Beneficial ownership in itself is merely a privilege, but the protection of the enjoyment of this privilege from third party interference can be a duty of the government. The *Algoma Lumber* case only contradicts to this on the surface. After all, the duty to protect is mentioned there as well: It is just in a different focus.

5. Handy & Harman v. Burnet[207]

Six men held 93.71 % of the shares of the corporation Handy & Harman, a New York corporation dealing in gold and special silver products. Another company, Hamilton & DeLoss, a Connecticut corporation, was organized to build a factory specializing in the manufacturing of certain products useful to Handy & Harman. The same six men who owned 93.71 % in Handy & Harman also owned more than 75 % of Hamilton & De Loss. De Loss was one of the six men while Hamilton was not. Hamilton had no shareholding in Handy & Harman but owned 20 % of Hamilton & De Loss. Hamilton was also named president of the latter corporation. He attended the stockholders meetings of both corporations but never voted against the majority of the stockholders. The financing of Hamilton's 20 % shareholding in Hamilton & De Loss was facilitated with the help of De Loss, a bank, and an individual named Higgins. For that purpose, the stocks were deposited with the bank as collateral security for the payment. When Hamilton failed to pay, De Loss took over the stock.

---

[205] COHEN'S HANDBOOK OF FEDERAL INDIAN LAW 293 (1945 ed.)

[206] *See infra* chapter "The Beneficial Ownership Concept Applied in Federal Indian Law", Sect. 3a).

[207] 284 U.S. 136 (1931).

Hamilton was paid a salary of US$10,000 p.a. by Hamilton & De Loss. Both corporations were operated as one business unit. During the taxable period in question, Hamilton and De Loss suffered a loss.

The Supreme Court had to decide whether, under Section 240 of the 1918 Revenue Act,[208] the two corporations Handy & Harman and Hamilton & De Loss would qualify as affiliated corporations and as such could file consolidated returns (which would facilitate an offset of the loss suffered by Hamilton & De Loss). In order to qualify for that affiliate status, the Act required in Sec. 240 (b) that "substantially all the stock of two or more corporations is owned or controlled by the same interests."

At the core of this case is a tax law question. According to Section 240 of the 1918 Revenue Act, affiliated corporations shall file consolidated tax returns. Corporations are considered affiliated if "substantially all their stock "is owned or controlled by the same interests."[209] The Court held that, in order to justify consolidated returns, "the[se] same interests are the beneficial owners in like proportions of substantially all the stock of each such corporation." The Court made clear that "carrying on of a business unit by two or more corporations does not, in itself, constitute affiliation."[210] What was of more importance to the Court was the equal distribution of stock along with the even influence of the stockholders in those corporations. The 20 % ownership of Hamilton and its complicated setup involving four parties (Hamilton, De Loss, the bank, and Higgins) constituted, the Court stated, "an indefinite and uncertain control of stock without title, beneficial ownership, or legal means to enforcing it, but resting solely on acquiescence, the exigencies of business, or other considerations having no binding force [. . .]."[211] The nature of the 20 % ownership on the stocks of Hamilton and De Loss was not sufficiently justifying the treatment of the entire enterprise as a consolidated unit.

The term *beneficial ownership* used in the quote above appears in the syllabus of the *Handy & Harman* case.[212] The fact that the term *beneficial ownership* was used next to the term *title* seems to suggest that the court differentiated between a general term for *legal* ownership and *beneficial* ownership. However, this would not make sense in view of the half-sentence that follows ("or legal means to enforce it"). How beneficial ownership as a *de facto* ownership could be enforced with *legal* means and what these means would be the Court did not answer. Once more the only conclusion left is that the Court did not deem it necessary to be more explicit about its use of the term *beneficial ownership*. Once more, *beneficial ownership* was used

[208] 40 Stat. 1081 (1918).

[209] *Handy & Harman*, 284 U.S. at 141.

[210] *Id.* at 140.

[211] *Id.* at 136.

[212] *Id.*

as a helpful term that catches a variety of scenarios which cannot be pinned down to a clear legal relationship.

The decision of the lower court[213] elaborated on the role of control over the stocks with control being considered the crucial element of shareholding which determined the influence on a corporation.[214] The lower court differentiated between two lines of cases: "One line holds that, when the corporations are operating as a business unit, actual control of the voting power of the minority stock is sufficient."[215] The other narrower line, held that: "[. . .] if control means something different from ownership of stock, it must at least be a control legally enforceable."[216] *In casu*, the court did not consider beneficial ownership as a position capable of legally enforcing control. Since De Loss did not legally own the stocks so long as they merely served as a security for the money owed by Hamilton, he did not have any legally enforceable control over Hamilton & De Loss Inc. with the result that while Handy & Harman was 93.71 % owned by the shareholders, their ownership on Hamilton & De Loss was significantly lower. The Supreme Court concurred with that analysis.

It may be noted here that the phenomenon of shareholder control via beneficial ownership became a very prominent issue, especially in cases where the ownership in shares was held indirectly, e.g., via a trust. Particularly the amendments to the Securities and Exchange Act[217] introduced by the 1968 Williams Act (amendment of sections 13(d) and 14 in 1968 (d)) had the purpose to introduce new disclosure obligations to investors. This became necessary not at least because, as POSNER put it:

> To the economist, [. . .], the coalescence of ownership and control is not a necessary condition of efficient performance.[218]

The disclosure obligations had the purpose to discipline the economist by at least increasing transparency and predictability. Beneficial ownership can be seen as a typical example of such missing coalescence of ownership and control. It thus had to be captured by the SEC Act. Circuit Judge Kaufman of the 2nd Circuit Court commented this endeavor:

> [. . .] at the legal outset, we are not confronted with the relatively simple concept of legal title, but rather with the amorphous and occasionally obfuscated concepts of indirect and beneficial ownership which pervade the securities acts.[219]

---

213 47 F.2d 184; see also Powerex Corp. v. Reliant Energy Services, Inc. 551 U.S. 224 (2007) (Breyer, J. dissenting) (explicitly mentioning beneficial ownership and control).

214 *See* also: Bath Industries, Inc. v. Blot, 427 F 2d 112 (7th Cir.1970); GAF Corp. v. Milstein, 453F 2d 712 (2nd Cir.1971).

215 47 F.2d 185.

216 *Id.*

217 15 U.S.C. § 78m(d).

218 POSNER, ECONOMIC ANALYSIS OF LAW, 181.

219 GAF Corporation v. Paul Milstein et al. 543 F. 2d 709, 713 (1971); see also AMP Inc. v. Allied-Signal Corp, 168 F.3d 649 (3rd Cir.1999) (providing a vivid example of such obfuscation by qualifying beneficial ownership as "outright ownership").

SUMMARY: Beneficial ownership was not defined in *Handy & Harman*. However, the case discusses the control aspect of beneficial ownership as a typical element of securities law that has become and still is extensively regulated.

6. Chicago, Milwaukee & St. Paul Railway Company v. Des Moines Union Railway Company[220]

This case involves a dispute between several railroad companies (complainants) and a company which was incorporated to run the operations of a railroad terminal in Des Moines (defendant). As regards the legal ownership, the complainants held the minority shares while Messrs. Hubbel and a Mr. Dodge,[221] officers and directors of the railroad companies, held a majority of five eighths of the shares. As regards the beneficial ownership situation,

> Complainants assert that they are the sole beneficial owners, having an equitable tenancy in common, and being entitled to the joint use of the property in perpetuity, [...][222]

The railroad companies base their sole beneficial ownership on an agreement concluded amongst them in 1882. In that agreement, the complainants contend that the terminal company was incorporated to hold the terminal property in trust as trustee for the railroad companies. The 1882 agreement contained detailed provisions regarding the concrete responsibilities for the operation of the terminal such as the organization of police control, supervision and maintenance, wheelage, spur tracks, and connection of the terminal with factories in the city.

The terminal company was incorporated in 1884 and the articles of the company recited the 1882 agreement details in full. The terminal company was organized as a "depot company" charged with the operation of the terminal. The 1884 articles also contained details about the share capital to be issued. Finally, the articles also provided that some fundamental decisions needed not only the approval of three-fourths of the shareholders, but also required consent of the railroad companies. The operational control shifted through the years from the railroad companies to the terminal company. At the beginning of that shift was the "financial embarrassment" of one of the railroad companies and concluded with the terminal company taking full charge of the operation of the terminal in 1888. Along with that development, the Hubbells acquired more and more shares in the terminal company until they became majority shareholders.

Their growing power and influence in the terminal company lead the Hubbells to insist that

[220] 254 U.S. 198 (1920).

[221] Dodge's legal position is not different from the Hubbells. So whenever the Hubbells are mentioned below, this will also imply to include Dodge.

[222] *Chicago, Milwaukee*, 254 U.S. at 200.

> [. . .] the proprietary [railroad] companies have lost their right to control the action of the terminal company, the Messrs. Hubbel as stockholders are entitled to control it and to have dividends out of its profits [. . .][223]

In essence, the Hubbells sought to use their powerful position in the terminal company to become legally and financially emancipated from the railroad companies. The railroad companies, unimpressed by this claim for independence and profits, claimed that the trust relationship with them as beneficiaries and the terminal company as trustee outweighed any corporate arrangements within the terminal company. The Court concurred with that view, stating that the shareholding was subordinate to the trust relationship which "dominated" all property interests in the terminal company. The stage thus being set with these facts. The question now arises, what role beneficial ownership plays on it.

Throughout the opinion on *Chicago Milwaukee*, the Supreme Court used the term *beneficial ownership* in several passages. The court also used the trust law terms *cestui que trust*[224] and *beneficiary*.[225] A consistency in the use of these three terms cannot be immediately discerned. Taking a closer look, the term *beneficial ownership* appears to subtly hint to the economic aspect of the trust arrangement, i.e. the joint investment of the railroad companies in a railroad terminal shared amongst each other, a leading theme throughout the entire decision. Each time the share of profit on the terminal is in focus, the term *beneficial ownership* or the more abstract term, *beneficial interest*, seems to be the preferred choice. When the focus is on the legal structure of the arrangement, the term *beneficiary* or its older synonym *cestui(s) que trust(ent)* is preferred.

The creation of a trust amongst the railroad companies with the terminal company as the trustee was another leading theme in *Chicago, Milwaukee & St. Paul Railway co. et al.* The court held that this creation of the trust did not depend on any "particular form of words", or, as Hudson put it: "there is no form of abracadabra that will bring the trust into existence",[226] so long as "reasonable certainty as to the property, the objects, and the beneficiaries"[227] were clear. This certainty was there since the property was with the railroad companies, the object was the terminal, and the beneficiaries were the railroad companies. The Court also did not consider later modifications of the arrangement regarding, e.g., the structure and financial basis of the terminal company, as a hindrance to the "continuance of

[223] *Id.* at 212; see also National Bank v. Insurance Co. *infra* Sect. 12 of this chapter.

[224] *Chicago, Milwaukee*, 254 at 220, 222.

[225] *Id.* at 208; the use of the latter two may be best explained with the statement from Hudson that "the tendency of [not only] English lawyers, to have more than one name for the same concept – arguably because it helps to maintain the mystique of the law and to ensure that the clients are sufficiently impressed by their counsel's knowledge of so much complicated terminology." Hudson, Equity And Trusts 14.

[226] Hudson, Equity And Trusts 31.

[227] 254 U.S. 196, 196, citing Colton v. Colton, 127 U.S. 310 (1888) (highlighting the psycho-economical motivation to provide for a beneficiary); Hudson, Equity And Trusts 47 f.; Uniform Trust Code Art. 4 § 402.

the trust."[228] Neither the changes of the beneficiaries in the trust.[229] nor organizational changes in the terminal companies[230] had a relevant impact on the trust's existence.[231] The Supreme Court summarized this by stating that

> from the very nature and terms of the trust, all the property and franchises of the terminal company were to be held for the benefit of the proprietary [i.e. the railroad] companies.[232]

The Court admitted that the Hubbells' and Dodge's shareholding in the terminal company entitled them, on the one hand, to participate in the benefits of the trust,[233] but, on the other hand, the profits from the terminal company presented no standalone value outside the trust arrangement. The "magnitude" of the stockholding was, under these circumstances, irrelevant. The Court also stated that the Hubbells and Dodge who served all as officers and directors of the terminal company were fully aware of their fiduciary obligations towards the trust regardless of their shareholding increasing over the years. In conclusion, the Supreme Court clearly gave the contractual agreements between the parties second priority. The main priority was with the trust arrangement.

SUMMARY: *Chicago, Milwaukee & St. Paul Railway* is a case about a business enterprise with competing corporate and trust law claims. Similar to the *Handy & Harman* case, *beneficial ownership* is an economically relevant but legally irrelevant element. Additionally, this case is the first case that could be found that clearly differentiates between *beneficial owners* and *beneficiaries*.

7. Montana Catholic Missions v. Missoula County[234]/ Bothwell v. Bingham County[235]

a) Significance

Montana Catholic Missions v. Missoula County is by far the most frequently quoted decision regarding beneficial ownership. This justifies an even more detailed analysis of this case. *Montana Catholic Missions* is mainly a tax law case not

---

[228] *Chicago, Milwaukee*, 254 U.S. at 209.

[229] The Court mentioned the composition of the beneficiaries *en passant* without giving it any further attention.

[230] *Id.* at 216 ("It is plain enough, and is conceded that the corporation could not, by merely altering its own internal organization, affect the interest of the *cestus que sent.*")

[231] For the change of beneficial ownership see also Jackson v. McIntosh, 12 F.2d 676, 1926; *In re Estate of McKim*, 111 N.M. 517, (1991).

[232] *Id.* at 210.

[233] *Id.*

[234] 200 U.S. 118 (1905).

[235] 237 U.S. 642 (1915).

dealing with federal Indian law topics directly.[236] Its generic nature (no specific federal Indian law terms are used), has made Montana Catholic Missions easily applicable to various fields of law:[237]

> The expression beneficial use or beneficial ownership, or interest is quite frequent in the law, and means in this connection such a right to its enjoyment as exists where the legal title is in one person and the right to such beneficial use or interest is in another, and where such a right is recognized by law, and can be enforced by the courts, at the suit of such owner or of someone in his behalf.[238]

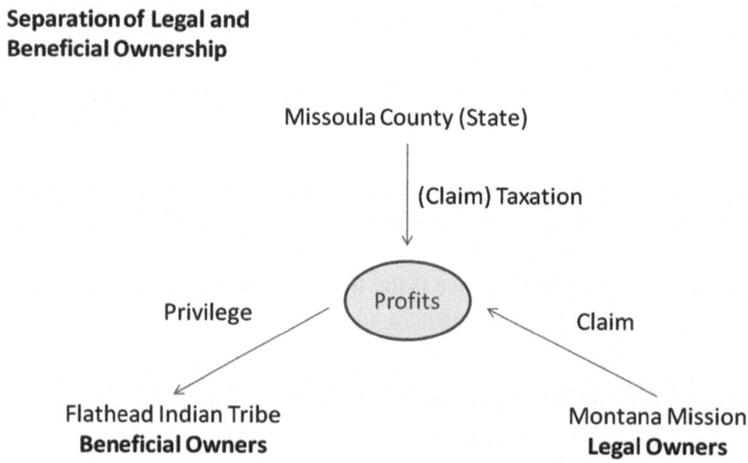

b) Facts

A Mission of Jesuits (hereinafter *the Mission*) ran a cattle farm. The proceeds of the farm were used for charitable purposes. The main purposes were the improvement and the education of the Flathead Indian's ('the Flatheads') reservation. The Mission was even appropriated government funds for these purposes. The State

[236] *Montana Catholic Missions*, 200 U.S. at 127.

[237] E.g. tax law (Portland General Electric, 237 Mont. 324; 773 P.2d, 1189 (1989)) or family and social security law (Christiansen v. Department of Social Security, Wn.2d 465, 131 P.2d 827 (1942); see generally WARDLE & NOLAN, FUNDAMENTAL PRINCIPLES OF FAMILY LAW 420 (2nd ed. 2006); Harrison v. Missoula, 146 Mont. 420; 407 P. 2d 89 (1965) (discussing public annexation of community property).

[238] *Montana Catholic Missions*, 200 U.S. at 128; see Portland General Electric Company v. Montana Dep't of Revenue, 237 Mont. 77; 773 P. 2d 1189 (1989) (containing an almost identical definition).

of Montana levied taxes on the profits of the cattle farm. When the Mission refused to pay these taxes, the State threatened to seize and sell part of the cattle. Caving in under that pressure, the Mission paid the taxes but then went to court to claim for recovery. The main argument of the Mission was that, since the Flatheads were the beneficial owners of the profits of the cattle farm, these profits were not subject to taxation "by or under state authority."[239] The Supreme Court, though "cordially" recognizing the charitable merit of the Mission, refused jurisdiction based on the ground that nothing in the case referred to the breach of either federal law or the federal constitution.

Apart from the above, *Montana* is a straight forward tax case. The Flatheads are the beneficial owners of the profits in focus. As such, they do not appear in court as a separate party to this tax litigation. In that sense, the Flatheads are mere bystanders. The outcome may have an economic effect on the Flatheads if the Mission has to pay taxes on the profits of the cattle farm, it will have less funds available to contribute to the Flatheads. However, there is no direct *legal* and particularly no property law effect that the Flatheads could experience. Simply put, the case is about whether the Mission has a duty to pay taxes on the profits of the cattle farm or not. The Flatheads are not legally affected by this. This fact is worth highlighting because, as has been and will be shown, it is typical for the status of beneficial owners that they are not involved in the strict legal aspects.

But what role does the beneficial ownership of the Flatheads play in resolving this case? Why does the Supreme Court find it necessary to generically define beneficial ownership?

The Mission argues that the profits from their cattle farm are solely used for charity, i.e. the Mission voluntarily does not claim these profits for its own purposes but donates them to the Flatheads.

c) *Definition of Beneficial Ownership*

The Flatheads are the only party that benefits from the profits of the cattle farm. In other words, the Flatheads beneficially own the profits. The parties do not disagree on the status of the Flatheads as beneficial owners. They instead disagree on the legal consequences of that status. The Mission claims that the status of the Flatheads as beneficial owners is not different from the status of "regular" owners with property vested in the profits. As the attorney for the plaintiff points out: "The case comes under the rule that property of Indians is not taxable by the State."[240]

---

[239] *Montana Catholic Missions*, 200 U.S. at 127.

[240] *Montana Catholic Missions*, 200 U.S. at 129 with further references; see also *infra* chapter "The Beneficial Ownership Concept Applied in Federal Indian Law", Sect. 4c).

aa) Right to Enjoyment

The above makes clear that the character of beneficial ownership is crucial to this case: If beneficial ownership is identical to ownership, then there is no taxability. If beneficial ownership is a type of ownership *sui generis*, then taxability may be given. The field is now prepared for an analysis of the Supreme Court's definition of beneficial ownership.

Regarding the interpretation of *right*, reference can be made to the extensive study in chapter "Beneficial Ownership as a Concept".[241] The term 'right' is used in this context in its general meaning as an abstract entitlement[242] and not as a concrete claim.[243] The present right is a right *in personam* (*certam sive determinatam*) as far as its companion the Mission is concerned. The right of the Flathead Indians ("the Flatheads") can be qualified as a privilege. The tribe is entitled to enjoy but has no duty *not* to enjoy the charitable contributions of the Mission. Correlatively, the Flatheads have no legal (although maybe a moral claim) against the Mission, e.g., to reach a certain level of education or develop the reservation to a certain extent. This legal disposition of the Flatheads is important to understand the underlying reasoning of the court. That the court consciously pondered on the Hohfeldian incidents is impossible because the decision predates HOHFELD's Fundamental Conceptions by over a decade. Nevertheless, a certain unarticulated hint to these upcoming conceptions can be detected as the analysis continues. By analyzing and defining beneficial ownership, the court discerns between regular claims and this peculiar kind of ownership that is qualified as *beneficial*.

Neither in dispute is the content of the right, the enjoyment. Generally, enjoyment is defined as the consumption of the beneficial use. The term *possession* is chosen here intentionally because the term *ownership* would insinuate a more powerful position of the Flatheads. Such beneficial use includes the right to profit and income there-from. The Supreme Court does not define enjoyment on such an abstract level. It just mentions what the enjoyment consists of in the concrete case: the consumption of the profits of the Mission's cattle farm for the purpose of education and reservation improvements. Since the content of the *enjoyment* is not in dispute, the court does not look deeper into this topic although such analysis and the conclusions thereof would be very helpful to answer the question as to what degree the enjoyment has to consist of in order to qualify as (tax free) property.

The entitlement of the Indians to enjoy the profits is not in dispute either. The Mission not only logically acknowledges the Flathead's entitlement to the profits of the cattle farm, but it even uses the Flathead's entitlement as the main argument against taxability. The core question thus remains whether a right of enjoyment sufficiently establishes a form of property which is out of reach of state taxation

---

[241] *See supra* chapter "Beneficial Ownership as a Concept", Sect. 2.

[242] Stanford Encyclopedia, http://plato.stanford.edu/entries/rights, 1.

[243] *Id.* at 4.

since "it is familiar law that a state has no power to tax the property of the United States within its limits.[244]"

bb) Recognized by Law

As a basis for a recognizable claim, the case mentions the Constitution, a treaty, a statute, property, or a contract.[245] The attorney for the Mission contends that "when federal jurisdiction is invoked on account of legislation claimed to impair the obligation of a contract"; there is no need to prove the existence of one of the five bases mentioned above. According to the Mission's attorney, it would suffice to simply prove an interest of the Indians.[246] The court disagrees, criticizing the attorney for not having mentioned any constitutional, treaty, or statutory provision that would be applicable to the rule contended by him. The court considers the case to be "simply a claim that the plaintiff is exempt from taxation on the cattle which it owns, because it is an institution of purely public charity [. . .]."[247] That simplicity of the case brings the court to the conclusion that the plaintiff was not able to establish any legally recognizable entitlement of the Flatheads to the profits:

> Taking the complaint as it is, it shows on its face that the Indians have neither any legal nor equitable title to the property, neither have they any legal or equitable right to beneficial use, [. . .].[248]

The court considers *equitable* or *legal title* on the profits as conditional to legal recognition. If the Flatheads had a right to the profits, they would have such title, but they do not for the simple reason that the Mission has no duty to donate its profits to the Flatheads: "The Plaintiff might refuse to spend another dollar upon the reservations [of the Flatheads][249]" and would face no legal consequences by doing so. Back to Hohfeld, the Flatheads may not have a duty to not enjoy the profits, but they also have no right to claim from the Mission what the Mission gives voluntarily. The Flatheads, in Hohfeld's terms, possess the *privilege* but not the right or *claim* to enjoy the proceeds given by the Mission. This situation of the Flatheads is characteristic for the situation of beneficial owners. They are entirely dependent on

---

[244] Wisconsin Central Railroad v. Price County, 133 U.S. 496, 504 (1889); see also the discussion of Bryan v. Itasca County, 426 U.S. 373 (1976), *infra* chapter "The Beneficial Ownership Concept Applied in Federal Indian Law", Sect. 4c).

[245] For the role and nature of recognized Indian as opposed to (not recognized) aboriginal title see *infra* chapter "The Beneficial Ownership Concept Applied in Federal Indian Law", Sect. 3a).

[246] The case law the attorney refers to is Railroad Company v. Citizens' Company, 166 U.S. 557 (1897) (contract); Bridge Proprietors v. Hoboken, 68 U.S. 116 (1 Wall.) (1863) (contract); McCollough v. Commonwealth, 176 U.S. 102, 118 (1898) (Constitution, treaty, statute). He does not mention any case law regarding property in that context.

[247] *Montana Catholic Missions*, 200 U.S. at 132.

[248] *Id.* at 135.

[249] *Id.* at 136.

their benefactor's goodwill. They can enjoy another's generosity but they cannot claim for it. Once the well runs dry, beneficial owners enjoy no legal protection.

cc) Enforceable by Beneficial Owner or Someone on Her Behalf

It is helpful to first remember the wording of the case at this point:

> Such a right [i.e. a "right" of beneficial ownership] is recognized by law, and can be enforced by the courts, at the suit of such owner or of someone in his behalf[250]

Beneficial use or interest is recognized by law and enforceable by a court. This leads to a Catch-22 situation. Beneficial ownership is only recognized if enforceable, but enforceability needs a right. The catch is that a right that is recognized by law is based on a *legal* and not on a *factual* title. As the *Montana* definition suggests, beneficial ownership appears in a situation where legal and factual title have to be distinguished. The beneficial owner is clearly the person holding the factual title. This leads to the conclusion that the beneficial owner's position will never be vested with an enforceable claim in a court of law except that the beneficial owner also disposes of a legal title. Once beneficial ownership is enforceable it ceases to be a mere factual entitlement. This dilemma will be further explored and resolved below under *National Bank v. Insurance Corp.*[251] What can already be determined at this point is that beneficial entitlements may not be enforceable directly, but indirectly. With this in mind, the position of the Flatheads and the Mission needs to be analyzed.

As stated above, the Flatheads are neither a party to the case at hand, nor are they represented by a third party on their behalf. As shown above, the Flatheads have no *claim* to receive the profits of the Mission's cattle business. They only have the *privilege* to enjoy the profits so long as they are voluntarily distributed to them by the Mission. The Mission, in turn, cannot legally represent the Flatheads not only because they have not been appointed, but because the *causa* is not directly legally related to the Flatheads. The plaintiff of the Mission tries to construe an agency relationship between the federal government and the Mission, claiming that the Mission was carrying out government duties. He refers to previous federal government appropriations for the cause of the Jesuit's efforts to educate the Indians. Again, the Supreme Court disagrees: "Congress has not constituted this corporation [i.e. the Mission] an agency of its own. [. . .] and even such appropriations ceased years ago."[252] Therefore the Mission, for lack of government assignment, does not enjoy state tax privileges.

---

[250] *Montana Catholic Missions*, 200 U.S. at 128.

[251] 104 U.S. 54 (1881); see *infra* Sect. 12.

[252] *Montana Catholic Missions*, 200 U.S. 138.

dd) Separation of Beneficial Use and Legal Title

The separation between beneficial use and legal title is the core element of beneficial ownership.[253] It is that peculiar split between two aspects of property which are normally united in one person, as LEFF so captivatingly describes:

> Most property, of course is held both legally and beneficially, i.e., the person with the title also has the right to use and enjoyment. Indeed so much is that taken for granted that it would be odd to describe the owner of a fee simple interest in real property as the "beneficial owner," or to say that he has the "beneficial enjoyment" [. . .]; he is just the owner and that he owns it for himself is just assumed.[254]

In this regard tax law and federal Indian law are an exception. The assumption of beneficial and fee simple ownership rests in one person must not be generalized in either of these two fields of law. There are cases in federal Indian law where beneficial and legal ownership are united in one person. In the case of *United States v. Sandoval*, for instance, the right of Pueblo Indians was recognized as fee simple ownership and thus united with the beneficial ownership.[255] In a more recent case, *City of Sherrill v. Oneida Indians*,[256] regular property status was even recognized against the will of the affected Indian tribe (the reason behind the Oneida's unwillingness to be recognized as regular land-owners lays in the tax exemption that Indian title holders enjoy).[257] But the rule remains that federal Indian law separates beneficial ownership from fee simple and allocates it to the Indians leaving fee simple with the government. This is one of the sources of all the conceptual questions surrounding beneficial ownership. As has been demonstrated on several occasions, a long non-linear history of precedents has made beneficial ownership even perceivable. The beneficial use in the case at hand is not hard to manifest and locate. The beneficial use is in the enjoyment of the support of the Mission. The decision lists an impressive amount of concrete objects which have been built by the Mission (at least partially) with the proceeds of the cattle farm: school buildings with dormitories, a blacksmith shop, a wagon shop, printing office, saddler shop, shoe shops, bakeries, and other shops of like character. It appears that a common community infrastructure has been built and made available by the Mission for the Flatheads. With regard to legal title the Court states

---

[253] Wolfchild v. United States, 559 F. 3rd 1228, n.5 (Fed. Cir.2009).

[254] Leff, *The Leff Dictionary of Law: A Fragment*, 94 YALE L.J., 2149 (1985).

[255] 231 U.S. 28 (1913) (recognizing fee simple title of the Pueblos because such title had been previously recognized by the Mexican Government); see also United States v. Candelaria, 271 U.S. 432 (1926) (upholding recognition yet restricting the right to alienate fee land, arguing that identical restrictions had already been applied under Mexican government).

[256] 544 U.S. 197 (2005); see also County of Yakima v. Confederated Tribes and Bands of Yakima Nation, (502 U.S. 251 (1992) (discussing taxability of repurchased land); Cass County Joint Waters Resource District v. 1.43 Acres of Land, 643 N.W. 2d 685 (ND 2002) (discussing state jurisdiction over land purchased by an Indian tribe in fee).

[257] *See generally* for the (state) taxability Bryan v. Itasca County, 426 U.S. 373 (1976), discussed *infra* in chapter "The Beneficial Ownership Concept Applied in Federal Indian Law", Sect. 4b).

> That prior to 1895 all property [. . .] was conveyed to the plaintiff herein, to hold the same in trust for the said Jesuit Fathers, and by such conveyance it now has the legal title to all of the cattle acquired by the said Jesuit Fathers on the said reservation and the increase thereof.[258]

What can be concluded from this is that regardless of all these extensions and improvements of the mission station in the beneficial interest of the Flatheads, the mission retained legal ownership and thus liable for the taxes.

ee) Beneficial Ownership Ad Interim

Montana Catholic Missions also refers to another situation where beneficial ownership comes into play by quoting *Central Pacific Railroad v. United States*,[259] a tax case which does not specifically mention or deal with beneficial ownership, but with the temporary taxability of possessory rights in land (Fig. 1).

> And one is also said to have the beneficial ownership of land who has done everything to entitle him to a patent from the government, and who therefore has the legal right to such patent, and all that remains to be done is for the proper officer to issue it.[260]

While in the previous definition, two parties, i.e. the de facto (beneficial) and the de jure (legal)] owner, are involved, this definition involves a single party who, in the course of time, legally transforms from a de facto into a de jure owner. Beneficial ownership is only a transition status between lack of title (patent) and the full title. The court does not elaborate on the legal implications of that interim status. It doesn't have to, because this kind of beneficial ownership clearly does not apply to the *Montana* case, which deals with two parties who are clearly identified as beneficial and legal owner respectively. Neither is there a time component nor a condition involved in *Montana*.[261] Instead, the Court refers to *Wisconsin Central Railroad v. Price County*,[262] and to *Central Pacific Railroad Co. v. Nevada*.[263] It is no coincidence that these two precedents involve railroad companies. Railroad construction did not only have an impact on the physical, but also on the legal landscape. Parcels of land were sold to the railroad construction companies and, at the same time, land patents were granted by the government to "encourage the settlement of the country."[264] These two elements of the government strategy would create issues between the property of railroad companies, private settlers, the states, and the government, but, of course, also tax issues. Both cases discuss the

---

258 *Montana Catholic Missions*, 200 U.S. at 124.

259 162 U.S. 512 (1896).

260 *Montana Catholic Missions*, 200 U.S. at 128.

261 In *Wolfchild v. United States*, 559 F. 3rd 1228 (Fed. Cir.2009), (mentioning *temporary occupancy* pending future legislation without further elaborating or even differentiating between occupancy and beneficial ownership).

262 133 U.S. 496 (1889).

263 162 U.S. 512 (1886).

264 *Id.* at. 508 (citing Winona & St. Peter Railroad Co. v. Barney, 113 U.S. 618, 625 (1885)).

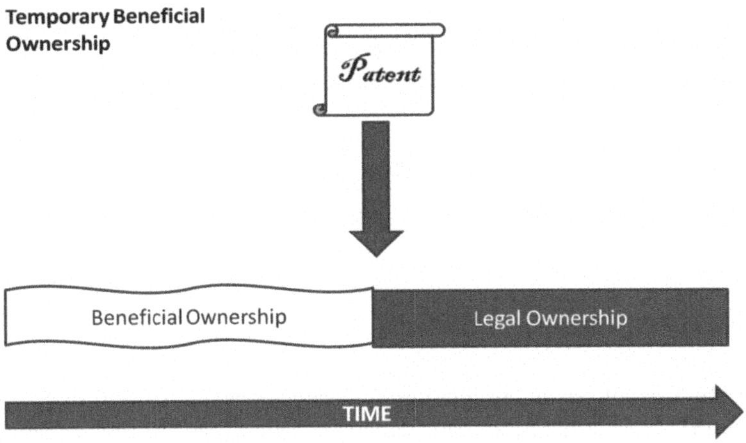

Fig. 1 Transition from Beneficial to Legal Ownership

taxability of certain categories of railroad land. The *Wisconsin* case speaks of an "a float"[265] status of the landownership. Like *Montana*, the railroad cases define the ownership status during that interim phase as beneficial ownership. The state of limbo between one legal situation and another provides the perfect soil for beneficial ownership.

The case *Bothwell v. Bingham County*[266] also deals with beneficial ownership as a temporary condition. In this tax law case, the United States sold a tract of land to the plaintiff Bothwell, which the County of Bingham, Idaho, levied taxes upon despite the fact that the government had not yet issued the patent that would constitute legal ownership on that land to Bothwell. Bothwell thus claimed mere beneficial ownership. The Supreme Court decided against the plaintiff, holding that:

> Where proceedings to acquire title to public land have reached the point where nothing remains to be done by the entryman[267] [*in casu* Bothwell] [. . .] the entryman is regarded as the beneficial owner and the land is subject to taxation.[268]

This case does not differ from the railroad cases discussed above. The fact that beneficial ownership was transferred from the United States to Bingham, leaving the former with only "the naked title",[269] is regarded a sufficient reason to derive legal consequences, i.e. taxability. The Supreme Court bases this on several precedents, including the *Wisconsin Railroad* case discussed above. These

---

[265] *Id.* at 509.

[266] 237 U.S. 642.

[267] "Entryman" is the technical term for a person who seeks to acquire public land.

[268] 237 U.S. 642, 642; see also Leff, *The Leff Dictionary of Law*, 94 Yale L. Rev. 2149 (1985).

[269] *Id.* at 647; for *naked title* see *infra* Sect. 8.

precedents are concerned with the conditions that have to be met to cause taxability without going into any details about the property law aspects.[270]

SUMMARY: Beneficial ownership can be used to describe a situation where legal ownership is in one person while the right (privilege) to enjoyment is in another (*Montana*). Beneficial ownership is also used to describe an "a float" status, an interim phase where fee is about to be achieved (*Bothwell*) and, more importantly, is nonetheless already subject to taxation.

8. Wells v. Savannah[271]

In 1790, the City of Savannah, Georgia, needed money. To fulfill that need, she auctioned off some of her real estate called "common lots" to private purchasers. The city offered various methods to pay for the auctioned lots. Apart from straight cash payments, a purchaser was also offered to

> agree with the city to pay in cash the balance of his bid over to valuation, called the increase money, and also to pay a ground rent of five percent upon the amount of valuation, payable quarterly.[272]

The payment method of interest in this case was the ground rent method. The class of purchasers that chose the ground rent payment method retained the lots so long as they, their heirs, or assigns paid the ground rent. The ground rent purchasers were also given the opportunity to buy out the lot by paying a sum to be determined by the leftover rent and the original valuation money. Should the ground renters fail to pay the rent, the community gained the power of "re-entry" into the lot. For almost 100 years, such arrangements were made between the city and many purchasers. As a particular incentive to enter a ground rent agreement with the city, no taxes were levied on the ground rent lots for decades. When the city changed its mind in 1878 and issued an ordinance which decreed the taxability of the ground rent lots, the ground renters went to court. The ground renters submitted committee reports of the city, deeds and witness statements that were to prove that their lots were not subject to city tax. They claimed for the 1878 ordinance to be declared void. Not all too impressed by the evidence put forward, Georgia Supreme Court Justice Peckham stated:

---

[270] *See* Witherspoon v. Duncan, 71 U.S. 210 (discussing original taxability of public lands once registered with ("entered at") the land office and a "certificate of entry" has been obtained); In Carroll v. Safford, 44 U.S. (3 How.) 441, 441 (1845) (holding that payment for the land accompanied with the necessary certification constitutes taxability, "although a patent has not yet been issued"); In Hussman v. Durham, 165 U.S. 144 f. (1897) (holding that legal and beneficial ("equitable") ownership remained with the government with the result that there was no passing of "tax title"); Bothwell v. Bingham, see *supra* Sect. 7c).

[271] 181 U.S. 532 (1901).

[272] *Wells, id.*

> The facts proved must show either a contract expressed in terms or else it must be implied from facts which leave no room for doubt that such was the intention of the parties and that a valid consideration existed for the contract. If there be any doubt on these matters, the contract has not been proven and the [tax] exemption does not exist.[273]

The judge considered the evidence submitted as insufficient. Neither was he receptive for the plaintiff's arguments regarding the interpretation of the language of certain city tax documents. For the judge it was also clear that the city's behavior was not a kind of *venire contra factum proprium*:

> Mere nonuser by a government of its power to levy tax, it matters not for how long it continued, can never be construed as a forfeiture of the power.[274]

Finally, the ground renters argued that their agreement with the city was a lease rather than a contract over the sale of property with the consequence that the property was still with the city and could therefore not be taxed. The Court did not agree for several reasons. For one, the possibility of the purchasers to still buy their lots even once they entered a ground rent agreement proved that their entitlement exceeded the rights granted in a regular lease contract. Furthermore, the city's right of reentry in case of failure on the ground renter's side to pay the rent had no bearing on the taxability. The Court held that their right was "in substance that of ownership." In addition to these considerations, the Court quoted over two pages of the opinion of Chief Justice BLECKLEY of the Georgia Supreme Court, the lower court entrusted with this case.[275] This unusually long quote was justified by its content.[276] Regarding the lease issue, Judge BLECKLEY added:

> The value of property consists in its use, and he who owns the use forever, [. . .], is the true owner of the property for the time being. This holds equally of a city lot or of all the land in the world.[277]

The emphasis here is on *use* and *value*. The term *use* is a long established term in the common law reaching back even further than the origins of trust law.[278] In a trust situation, the beneficiary has the use while another person has the legal title. As this case is not dealing with a trust, the term *use* can be taken for what it is in its most common form, the enjoyment of and profit from a thing. The judge's deliberations on the *value* of the property explain this. Naturally, corporeal property like the ground rent lots has a certain value. The value is a decisive element here because the State of Georgia taxes *ad valorem*, meaning that taxability is connected

---

[273] *Id.* at 539 f.

[274] *Id.*

[275] *Wells*, 181 U.S. 531, 546 with further references.

[276] *See* also Wright v. Central Georgia Railway Company, 236 U.S. 674 (1915), in which Justice HOLMES uses parts of the same quote.

[277] *Wells*, 181 U.S. at 545.

[278] It originates in the Latin *ad opus*; HUDSON, EQUITY AND TRUSTS 14.

to the person who "sustains the losses of depreciation in value, and [...] takes the benefit of appreciation."[279] In other words, the person who owns the risk of appreciation or depreciation of the corporeal property is liable for the taxes. The flexible value of the property thus stood in contrast with the fix rental fee and the fixed purchase price of the lots. As has been shown, the flexible value of the lots stayed with the ground renters while the city had only a claim for the fixed amounts (rent, purchase price). A lessee by definition does not bear the value risk of the property she rents. It is by definition the owner who bears that risk. The contractual agreement between the city and ground renters clearly provides for the former to bear the value risk of the ground lots which makes the renters the owners.

Beneficial ownership was used here by the ground renters to construe the city's participation in the value of the ground rent lots. If the city participated in the value of the ground rent lots, taxing the ground renters would be hard to justify. The city would receive rent and tax money on the same lot from the ground renters. The city would reach beneficial owner status, and

> Whoever beneficially owns the value must pay the taxes. This rule is without exception.[280]

But the Judge would not accept this argument. He writes,

> Not an iota of beneficial ownership in the city lots now in question abides in the municipality.[281]

The judge further held that the city had but the naked title on the lots, and the only purpose of the lots was to serve as security.

> The city but retained a qualified and wholly unproductive title as security for the purchase money, and until that shall be paid, as security also for the annually accruing compensation under the name of ground rents in lieu of interest on that money.[282]

The term *naked* or *bare* legal title appears quite frequently in cases which mention beneficial ownership.[283] It is used to describe the position of the party or entity which does *not* beneficially own the object of property but also, as in this case at hand, remains legally inactive for a specific reason.[284]

SUMMARY: The *Wells v. Savannah* case adds an economical aspect to the beneficial ownership concept; the participation in the value of the property. There

---

[279] *Wells*, *id.* at 545.

[280] *Wells*, *id.*; this holding was revised in Montana Catholic Missions v. Missoula County only four years later.

[281] *Id.* at 546.

[282] *Id.*

[283] First State Bank v. United States, 92 F.2d 132 (9th Cir.1937); Guaranty Trust Co. v. Atlantic C. E.R. Co, 138 F. 517 (9th Cir.1905); Aurbach v. Gallina, 753 So. 2d 60, 62 (Fla. 2000) (stating that "mere naked title could repose in one entity but 'beneficial ownership' on another"); Farmers' & Mechanics National Bank v. King, 57 Pa. 202, (1868) ("*naked legal right* with the beneficial ownership in another"); In re Estate of Massouras, 16 Wis. 2d 304, 312, 114 N.W.2d 449 (1962).

[284] Compare with *Handy & Harman*, see *supra* Sect. 5, in which the reason, similar to here was that the property was used merely as a security.

was the special contractual arrangement of the parties with its complex combination of contractual and property claims (auction, rent, sale, security) and municipal entitlements (taxes, re-entry). But at the end the deciding element was the Georgian tax law with its *ad valorem* approach. The U.S. Supreme Court brushed all the arguments of the ground renters aside and decided for their tax liability by determining the ground renters as the beneficial owners of the taxable property. What constituted the ground renters as beneficial owners was, in the Court's opinion, the fact that they bore the value risk of their lots.

9. Union Stock Yards Bank v. Gillespie[285]

The deliberations of the Supreme Court on beneficial ownership in this decision are entirely based on *National Bank v. Insurance Company*,[286] a case which will be discussed in detail below. There is, however, one *obiter dictum* of the Court that is noteworthy:

> The right of an owner of property is not limited to the property itself, but extends to everything which is its direct product or proceeds.[287]

In all the case material that was reviewed, no articulation of the origin of beneficial ownership as concise and comprehensive could be found. The most prominent definition of beneficial ownership in *Montana Catholic Missions v. Missoula County*[288] is in essence based on this separation between "property itself" and "its direct product or proceeds."[289] The qualification of the enjoyment of direct product and proceeds is not further analyzed in this case.

10. Drexel v. Berney[290]

A Mr. Robert Berney, the decedent, a U.S. citizen, married to Louise Berney, a French citizen, died in Paris, France in 1874. Amongst other assets, the decedent left stocks and bonds kept safe in New York, London, and Paris.

---

[285] 137 U.S. 411 (1890).

[286] 104 U.S. 54.

[287] 137 U.S. 414.

[288] 200 U.S. 118.

[289] In the case itself, the Supreme Court Justice Brewer quickly added that this dictum did "not represent the questions involved in this case, [and] a more detailed statement of the facts is requisite." Quid hoc? One almost gets the impression that the Judge himself was so impressed by the ingenious sentence he had just created that he worried to lose the focus on the case at hand. Whatever the motivation behind this statement and its immediately following play down was, the brilliancy remains.

[290] 122 U.S. 241 (1887).

In his will and an amendment thereto, a *codicil*, dated from the year of his death, the decedent had bequeathed his estate to several executors of his will: Louise Berney (the widow), James Berney (his brother), Messier de St. James (a French citizen), and two other persons who did not play a prominent role in the case. The executrix and the executors were to create a trust of the decedent's residuary estate and serve as trustees. The widow (executrix) and other family members, mainly nieces and nephews of the decedent, were to be the beneficiaries.

After her husband's death, Louise Berney, the executrix, presented the will to the proper authorities in France and a notary was appointed. A few months later and "before anything else was done",[291] James Berney also submitted the will and *codicil* to the proper court in Montgomery, Alabama. The court assumed full jurisdiction over the case and decreed that the decedent was a resident of Alabama. The court also named James Berney to be the sole executor of the decedent's estate. In his newly acquired position as sole executor, James Berney gave Messier de St. James, a French lawyer, the power of attorney to start the liquidation of the overseas property of the decedent. Louise Berney and the other heirs were fully aware of the actions of James Berney and did not oppose. The purpose of these actions was to "secure immunity of the decedent's estate from taxation in France."[292]

The asset of particular interest in the case is a transaction involving a large single position of $200,000 in U.S. registered bonds deposited in London, England. Louise and James arranged with the help of St. James to have these registered bonds converted into bearer bonds. This transaction was facilitated via an agent in London and Drexel, a New York bank, the appellant in this case under the supervision of St. James. Drexel converted the bonds as instructed by St. James and transferred the proceeds to him, but St. James "had converted the coupons to his own use." The executors on behalf of the heirs filed a lawsuit which eventually resulted in a full discharge of St. James. St. James died shortly afterwards.

With St. James dead and discharged[293] but with the heirs still not in possession of the $200,000,[294] Louise and her "confederated" relatives now filed suit against Drexel, the New York bank that was involved in the bond transaction. They claimed that the Alabama probate decision and all the appointments and decrees based on it were invalid, because the decedent was domiciled in France and, hence, French law should be applied and the courts of France should have jurisdiction over the case. The intention behind this was clear: if the wrong court decided over the inheritance, all the transactions that followed based on that decision would be void, including the bond transaction carried out by Drexel. Drexel could thus be held liable for having paid out the proceeds of the bond transaction to St. James with no legal

---

[291] *Id.* at 244.

[292] *Id.*

[293] *Drexel*, 122.U.S. at 247.

[294] "Because St. James has since died, and because of the laws and customs of France, complainants cannot ascertain the precise details of the transaction." *Id.* at 246.

cause. Furthermore, the heirs claimed that according to French law, the only executrix of the decedent's estate was Louise. Drexel replied that the entire claim of Louise and the heirs was based on a series of, "false representations" and "fraudulent suppression of facts."[295] Drexel also claimed that, even if French law would apply, Louise Berney would not be entitled to represent the other heirs before a clear accounting had been made between her and the heirs' entitlements. These claims along with others were submitted by Drexel in a bill in equity seeking relief by an injunction against Louise and her allies. The Circuit Court dismissed the bill and Drexel appealed to the Supreme Court.

Supreme Court Judge MATTHEWS opined:

> The only ground here urged in support of the decree [to dismiss the bill] and the demurrer[296] to the bill is that the complainants [Drexel] have a complete and adequate defense at law, and that consequently they do not bring themselves within the jurisdiction of a court of equity.[297]

This quote is representative of the opinion of the Supreme Court. The court focused on the question of jurisdiction, whether a court of equity could be invoked if there was already a court of law available to the appellants (Drexel). The Court concurred with this view for reasons that do not need to be further elaborated here because, as has been mentioned in the chapter on equity, jurisdictional questions regarding courts of equity and courts of law are, apart from few exceptions,[298] of mere historical interest here.[299] What catches one's attention though is the following quote:

> Equity will look through the form of the transaction and adjust the equities of the parties with a view to its substance rather to its form [. . .].[300]

And it is immediately after this quote that the Court mentions beneficial ownership for the first and only time in this case:

> In such cases, equity looks to the beneficial ownership of the debt.

This sentence is a variation of the fundamental principle of equity that *Equity looks to the intent rather than to the form.*[301] The philosophy behind this principle is to give equity the function to look through legal constructions which fence off arguments that in a strict legal sense would be inadmissible but would still be equitable in a general sense. In the present case, the Supreme Court reached the

---

[295] *Id.* at 247.

[296] A demurrer is a formal refusal of a party in a litigation to reply to the statements of the counterparty.

[297] *Drexel*, 122 U.S. at 252.

[298] Delaware, New Jersey, South Carolina, and Tennessee. On the federal level, the courts of bankruptcy also operate as courts of Equity, see n.286.

[299] *See supra* chapter "Common Law, Equity, and Beneficial Ownership".

[300] *Drexel*, 122 U.S. at 254.

[301] HUDSON, EQUITY AND TRUSTS 11.

conclusion that the distribution of the decedent's estate amongst Louise Berney and the other heirs was not yet sufficiently substantiated, and, if French law would be applied to the case, it could thus far only be established that Louise as the wife of the decedent would be entitled to a different potentially larger share. According to the Court, Louise's individual claim thus may give her a share of the inheritance, but at the same time prevented her from claiming also on behalf of the other heirs who had a different beneficial interest in the estate of the decedent. In other words, the court was of the opinion that Louise was not empowered to wear two hats at the same time, one hat of an individual heir and one of the executrix representing the beneficial interests of the other heirs. The as yet undetermined amount that each heir is entitled to inspired the court to use the term *beneficial ownership*, a term

> wide enough to encompass the interest of one who has a potential but certain right, *e.g.*, one who is kept from total ownership only by some trivial technicality [. . .].[302]

Similar to the *Bothwell v. Bingham County* and the railroad cases discussed further below, in *Drexel v. Berney* the Supreme court had to deal with an "a float status" of the property entitlements of the parties involved. The main difference between these cases is that this status of limbo was to be ended in *Bothwell* by the authorities while in *Drexel v. Berney* it was by the claimant parties themselves through better substantiation of their individual claims. In both cases however, the court chose to use the term *beneficial ownership* to accurately describe the property situation in this interim phase.

11. Laughlin v. Mitchell[303]

Laughlin v. Mitchell was decided by the Supreme Court in the same year, 1887, as *Drexel v. Berney* discussed above. Both cases deal with probate, but these are the only similarities. While *Drexel v. Berney* mainly deals with jurisdictional issues, *Laughlin v. Mitchell deals* with the substantial issue, the inheritance itself. Particularly of interest for the purposes of this thesis, beneficial ownership plays a different role in these cases.

The *Laughlin* case is about a family dispute over an impressive plantation estate called *Diamond Place*, situated in Warren County, Mississippi. The key figures are a grandfather and father, a widow and wife with her two husbands, grandchildren, and several creditors. The property in dispute consists of twelve hundred acres of land,[304] "certain slaves, horses, mules, colts, cattle, sheep, and hogs"[305] and, of course, money. A dead husband and an ill patriarch who finally died as well already

[302] Leff, *The Leff Dictionary of Law*, 94 YALE L. REV. 2149 (1985).

[303] 121 U.S. 411 (1887).

[304] Approx. 4.5 km^2.

[305] *Laughlin*, 121 U.S. at 415.

describe this case best as a civil war epic family drama. The Supreme Court dwells on the dramatic story of the case in a way that leaves very little room for actual legal reasoning. Only one of the ten pages discusses the legal aspects of the case and the content of this one page is scattered all over the decision which consists of various fact summaries and pleadings held in lower courts. The term *beneficial ownership* appears only once in a recited plea of the oratrix,[306] (a Mrs. Laughlin, introduced above as the widow and wife, against a Mr. Mitchell, presumably her nephew):

> that the beneficial ownership and title to said property be decreed, as against said Joseph E. Davis [her father], deceased, and his devises be in your oratrix.[307]

What happened? Mrs. Laughlin's first husband, David McCaleb, was the original owner of the *Diamond Place*. The couple lived on the property and ran the plantation. In 1846, when the couple was in financial distress, they were forced to auction off the *Diamond Place*. Laughlin's father stepped in and bought the *Diamond Place* which allowed Laughlin and her husband to stay on thc property. In 1847, Laughlin's first husband died. She married again 1 year later, and stayed on the *Diamond Place* and ran the plantation together with her new husband Edmund C. Laughlin. In the years that followed, the plantation ran successfully which enabled the couple to repay Laughlin's father the debts that had incurred in the past. Laughlin approached her father on several occasions, asking him to convey the title on the *Diamond Place* to her. Her father instead presented her a lease contract "for her life in consideration of natural love and affection and 100$", keeping "legal and equitable title and the right of property in and to the land"[308] to himself. In essence, Laughlin and her husband, by signing the treaty, would take on the responsibility to continue to manage the plantation "in a proper and husband like manner" and at the end of the lease would surrender the property back to the father or his heirs respectively. Laughlin tried to remind her father of his promise that, once she and her husband had paid off their debts, she would be given fee simple on the *Diamond Place*. Her father insisted on the lease and replied: "I think it best for you." The lease contract was signed and put on public county record by the Laughlins in 1858, more than 10 years after the father had purchased the *Diamond Place*.

In 1869, an offer of the father to sell the place to Laughlin and her husband was refused. The two considered the price as far too high. In the same year, the father made his will in which he devised the property to Laughlin for her life and after her death to a Joseph D. Mitchell, one of his grandsons. The father died in 1870 and a legal dispute arose between Laughlin and Mitchell over the inheritance.

Mitchell insisted on the execution of the will, claiming that Laughlin was still bound by the lease contract and, thus, had no legal title on the *Diamond Place*. Laughlin claimed that her deceased father, by buying the place and letting her and

---

[306] A female complainant in an equity pleading.

[307] *Laughlin*, 121 U.S. at 417.

[308] *Laughlin*, 121 U.S. at 411; the differentiation between legal and equitable title *and* the right of property can be best explained with the most obvious interpretation: *Right of property* is used to denominate chattel.

both her husbands' live on it and manage it, had created a *trust* with her as the beneficiary. After he died she demanded to be entitled to, as already quoted above, "beneficial ownership and title."[309]

The Supreme Court did not delve into the legal complexity of the case and more or less reiterated the opinion of the district court. Like the lower court, the Supreme Court considered the evidence sufficient that Laughlin was fully aware of the facts in relation to her title to the *Diamond Place* and of the validity of her and her husband's signature on the lease agreement. And finally, with the lease contract in force for 10 years, Mitchell was entitled to believe that his grandfather had the right to dispose over the *Diamond Place*. This lead to the Court's holding that: "no ground is shown for setting aside the lease, and that the decree of the circuit court must be affirmed."[310]

The *Laughlin* case discussed four possible bases for the entitlements to the property in dispute: contract, inheritance, equity, and beneficial ownership.

a) Contract: Lease

The Lease contract contained an arrangement between the father and the Laughlins. The document was signed by both Laughlin and her husband and duly filed with the local registry. It provided the legal basis for the relationship between the father and the Laughlins for over a decade.[311] In it, the father conveyed the *Diamond Place*, real and personal property to Laughlin "for and during her natural life."[312] Neither an *inter vivos* nor a *post mortem* transfer of the title to the property could be discerned by the court.[313] Laughlin's title under the lease thus was limited to privileges such as occupancy and use but did not include the power to freely change the ownership situation by, e.g., granting property entitlements to her husband. Consequently the lease was an obstacle to Laughlin's claim to simple fee title on the *Diamond Place*, an obstacle that needed to be removed. The Laughlins thus contended to have been forced into the lease by the father but were unable to provide sufficient evidence for this allegation of duress.

b) Inheritance: Will

The will of the father entitled the daughter to the *Diamond Place* "for and during her life, with full enjoyments of the profits and privileges, thereunto belonging."[314]

---

309 *Id.* at 417.

310 *Id.* at 421.

311 *Laughlin*, 121 U.S. at 411.

312 *Id.* at 419.

313 *Id.* ("[...] it not clearly appearing whether this (title to property) was to be in fee or for life.").

314 *Id.* at 412.

Another clause speaks of the daughter's "life estate."[315] The provisions in the will were in line with the lease as far as the description of Laughlin's property title is concerned. The father expressly entitled his daughter to the *life estate* while, in a separate clause, he gave to his grandson the *Diamond Place* "to hold enjoy the same in fee simple" upon the death of his daughter. So long as the daughter was alive, the grandson was not entitled to the property. The *life estate* position of the daughter was limited in time. It would only last as long as she was alive. Laughlin would also be limited with regard to her power to dispose of the property. As in the lease, Laughlin would have only had certain privileges such as occupancy, use, and operation of the *Diamond Place* but she would have no power to alienate the property or giving her husband life estate.[316]

c) Equity: Trust

Laughlin claims in court that her father, by buying the property of her first husband and along with several oral assurances and promises, had impliedly created a trust to her benefit and upon his death, she would become the sole successor in title.[317] The Court did not see this argument as sufficiently established by evidence.[318] The decision does not offer enough facts to the trust argument that would allow a detailed analysis of the consequences. This only leaves room for speculation on that scenario. What can be stated nevertheless is that even if the Supreme Court had followed the trust argument, Laughlin would have "only" become the *equitable* owner of the *Diamond Place* and the power to dispose of the property after the Settlor's death would have been vested with the *legal owner*, the trustee (whoever that may have been).

d) Beneficial Ownership

As has been shown on several occasions in this thesis, beneficial ownership is, technically speaking, never a legal basis. Beneficial ownership is rather woven into

---

[315] *Id.*

[316] *See* Hohfeld, *Fundamental Legal Conceptions*, 26 YALE L.J., 746 (1917) (providing a good summary of privileges and powers emerging from real estate property).

[317] HUDSON, EQUITY AND TRUSTS 31; see also Chicago, Milwaukee & St. Paul R.C., *supra* Sect. 6 of this chapter.

[318] The Court considered sufficiently established that the father "[...] purchased the property with the purpose of letting the plaintiff and her husband remain on the plantation and control it, and the property upon it, intending to hold the legal title to all of and make himself personally responsible for the expenses of the plantation, the income to be applied to pay those expenses and the personal expenses of this daughter and her husband, and the remainder of it to the payment of the purchase money for which he was personally liable, and intending, when this was done, to convey, or secure by his will, to her a title to the property, it not very clearly appearing whether this was to be in fee or only for life"; *Laughlin*, 121 U.S. at 419 f.

the three bases described above. Beneficial ownership is an economical *de facto* element and best defined as a privilege but never as a right or claim. Some content of Laughlin's beneficial ownership has already been described (occupancy, enjoyment of proceeds, operation of the plantation, etc.).[319]

But why would the father legally limit his daughter's position to these privileges? What kept him from giving her simple fee title? The answer can be found in his statement: "I think it best for you."[320] This hardly unusual statement of the paternalistic era of the nineteen-hundreds seemed the leading theme of all the legal arrangements that the father did or did not make in the interest of his daughter. From the beginning, when she and her first husband were in financial troubles, the father stepped in as the *deus ex machina*. But, unlike the ancient Greek figure, he appeared in the middle of the play and did not leave the stage until he died. The husbands of his daughter he considered merely supporting acts. There is no mention of any important interaction with them. After he had rescued the daughter and her first husband from the first misery, he had installed himself a power position which would rule his daughters' and her husbands' lives. His motivation was to provide for a material and legal arrangement for his daughter which was to ensure that she was entitled to *live on and from and manage* the *Diamond Place* for the rest of her life. The full equitable and legal entitlement of the daughter did not seem necessary to him to ensure this. He preferred keeping such entitlement to himself. Having his daughter and her second husband sign a lifelong lease, i.e. a contractual agreement with only personal but no property claims, would keep him in charge and the Laughlins on a short leash.

Admittedly, there is not much if any legal analysis in this description of the father's motivation. But these observations are nonetheless important as they point to a phenomenon that is representative for an entire group of cases: That phenomenon is the reluctance to give up legal power over the counterparty. This can be best achieved by giving the counterparty privileges while reserving the rights or claims. By granting merely beneficial ownership, the legal situation remains unchanged.

Similar arrangements based on the same paternalistic element can be observed in federal Indian law cases: tolerate the Indians as occupants of the land, allow them to sell their chattels, but reserve the fee simple. Not just this mechanism, but also the well-meaning paternalistic attitude of "I think it best for you", as will be[321] shown throughout this thesis is a clandestine principle in federal Indian law as well.[322]

SUMMARY: Beneficial ownership in the *Laughlin v. Mitchell* case is representative of an entire case group which deals with an entity or person preserving its

---

[319] The list of content is virtually indefinite, HOHFELD, *id.*, The elements listed serve only as vivid examples.

[320] *Laughlin*, 121 U.S. at 416.

[321] *See infra* chapter "The Beneficial Ownership Concept Applied in Federal Indian Law", Sect. 4b).

[322] *See* also regarding family and ownership Aurbach v. Gallina, 753 So. 2d 60, 62 (Fla. 2000) ("To analyze the family dynamics to determine all the 'beneficial' owners of a car is to impose a fuzzy legal standard [. . .]").

legal power position by vesting its weaker counterpart with mere privileges as opposed to fully fledged rights.

12. National Bank v. Insurance Company[323]

This oldest decision of the U.S. Supreme Court, *National Bank v. Insurance Company* dates back to 1881, the same year Oliver Wendell Holmes, Jr. first published *The Common Law*. (Holmes was still years away from becoming a member of the Supreme Court at that time.[324])

The case deals with a bank account which was opened for a Mr. A.H. Dillon Jr., General Agent of the Connecticut Mutual Life Insurance Company (the Insurance Company), at the Central National Bank (the Bank). Dillon used the funds on the account for business purposes, namely bi-monthly remittance of premium revenue by check. His commissions as an agent were also paid into this account. When Dillon was in financial distress, he tried to fix the situation with a loan and notes. Dillon also used the premium and commission funds on the account for various purposes. Finally, when he drew a check for the Insurance Company for premium remittance and when the Insurance Company presented the check to the Bank for payment, the Bank refused to pay "on the grounds that there were no funds to the credit of the drawee sufficient to pay it."[325] In the aftermath the Bank went bankrupt. The Insurance Company went to court requesting, as the beneficial owner (!) of the account, an injunction to halt the liquidation proceedings until "a sufficient amount to satisfy the complainant's demand"[326] would be retained.

This earliest U.S. Supreme Court decision that could be found introduced beneficial ownership without pomp and circumstance. The term was used as if it was a part of the regular *jargon*. There are several reasons for this. For one, the term *beneficial owner* appears in the state courts already five decades earlier than in the federal courts.[327] Furthermore, the court based its opinion on the authority of an earlier state decision in which the term was already used, *Farmers' & Mechanics' National Bank v. King*,[328] a decision of the Pennsylvania Supreme Court of 1868. The Judge who wrote the opinion in *Farmers'* was William Strong (1808-1895). Justice Strong was elected in the U.S. Supreme Court in 1870, i.e. 2 years after he wrote this opinion.[329] In the *Farmers'* decision, Strong had stated that

[323] 104 U.S. 54 (1881).

[324] Holmes joined the Supreme Court in 1902.

[325] *National Bank*, 104 U.S. at 58.

[326] *Id.* at 60.

[327] Leadman v. Harris, 14 N.C. 144 (1831); see *supra* note 75.

[328] 57 Pa. St. 202, 205, (1868).

[329] The *Farmers'* decision was published in the same year Strong retired from the Pennsylvania Supreme Court (1868) and the *Insurance Company* decision was published one year after Strong retired from the U.S. Supreme Court (1881).

> equity will follow a fund through any number of transmutations, and preserve it for the owner so long as it can be identified. [. . .] If money has been converted by a trustee or agent, the legal right may have been changed, but equity regards the beneficial ownership.[330]

The choice of a slightly changed version of the maxim that *equity follows the law* indicates that the term *beneficial ownership* was used here as a synonym for *beneficiary*. Furthermore, the Court granted the owner of the funds an *equitable* claim on the funds deposited in the account that has been opened in the name of a trustee. As has been shown, equitable claims are never based solely on beneficial ownership.

The court further considered Dillon as a trustee of the Insurance Company. It stated that "the relation of Dillon to the insurance company was one of confidence and trust."[331] "He must, we think, be regarded and treated as a trustee."[332] The Insurance Company, on the other hand, was considered as a beneficiary of at least that part of the funds that were related to the premium remittance. Also, "the beneficial owner is entitled to the proceeds, whatever be their form."[333] With this additional holding, the court referred to another equity maxim: *Equity looks to the intent rather than to the form*.[334]

At the time the decision was made, the more common term for *beneficiary* was the ancient law-French term *cestui que trust*, *cestui que use*, or *cestui que vie*.[335] In fact, the term *cestui que trust* appears once in the opinion in a quote where it was clearly used as a synonym to the term *beneficiary*.

Finally, the Court used the term *beneficial owner* consistently on several occasions as a synonym of the term *beneficiary*. This is not unusual and can be observed in academic works of the days. Scott even goes this far to state that:

> Even in Bacon's day a court of law [. . .] recognized that it was the *cestui que trust* [beneficiary] who is beneficial owner.[336]

Scott's statement goes deeper than the first impression may suggest. At the very end of his article he states:

> When it is necessary for the protection of the *cestui que trust*, equity will recognize that he is in very truth the beneficial owner of the trust property.[337]

To call the beneficiary the *beneficial owner in very truth* appears confusing only on the surface. As explained on several occasions, beneficial ownership is a *de facto*

[330] *National Bank*, 104 U.S. at 69; underline added by author.

[331] *Id.* at 70.

[332] *Id.* at 71.

[333] *National Bank*, 104 U.S. at 68.

[334] *See also* Ohio Valley National Bank v. Hulitt 204 U.S. 162, 168 (1907) ("[. . .] the law looks through subterfuges and apparent ownerships and fastens the liability upon the shareholder to whom the shares really belong.").

[335] Medieval French for *cestui a que use le feoffment fuit fait*: The person to whom the feoffment, (i.e. transfer of full title (fee simple) on property) was made.

[336] Scott, *The Nature and Rights of the "Cestui Que Trust"*, 16 Colum. L. Rev. 276 (1917).

[337] *Id.* at 290.

ownership based upon concrete economic circumstances. In that sense, beneficial ownership is the basic economic layer on which legal layers can be built upon. Thus, the status beneficial owner and beneficiary can rest in one and the same person. However, to say that the beneficiary is *in very truth the beneficial owner* is only true to an extent because it would be false to state that the beneficial owner is in truth the beneficiary. This is not always considered when beneficial ownership is used as a synonym for beneficiary or *cestui que trust*.

SUMMARY: The first time the term *beneficial ownership* concept appeared in a U.S. Supreme Court Decision it is not defined but simply used as a synonym to the term *beneficiary*.

13. Summary Findings

- Beneficial ownership is a factual element that, together with other factual elements, *can* overrule legal ownership (*Hellenic Lines v. Rhoditis*)
- Beneficial ownership is a privilege, not a right (*United States v. Algoma Lumber Co.*)
- Beneficial ownership is built on the notion that property extends not only to itself, but also to its direct products and proceeds (*Union Stock Yards Bank v. Gillespie*)
- The protection of beneficial ownership is a self-declared (non-correlative) responsibility of the government (*United States v. Shoshone*, *Tooahnippah v. Hickel*)
- Beneficial ownership is an important factor in discussions about control over an entity (*Handy & Harman v. Burnet*)
- Beneficial Owner and Beneficiary are not synonyms (*Chicago, Milwaukee & St. Paul Railway Co. v. Des Moines Union Railway Co.*; *National Bank v. Insurance Co.*)
- Beneficial Ownership is applied in some cases as an interim "floating" legal status (*Bothwell v. Bingham County*, *Montana Catholic Missions v. Missoula County*; *Drexel v. Berney*)
- Beneficial ownership is a term frequently used to describe a situation where the beneficial use and legal title are separated (*Montana Catholic Missions v. Missoula County*)
- Characteristic privileges emerging from beneficial ownership include enjoyment, occupancy, and use (*Laughlin v. Mitchell*, *Montana Catholic Missions v. Missoula County*; *Chicago Milwaukee & St. Paul R.C. v. Des Moines U.R.C*; *Handy & Harman v. Burnet*; *Wells v. Savannah*)
- In several cases a certain paternalistic notion can be observed in the more powerful party. In these cases, beneficial ownership privileges are granted instead of conveyance of fee simple (*Laughlin v. Mitchell*, *Tooanippah Goombi v. Hickel*; *United States v. Algoma Lumber Co.*; *United States v. Shoshone Tribe of Indians*). As the following chapter will show, this is particularly true in federal Indian law cases.

Fundamental Aspects of Federal Indian Law

1. Introductory Note on the Moral Aspect

An introductory note may be appropriate here before starting the analysis of the role of beneficial ownership in the context of federal Indian law. The way the "Indian problem" was managed, according to one author, "broke Indian hearts for generation after generation."[338] Many historical events and many actions and omissions of the U.S. are perceived today as not only unjust, but even immoral. It seems to have become public opinion that the U.S. government failed to find a fair solution which would guarantee the prosperous co-existence of Native Americans with their fellow citizens. For the purpose of this thesis any further investigation will be discontinued here with a statement of Chief Justice Rehnquist[339]:

> That there was tragedy, deception, barbarity, and virtually every other vice known to man in the 300 year history of the expansion of the original 13 Colonies into a Nation which now embraces more than three million square miles and 50 States cannot be denied. But in a court opinion, as a historical and not a legal matter, both settler and Indian are entitled to the benefit of the Biblical adjuration: 'Judge not, that ye be not judged'.[340]

The purpose of this thesis is to analyze a concept and its application in a specific field of law. To interpret the historical and political environment from a moral perspective shall be left to those who feel the calling to do so. They are, however, well advised to proceed with the caution and sensitivity that our forebears are so often criticized for lacking.

---

[338] John Collier (1884–1968), Commissioner of the Bureau of Indian Affairs (1933–1945) quoted in Cohen's Handbook of Federal Indian Law Chapter VII (1945 ed.).

[339] William Hubbs Rehnquist (1924–2005), 16th Chief Justice of the Supreme Court of the United States.

[340] United States v. Sioux Nation of Indians, 448 U.S. 371, 438 (1980).

M. Reinhard-DeRoo, *Beneficial Ownership*, DOI 10.1007/978-3-319-01686-3_6,

2. Why Federal Indian Law?

The field of federal Indian law is based upon more than 4,000 treaties and statutes and upon thousands of judicial decisions and administrative rulings[341] dealing with the relationship between the U.S. and its indigenous citizens.[342] This field of law may not come to mind spontaneously in the context of a thesis on beneficial ownership. However, one may only recall the land disputes involving Native Americans to understand that property law is a central element of federal Indian law. This alone justifies a closer look into parts of that area of law. Specific fundamental aspects of this area of public law have thus been chosen for several important reasons:

- Federal Indian law is the field of law in which the U.S. Supreme Court frequently mentions beneficial ownership.
- Federal Indian law invites a comparison of the ownership concepts of the European Americans with the ownership concepts of the heterogeneous group the over 500 tribes of the so-called *First Americans*.[343]
- Federal Indian law and particularly its origins are based on the legal environment of an era of property redistribution. As opposed to the Old World with its century old legal traditions, the New World was given the chance to a new start, setting off a major redistribution experiment, and distribution of scarce resources is what property law is all about.[344]
- Federal Indian law deals with concrete objects like forests, lakes, land (e.g. *United States v. Algoma Lumber Co.*,[345] *United States v. Dann*[346]), hunting and fishing grounds (e.g. *Montana v. United States*,[347] *United States v. Dorwin Aam*[348]), and mining (e.g., *United States v. Sioux Nation of Indians*[349]). Federal Indian law also deals with very existential human situations like war, migration, trade, and the human condition as such rather than with virtual transactions and interactions between legal entities.

---

[341] COHEN'S HANDBOOK OF FEDERAL INDIAN LAW Chapter VIII (1945 ed.).

[342] Indians received U.S. citizenship in 1924 based on the Indian Citizenship Act, 8 U.S.C.A. § 1401(b).

[343] The question about the ethnicity of the first inhabitants of the North American continent has been subject to controversy since the discovery of the Kennewick Man, a 9000 year-old skeleton discovered in Washington State, Sawyer, *Kennewick Man*, 280 SCIENCE 18 f. (1998); see generally WALDMAN, ATLAS OF THE NORTH AMERICAN INDIAN 1 ff. (3rd ed.2009) (providing background information regarding the pre-colonization era).

[344] MATTEI, BASIC PRINCIPLES OF PROPERTY LAW 6.

[345] 305 U.S. 415 (1939).

[346] 470 U.S. 39 (1985).

[347] 450 U.S. 544 (1981).

[348] 887 F.2d 190 (9th Cir.1989); see also Parisi, *Entropy in Property*, 50 AM. J. COMP. L., 597 (2002).

[349] 448 U.S. 371 (1980); for the Roman law principle: "*Cuius est solum eius est usque ad coelum et usque ad inferos*"; see Parisi, *id.* at 606 f. (2002).

- The history of federal Indian law is also the history of a great variety of property law concepts reaching from brutal conquest to sophisticated trust relationships.

These elements visualize legal problems in a more evident way than other fields such as securities law or trust law would.

3. Cultural Differences

a) Stereotypes

Law develops organically and its nutrients range from proactive regulation to simple forgetfulness. Historical, economic, educational, and social backgrounds, as well as language (along with other elements) provide the cultural soil in which laws are planted.

The study of the cultural aspects of federal Indian law is more complex than one may expect. A great error lies in the perception that only two cultures are involved in federal Indian law, the culture of the United States and the culture of the Native Americans. As has already been indicated, there are hundreds of tribes of different cultural heritage and traditions. Misconceptions of the Indian culture lead to stereotypes as described by COHEN:

> Common opinion pictures the original American dressed in feathers and wampum, his belt adorned with scalps, mounted on a horse, gazing after buffalo. This picture blurs over the fact that many Indians, before white contact, were farmers and fisherman who had never seen feather head-dresses, wampum, scalps, or buffalo, that Indians ever rode a horse before Spaniards brought horses into North America, and that the special combination of striking Indian peculiarities which the modern "circus Indian" embodies did not exist before the rise of modern American showmanship.[350]

The past 50 years since this observation was documented only changed insofar as the modern showmanship now also includes moving pictures.

b) Lyng v. Northwest Indian Cemetery

Few cases are as representative of the still existing major cultural differences between the United States and its native inhabitants as *Lyng v. Northwest Indian Cemetery*.[351] The case involved a dispute over a timber harvesting project of the federal government. The project also included the construction of a road through the so-called Chimney Rocks area which had been worshipped for at least two

[350] COHEN'S HANDBOOK OF FEDERAL INDIAN LAW Chapter IX (1945 ed.).

[351] 485 U.S. 439 (1988).

centuries by several Indian tribes as a place of high spiritual value. The Indians claimed that their constitutional rights to free exercise of religion were impaired.[352] The Supreme Court held that "the Free Exercise Clause is written in terms of what the government cannot do to the individual, not in terms of what the individual can exact from the government."[353] The court referred to *Bowen v. Roy*, which held that social security numbers used by states to administer welfare programs would not violate the religious freedom of certain Indians who believed that such numbering would hurt their spiritual integrity.[354]

> Accordingly, we explained that *Roy* could no more prevail on his religious objection to the Government's use of a Social Security number for his daughter than he could on a sincere religious objection to the size or color of the Government's filing cabinets.[355]

The Court's main concern was that, by admitting the claim of the Indian tribes, it would set a precedent prohibiting government activities based on Indian religious beliefs. Such religious beliefs would, as a consequence, "require *de facto* beneficial ownership of some rather spacious tracts of public property."[356] For once, the Supreme Court mentions beneficial ownership here in connection with a spiritual value, a spiritual value, most notably, with enormous impact on the federal government's right to use its own property. The majority opinion written by Justice O'CONNOR does not address this aspect but rather discusses the relationship between the government and the Indians from an administrative law perspective. The main concern under this premise is more or less an impact analysis with the outcome that building the road and cutting the timber merely affects the land but not the religious freedom of the Indians.

Justice BRENNAN in his dissent calls "such reading [...] wholly untenable [...] demonstrated by the cruelly surreal result" that even if government action lead to the virtual destruction of a religion, this could still not be prevented by the constitutional right of free exercise.[357] BRENNAN criticizes the Court for not sufficiently considering the fact that "Native American faith is inextricably bound to the use of land."[358]

SINGER assumes that the Court based its conclusion in part on the Jewish and Christian idea that faith can be practiced anywhere.[359] This assumption does not seem entirely accurate. If the Wailing Wall in Jerusalem or St. Peter's square in

---

[352] U.S. Const. amend. I; Bowers & Carpenter, *Challenging the Narrative of Conquest* 492 ff. (providing essential information regarding religious beliefs and culture of the Indians).

[353] *Lyng*, 485 U.S. at 440.

[354] 476 U.S. 693 (1986); see generally 92 Stat. 469 (1978), 82 Stat. 77 (1968).

[355] *Lyng*, 485 U.S. at 470 ff. (Brennan J., dissenting).

[356] *Id.* at 453.

[357] *Id.* at 472.

[358] *Id.* at 460 f.

[359] Singer, *Property and Coercion in Federal Indian Law*, 63 S. CAL. L. REV. 1832 (1990); Justice BRENNAN also discusses the different Jewish/Christian idea without insinuating that his colleagues were motivated by such a perspective.

Rome were to make way for a highway, the reaction of most Jews or Christians would not be different than the Indian's reaction in *Lyng*. Of course, churches and temples of lower significance have been and are being destroyed or put to different uses regularly, but these are only locations of lower significance. The Supreme Court's description of the Chimney Rock area, referred to by the Indians as *the High Country*, demands a comparison with Jewish or Christian sites of the highest caliber.[360] Finally, it may be added that a group of agnostic or atheist judges would hardly be more sympathetic to the idea of sacred, untouchable territories.

The judges' decision was much more likely motivated by the other characteristic idea of the western civilization that land is to be owned and made use of. Justice BRENNAN speaks of the "longstanding conflict between two disparate cultures - the dominant Western culture, which views land in terms of ownership and use, and that of Native Americans, in which concepts of private property are not only alien, but contrary to a belief system that holds land sacred."[361] The central idea underlying the belief system already of the early English colonizers was to "settle near natives who have too much property but too little skill to use it productively."[362] This idea had greater influence on the Court than Jewish or Christian belief that religious practice is not land-tied. After all, the government action that the Indians tried to prevent was intended to make the Chimney Rock area more productive.

What is particularly interesting with regard to this thesis is the Court's use of the term *beneficial ownership*. The term is only used twice in the opinion. First, in the aforementioned quote speaking of Indian beliefs potentially requiring *de facto* beneficial ownership in order to remain intact, and secondly in Judge BRENNAN's interpretation of the same quote. The interpretation argues that the Court's belief that said *de facto* beneficial ownership could be exacted from the government.[363] For once, the term beneficial ownership is used here to describe the interests of the government. Unfortunately, the Court does not further elaborate on the content or nature of the government's beneficial ownership.

c) Indian Status

In 1873, long before COHEN, FRANCIS A. WALKER, a former Indian Commissioner warned of oversimplification, but also admitted to a certain necessity to categorize the Indians:

---

[360] *Lyng*, 485 U.S. at 443.

[361] *Id.* at U.S. 473.

[362] O'Melimn, *The Imperial Origins of Federal Indian Law*, 31 Ariz. L. REV. 1221 (1999); Frickey, *Domesticating Federal Indian Law*, 81 MINN. L. REV. 88 f. (1996) ("When stripped of its First Amendment veneer, however, the Court's view of the case boiled down to an assessment of competing property interests").

[363] *Lyng*, 485 U.S. at 458.

> Equally obdurate must one be to the seductions of Indian ethnology, except so far only as it may simplify the classification of the present Indian population to refer tribes and bands to recognized groups or families, for the better or briefer characterization of their qualities and affinities.[364]

Indian status, be it as a collective or as individuals are operational key elements of any federal Indian law case.[365] They are also a condition for claims and entitlements. "Eligibility for a range of federal services and benefits pursuant to treaties, statutes, or other agreements often has necessitated determinations of tribal status."[366] The history of Indian status has changed constantly and was not systematically defined and administered until the twentieth century.[367]

A good example for the (at times) drastic change in Indian status and the implications on Indian ownership is the Termination Policy of the 1950s. The legislation based on this policy was intended to break up the tribes and vest the same rights and responsibilities in Indian individuals as in "regular" U.S. citizens.[368] Termination legislation provided for substantial change in Indian's property rights representing the "most concerted drive against Indian property"[369] since the Indian Relocation Policy of the 1830s.[370]

One of the largest terminations was the one of the Klamath tribe of Oregon. Pursuant the Klamath Termination Act,[371] tribal property was to be sold and the

---

[364] WALKER, THE INDIAN QUESTION 15.

[365] For the recognition of tribes see COHEN'S HANDBOOK OF FEDERAL INDIAN LAW 5.02[3] (2005 ed.); see *infra* chapter "The Beneficial Ownership Concept Applied in Federal Indian Law", Sect. 2. for the differentiation between collective and individual property.

[366] COHEN'S HANDBOOK OF FEDERAL INDIAN LAW §3.02 [6][f], § 5.03[2] (2005 ed.); see *e.g.* the Snyder Act (25 U.S.C § 13 (1921)) and the Johnson-O'Malley Act (25 U.S.C. §§ 452–456 (1934)) (providing both for health care, housing, educational and other services).

[367] Since 1977, the Office of Federal Acknowledgment (OFA) is responsible for the administration of the federal recognition of Indian tribes. Individual tribal membership is in essence granted by a federally recognized tribe; LaPier v. McCormick, 986 F.2d 303,305 (9th Cir.1993); Joint Tribal Council of the Passamaquoddy Tribe v. Morton, 528 F 2d 370 (1st Cir.1975); CLINTON et al. eds., AMERICAN INDIAN LAW: NATIVE NATIONS AND THE FEDERAL SYSTEM 391(5th ed. 2005).; Toro, "*A People Distinct From Others*": *Race and Identity in Federal Indian Law and the Hispanic Classification in OMB Directive No. 15*, 26 TEX. TECH. L. REV. 1219, 1271 f., n.112 (1995); see Morton v. Mancari, 417 U.S. 535, 555 (1974); see generally Goldberg, *What's Race Got to Do With It? The Story of Morton v. Mancari* 81 ff. (discussing the development of the relationship between "regular" citizen and Indian status).

[368] CANBY, AMERICAN INDIAN LAW IN A NUTSHELL 27 (5th ed. 2009); for the political motivation behind the Termination Policy era, see: Berger, *Sheep, Sovereignty, and the Supreme Court: The Story of Williams v. Lee* 363.

[369] DEBO, ANGIE, A HISTORY OF THE INDIANS OF THE UNITED STATES, 349.

[370] The Termination Policy was repudiated in the 1970s. See generally COHEN'S HANDBOOK OF FEDERAL INDIAN LAW § 3.02[8][b] (2005 ed.) for the impact of the repudiation.

[371] 25 U.S.C. § 564 (1988 & Supp. V. 1993).

proceeds to be distributed amongst individual Indians.[372] One of the key provisions § 564c, provides that:

> [. . .] ***rights or beneficial interests*** in tribal property of each [Indian] person [. . .] constitute personal property [. . .].[373]

As already observed in the discussion of *United States v. Algoma Lumber Co. et al.*,[374] this juxtaposition of rights and beneficial interests is not unusual. *Algoma* even uses the term beneficial *ownership* instead of *beneficial interests*.[375] The logic behind this juxtaposition can be explained with the fact that there would be no need to mention rights and beneficial interest separately if both terms were conceptually identical. HOHFELD's description of privileges, those incidents which cannot be claimed but merely enjoyed until revoked, fits here as well.

Uncertain Indian status causes uncertain property status. The recognition of Indian status thus bears consequences on property. Cases which address this phenomenon will be discussed below in the chapter "The Beneficial Ownership Concept Applied in Federal Indian Law".[376]

d) Diversity and Uniformity

According to COHEN.[377] the federal government started a uniform approach to the Indians in what would become federal Indian law in 1789, the year of the French Revolution, almost 300 years after Columbus set foot on the New World. Although it would be difficult to construe a connection between these crucial historical events in France and the United States, it seems quite remarkable that the same year, 1789,

---

[372] *See infra* chapter "The Beneficial Ownership Concept Applied in Federal Indian Law", Sect. 3. for the differentiation between communal and individual Indian ownership.

[373] Emphasis added.

[374] 305 U.S. 415, 421 (1939).

[375] *Id.* 421.

[376] Choate v. Trapp, 224 U.S. 665, 675 (1912) (confirming tax free status of Indians with allotments) see *infra* chapter "The Beneficial Ownership Concept Applied in Federal Indian Law", Sect. 2b); United States v. Sandoval, 231 U.S. 28 (distinguishing between Pueblo Indians and "wild" Indians) see *infra* Sect. 3c) of this chapter; Wolfchild v. United States, 559 F. 3rd 1228 (Fed. Cir.2009) (discussing beneficial ownership of the heirs of a group within the same tribe) see *infra* chapter "The Beneficial Ownership Concept Applied in Federal Indian Law", Sect. 2a); United States v. Dann, 470 U.S. 39 (1985) (recognizing individual aboriginal title in a group of Indians) see *infra* chapter "The Beneficial Ownership Concept Applied in Federal Indian Law", Sect. 2a); Cramer v. United States, 261 U.S. 219 (recognizing title of a group of individual Indians) see *infra* chapter "The Beneficial Ownership Concept Applied in Federal Indian Law", Sect. 2b); *The Cherokee Trust Funds* case, 117 U.S. 288 (1886) (declining entitlement to trust funds of a band of former members of an Indian tribe that resisted removal to the west and became regular citizens of North Carolina); see also *infra* chapter "The Beneficial Ownership Concept Applied in Federal Indian Law", Sect. 2a).

[377] COHEN'S HANDBOOK OF FEDERAL INDIAN LAW 68 ff. (1945 ed.).

symbolically marks the beginning of a new era of emancipation in one culture, marks the jump-start of "the essential administrative machinery for dealing with Indian affairs"[378] in another culture.

With the increasing power and influence of the federal government over Indian affairs, statutory laws providing general rules applicable to all Indian tribes regardless of their cultural background were implemented. In 1935, a generic definition of Indians was introduced in which "[An Indian is] any person of Indian descent who is a member of any recognized Indian tribe and now under Federal jurisdiction" is considered to be an Indian. This, according to COHEN, shows the government's intention to shift its focus from racial to socio-political groups.[379]

4. Law, Property, and Language

Reference has already been made to the rich variety of languages that are spoken by the different Indian tribes. To study the linguistics and extract different views on legal concepts would be nearly impossible. The Supreme Court considers language as the first barrier to the Natives' comprehension of property concepts.

> We doubt if any interpreter could intelligently translate the contents of a writing that deals with the property concept for the Indians did not have a word for it. People do not have words to fit ideas that have never occurred to them. [. . .] Acquisitiveness, which develops a law of real property, is an accomplishment only of the "civilized".[380]

The fact that Judge JACKSON[381] put the word *civilized* in quotations hints to a certain unwillingness to compare the degree of peoples' civilization.

Also, the judge chooses the word *acquisitiveness*, a word that is not a technical legal expression but rather the descriptive state of eagerness to possess and profit from a thing, as the core element dividing "civilized" European and Indian understanding of property. This hardly originates from a utopian view of noble savages being too imposing to quarrel over vile issues like property. It rather recalls BENTHAM's idea of property as a product of the law (and the law, of course a product of civilization):

---

378 *Id.*

379 *Id.* at 5; see generally Toro, "*A People Distinct From Others*", 26 TEX. TECH. L. REV. 1219, 1272 (1995) (suggesting new guidelines for reforming racial and ethnic classifications); see also *infra* chapter "The Beneficial Ownership Concept Applied in Federal Indian Law", Sect. 2a).

380 Shoshone Indians v. United States, 324 U.S. 335, 357 (1945).

381 ROBERT H. JACKSON, 1892–1954. In the same year *Shoshone* was published, Justice Jackson took a leave of absence from the Supreme Court to serve as United States Chief of counsel for the prosecution of Nazi war criminals. JACKSON is remembered as being highly influential on the development of due process.

> Property and law are born and must die together. [. . .] Take away the laws and all property ceases.[382]

Even more subtle, BECCARIA, the great Italian reformer whose ideas were highly influential on BENTHAM,[383] was willing to consider property as a "terrible, maybe even unnecessary right ("terribile, e forse non necessario diritto"[384])."

To this interdependency between law and property, Justice JACKSON reflects on the interdependency between written language and the law. This results in the following syllogism:

- *IF property is/depends on law*
- *AND law is/depends on language*
- *THEN property is/depends on language.*

If language is a product of civilization, then JOHN LENNON's imperative ("imagine no possessions") becomes less utopian since there are people without concepts of property. BENTHAM brings the example of savages who are condemned to hide and protect their goods (e.g., hunting prey) day and night from thieves and intruders.[385] Still today, Indians are perceived as having no property concept of their own in their culture:

> Today, tribal lands are "owned" by Native Americans, but the cultural meaning of land precludes its treatment as a mere commodity.[386]

What does this *cultural meaning* consist of and what role does it play for the Native American conception of property? The following section is intended to shed some light on this question.

5. The Native American Property Concept

ROBERT A. WILLIAMS, a man of "magnificent scholarship" wrote a fascinating account of the history of western foundational legal concepts and discourses of native people.[387] The book is entitled *The American Indian in Western Legal Thought.*[388] Philosophical concepts from Aristotle (conception of natural justice), Thomas Aquinas (all humans possess reason), and John Locke (reflections on natural

---

[382] BENTHAM, Works, 557; see generally DUBE, The Theme of Acquisitiveness in Bentham's Political Thought, New York 1991 (providing background information on the nature and origin of acquisitiveness).

[383] Grechenig & Gelter, *The Transatlantic Divergence in Legal Thought*, 31 HASTINGS INT'L & COMP. L. REV. 320 (2007).

[384] BECCARIA, DEI DELITTI E DELLE PENE; 556. *Bentham*, Works, 558 disagrees with this view, seeing the source of evil not in the law but in people's greed for possession.

[385] BENTHAM, WORKS, 556.

[386] CARRUTHERS/ARIOVICH, 30 ANN. REV. SOC., 26 (2004).

[387] Singer, *Property and Coercion in Federal Indian Law*, 63 S. CAL. L. REV. 1838 (1990).

[388] *See* bibliography.

law and property); theological concepts from the Popes Urban II (*Lebensraum* argument of the crusades), Innocent IV (jurisdiction of the Holy See over all men); legal precedents like Calvin's Case (differentiating between friendly aliens and perpetual enemies); legal opinions like Camden/Yorke (reducing the ultimate title of the Crown in certain colonies) are only a few examples of the incredible wealth of great ideas and terrible mistakes that have preoccupied the western legal mind for millenniums.

WILLIAMS' account, however, only represents the western view. A book entitled *The Western Conqueror in American Indian Legal Thought* does not exist. There are, nevertheless, statements of famous Indians which are useful in coming to a better understanding of Native American legal thought.

a) Statements of Indians

CHIEF SEATTLE purportedly sent a letter to President FRANKLIN PIERCE in 1855[389]:

> How can you buy or sell the sky, the warmth of the land? The idea is strange to us. If we do not own the freshness of the air and sparkle of the water, how can you buy them?[390]

Historians have established in recent years that this letter between a great chief and a President is "[...] a unhistorical artifact of someone's fertile literary imagination."[391] Considering the fact that CHIEF SEATTLE was illiterate (as were most Indians of the nineteenth century), there is a high likelihood that the letter was written by a white man. The lacking historical authenticity of the document contrasts its significance. After all, the letter has served as one of the most prominent sources for the common perception on Native American thought about (property) rights until today. This artificial letter between two leaders of the nineteenth century can serve as an example that the Europeans, consciously or subconsciously, dominated the cultural and legal perception of the Native Americans.

---

389 CHIEF SEATTLE, ('Si'hal', ca. 1780–1866), Leader of the Duwamish ('Dkhw'Duw'Absh') Indians; President *Franklin Pierce* (1804–1869).

390 SWANN/KRUPAT, RECOVERING THE WORD: ESSAYS ON NATIVE AMERICAN LITERATURE, 525; "Objects possessing powerful, noncommercial social meanings are often deemed inappropriate for ownership. For example, traditional Native American conceptions of land clashed with those of European settlers, who viewed land as private property", CARRUTHERS/ARIOVICH, 30 ANN. REV. SOC., 26 (2004).

391 "A search of the records of the Bureau of Indian Affairs and of the Office of the Secretary of the Interior in the National Archives and the presidential papers of Franklin Pierce in the Library of Congress has not uncovered even a trace of such a letter. [...] no source for the text of the 1855 letter has ever been discovered." Clark, "*Thus spoke Chief Seattle*", 18 Nat'l Archive, 2 (1985); for the historical speech of Chief Seattle in 1854, see Arrowsmith, William, *Speech of Chief Seattle*, 8 Arion [Boston University], 461 ff. (1969); FURTWANGLER, ANSWERING CHIEF SEATTLE 10 ff.

There are, nevertheless, authentic statements from Indians regarding Indian property which appear to be in a similar tone like the artificial statement of Chief Seattle e.g. the Comanche Leader Ten Bears' plea:

> I was born on the prairie, where the wind blew free and there was nothing to break the light of the sun. I was born there where there were no enclosures and where everything drew a free breath. I want to die there and not within walls.[392]

Another example is the statement from Lakota author Standing Bear trying to explain the perspective of the white man from a Native American perspective:

> The white man does not understand the Indian for the reason that he does not understand America. He is too far removed from its formative process. The roots of the tree of his life have not yet grasped the rock and soil. The white man is still troubled with primitive fears; he still has in his consciousness the perils of this frontier continent.[393]

There are some common elements in all the statements that have been reviewed. All these elements circle around the white man's incapability to understand the significance of a spiritual connection to nature and the respect for ancestors. In view of the recently decreasing self-confidence of the western civilization due to heightened sensitivity to environmental issues and diverse cultures, an increasing understanding of the Indian's concerns expressed in their statements seems to develop. Whether this heightened sensitivity will ever translate into hard law remains to be seen. Great vision and wisdom as expressed in the examples above would only be suitable topics for a constitution. How these would be implemented on the lower, more concrete levels of legislation is another question.

In sum, the statements of famous Native Americans only allow conclusions regarding their genuine relationship to nature and its resources.

b) Canons of Construction

Clear dominance of the European-American legal conception over Indian legal matters manifests itself in the *Canons of Construction* which provide that ambiguous provisions are to be interpreted in favor of the Indians: In case of doubt, the Indian understanding prevails.[394] In *Shoshone Indians v. United States*, the Supreme Court held that

---

[392] CLINTON et al. eds., AMERICAN INDIAN LAW: NATIVE NATIONS AND THE FEDERAL SYSTEM 137 (4th ed. 2005).

[393] *Id.*

[394] Worcester v. Georgia, 31 U.S. 515, 528 (1832); Shoshone Indians v. United States, 324 U.S. 335, 362 (1945); Jones v. Meehan, 175 U.S. 1, 11 (1899); Minnesota v. Mille Lacs Band of Chippewa Indians, 526 U.S. 172 (1999); COHEN'S HANDBOOK OF FEDERAL INDIAN LAW § 2.01 ff. (2005 ed.); CLINTON et al. eds., AMERICAN INDIAN LAW: NATIVE NATIONS AND THE FEDERAL SYSTEM 203 (4th ed. 2005); Blurton, *Canons of Construction, Stare Decisis, and Dependent Indian Communities*, 16 ALASKA L. REV. 41 (1999).

> the Indians [. . .] are a weak and dependent people who have no written language and are wholly unfamiliar with all the forms of legal expression [. . .] the treaty must therefore be construed not according to the technical meaning of its words to learned lawyers, but in the sense in which they would naturally be understood by Indians.[395]

The canons of construction have been created in *Worcester v. Georgia* with the purpose to limit the United States' right of conquest.[396] The canons are based on the special trust relationship between the United States and its native inhabitants.[397] The canons of construction require that treaties and statutes "are to be construed liberally in favor of the Indians, with ambiguous provisions interpreted in their benefit."[398] The canons of construction are very frequently applied by the courts.[399] When the Supreme Court made an exception to this rule in *Alaska v. Native Village of Venetie*,[400] it was harshly criticized.[401]

The case *Minnesota v. Mille Lacs Band of Chippewa Indians*,[402] serves not only as a good example for the remaining vital importance of the canons of construction.[403] The case also demonstrates the relevance of the canons with regard to the beneficial ownership concept. The case concerned the interpretation of treaty based land cessions in the mid-1900s. The Supreme court applied the canons of

---

[395] *Shoshone*, 304 U.S. 111 (1938); see *supra* chapter "Beneficial Ownership Used in U.S. Supreme Court Decisions", Sect. 4 with further references.

[396] Worcester v. Georgia, 31 U.S. 515, 582 (1832); Blurton, *id.* at 40 n.15 (1999); Williams, David, *Legitimation and Statutory Interpretation: Conquest, Consent, and Community in Federal Indian Law*, 80 Va. L. Rev. 413 (1994).

[397] *See infra* chapter "The Beneficial Ownership Concept Applied in Federal Indian Law", Sect. 4b); Skibine, *The Chevron Doctrine in Federal Indian Law and the Agencies' Duty to Interpret Legislation in Favor of Indians*, 11 St. Thomas L. Rev. 23 f. (1998).

[398] County of Yakima v. Confederated Tribes & Bands of the Yakima Indian Nation, 502 U.S. 251, 269; in Chickasaw Nation v. United States, 534 U.S. 85 (2001) the Supreme Courts seems to consider the application of the canons to treaties more important than their application to statutes; in that regard see *also* Weisz, *Constitutional Law – Federal Indian Law: The Erosion of Tribal Sovereignty as the Protection of the Nonintercourse Act Continues to be Redefined More Narrowly*, 80 N.D. L. REV. 217 (2004).

[399] *E.g.* in: Jones v. Meehan, 175 U.S. 11 (1899); Choate v. Trapp, 224 U.S. 665, 675 (1912); Choctaw Nation v. United States, 318 U.S. 423, 431 f.; Choctaw Nation v. Oklahoma, 397 U.S. 620 (1970); Bryan v. Itasca County, 426 U.S. 373 (1976); White Mountain Apache Tribe v. Bracker, 448 U.S. 136 (1981); good examples for the vital use of the canons in lower courts is Reich v. Great Lakes Indian Fish and Wildlife Communion, 4 F. 3rd 490, 495 f. (1993); Williams v. Babbitt, 115 F. 3rd 657 (9th Cir.1997); Cohen's Handbook of Federal Indian Law § 2.02[1] (2005 ed.) with further references.

[400] *See* 522 U.S. 520 (1998) (interpreting two federal Indian law statutes, Alaska Native Claims Settlement Act (ANCSA), 43 U.S.C. §§ 1601 ff. (1994); 18 U.S.C. § 1151(b) (1994) without paying any regard to the canons of construction).

[401] Blurton, *Canons of Construction, Stare Decisis, and Dependent Indian Communities*, 16 Alaska L. Rev. 54 (1999).

[402] 526 U.S. 172 (1999).

[403] Cohen's Handbook of Federal Indian Law *id.*

construction to Article 1 of the respective treaty,[404] a catch-all clause which contained the complete relinquishment and conveyance of "any and all right, title, and interest, of whatsoever the nature the same may be [..]."[405] The claimant contended that the clause included the cession of beneficial incidents (*in casu* hunting and fishing rights). The beneficial incidents were referred to in the case as *usufructuary* rights or *usufructuary* privileges without further elaboration on their nature. The Court stated that:

> It is difficult to believe that in 1855, the Chippewa would have agreed to relinquish the usufructuary rights they had fought to preserve in 1837 without at least a passing word about the relinquishment.[406]

In spite of the multitude of legal terms (right, title, and interest, of whatever nature) describing the ceded entitlements of the Chippewahs, the Supreme Court cut to the chase. The Court simply found it not believable that the Indians intended to give up their hunting and fishing privileges. For once, legalese lost the battle thanks to the canons of construction.

As fair and correct this federal Indian law version of *interpretatio contra stipulentem* might be, the canons of construction are also telling of the actual power situation. To become the systematically preferred party in case of ambiguity can only be granted by the party with the power to do so.

c) Conclusions

Considering the above, it does not seem surprising that all the doctrines and definitions surrounding Indian tribes, Indian country, Indian rights (including Indian title), and even the interpretation of Indian misery have (to a large extent) been in the domain of the daughters and sons of American immigrants. It can be concluded from the above that, from noble savage reveries to the dry law, the property concepts of the multitude of Native American tribes are entirely dominated by European-American cultural understanding, and such understanding being the root of the laws applicable to Indian matters.

---

404 10 Stat. 1166 (1855).

405 *Mille Lacs*, 172 U.S. at 184.

406 *Id.*

6. Historical Doctrines

a) Basis

There is neither a need nor space to give a full account of the history of federal Indian law.[407] The basis for the doctrines which shall be discussed in the following is the so-called *Marshall Trilogy*, three Supreme Court decisions of the early nineteenth century.[408] These decisions do not only provide an extensive recount of the history of the relationship between the United States and its aboriginal inhabitants, but no other group of cases has permanently shaped the fundamental understanding of the legal relationship with the Native Americans as the *Marshall Trilogy* and its underlying doctrines have. Even today, nearly all federal Indian law cases and academic publications quote Marshall trilogy cases at least once. This incredible significance of the trilogy renders a thorough description of the historical and political context necessary.

b) The 1830s

aa) A Defining Period

In many regards, federal Indian law had its defining moment in the 1830s, a time when the U.S. Supreme Court had the difficult task to analyze and decide upon the new Removal Policy of the U.S. The goal of this policy was to remove the Indians from their original habitat and dislocate them to *Indian Country* west of the Mississippi. The reasons for that policy were manifold. Key reasons were the increasing population of the older states of the Union, discovery of minerals on Indian territory, and cultural and social differences that were thought to be resolved easier by leaving the Indians on their own.[409]

---

[407] COHEN'S HANDBOOK OF FEDERAL INDIAN LAW § 1.01 ff. (2005 ed.) (providing a detailed History of Federal Indian Law). Published for the first time in 1941, edited and amended continuously, the *Handbook* is simply the hornbook of federal Indian law. The original author, FELIX SOLOMON COHEN (1907–1953), a Harvard Graduate and Professor of Columbia University, later in his short career worked for the administration of FRANKLIN D. ROOSEVELT in the Department of the Interior where he authored the so-called Indian New Deal and became Chief of the Indian Law Survey. COHEN has been encountered on several passages of this thesis already as one of the leading scholars of the Legal Realism movement. His Columbia Law Review article *Transcendental Nonsense and the Functional Approach* 35 COLUM L. REV, 809 (1935) is a still frequently quoted masterpiece of its own kind. See *supra* notes 6, 32, 42, 58, 62, 72, 122, 124, 149.

[408] Johnson v. M'Intosh, 21 U.S. 543 (1823), Cherokee Nation v. Georgia, 30 U.S. 1 (1831), and Worcester v. Georgia, 31 U.S. 515 (1832).

[409] COHEN'S HANDBOOK OF FEDERAL INDIAN LAW 53 (1945 ed.).

bb) The Role of the Marshall Court

The Supreme Court under Chief Justice MARSHALL was given the difficult task to review the legal aspects of this epochal change of policy which was about to abolish many treaties and agreements that had been concluded with the Indians since the early colonization period. The dimensions of this new policy invited the Marshall Court to address the general historical conceptual questions surrounding the legal relationship with the Indians. The Court accepted this invitation with great enthusiasm and built a foundation for federal Indian law which, in many regards, remains intact. This is not to say that, after that era, the court has never addressed the general aspects of Indian Law again,[410] but the landmark character of three specific cases has never been surpassed.

cc) The Marshall Trilogy

Three leading cases, all of them dating back to the early nineteen hundreds and all of them issued by the Marshall Court (though not directly), touch on the subject of this thesis with their *dicta*.

The Supreme Court was fully aware of the "Indian Question."[411] More and more European settlers had arrived in the U.S., most of them eager to contribute to the prosperity of the young nation. At the same time, relationships with the Indians remained complicated and tainted by conflicts over cultural differences and, of course, newly discovered land and resources. In this politically delicate situation, a simple case-by-case management would not provide for sustainable solutions.

Therefore, the court took a step back and set the tone by addressing more general questions regarding the status of federal and state government and of the Indians. By doing so, answers regarding the rights, privileges, powers, and immunities of the Indians could be developed. This renders the three cases, *Johnson v. M'Intosh,*[412] *Cherokee Nation v. Georgia*[413] *and Worcester v. Georgia,*[414] the most significant cases in respect of these relationships.[415]

The *Marshall Trilogy* also marks the transition of the Indian tribes from sovereign foreign nations bound only by treaties to the European colonial powers and the young United States, to wards of the United States protected from state interference

---

[410] *See e.g.* United States v. Sioux Nation of Indians, 448 U.S. 371 (1980).

[411] "Indian Question" is a term that has been already used in the 19th century by *FRANCIS WALKER* (see Bibliography) but also in the 20th Century by COHEN'S HANDBOOK OF FEDERAL INDIAN LAW 19 (1945 ed.).

[412] 21 U.S. 543 (1823).

[413] 30 U.S. 1 (1831).

[414] 31 U.S. 515 (1832).

[415] Twibell, *Rethinking Johnson v. M'Intosh (1823): The Route of the Continued Forced Displacement of American Indians Despite Cobell v. Norton (2001)*, 23 GEO. IMMIGR. L.J., 129 ff. (2008).

but also kept in tutelage by the federal government. The interpretation of these historical developments that still follow the *Marshall Trilogy* constantly centers around the core questions addressed and key doctrines developed in these cases. This counts in particular for the questions surrounding the U.S. government's definition of Indian property.

c) The Doctrine of Discovery: Johnson v. M'Intosh

aa) Motivation Behind the Doctrine

MARK TWAIN has summarized the essence of the property dispute between the European settlers and the Native Americans as follows:

> When the English, the French, and the Spaniards reached America, the Indian tribes had been raiding each other's territorial clothes-lines for ages, and every acre of ground in the continent had been stolen and re-stolen 500 times. The English, the French, and the Spaniards went to work and stole it all over again; and when that was satisfactorily accomplished they went diligently to work and stole it from each other.[416]

The first era of encounter between the European conquerors and the native inhabitants of the American continent is often referred to as the *Age of Sovereignty* (1608–1830). This simultaneously marks the era of first encounter and attempts to clarify situations between the European and the Native American civilization. If the expression *Clash of Civilizations* has ever been used accurately, then it would have certainly been in this context.[417] The conquerors from the east coast of the Atlantic were vested by their rulers with the legal and military power to discover and subjugate the rest of the undiscovered planet.[418] Europeans were motivated by the dream of wealth, the desire for adventure, and the mission of bringing the light of Christian faith to the darkest corners of the world. This motivation appears in many ways as bold as the modern western civilizations' dream of global wealth and the mission of bringing human rights to all the nations of the planet.[419]

---

[416] TWAIN, FOLLOWING THE EQUATOR 276.

[417] Riley, *The Apex of Congress' Plenary Power* 221.

[418] *See generally* WILLIAMS, ROBERT A., THE AMERICAN INDIAN IN WESTERN LEGAL THOUGHT, THE DISCOURSES OF CONQUEST 121 ff.

[419] "Die Entdeckung des vierten Kontinents, der beiden Amerikas, [war] eine mehr als nur geographische Sensation. Sie spiegelte sich in zahllosen Äusserungen eines neuen theologischen und merkantilen Appetits wider." (*The discovery of the fourth Continent, the Americas, was not only sensational from a geographical perspective. It also fueled in many ways a theological and mercantile appetite* [translated by author]); SLOTERDIJK, IM WELTINNENRAUM DES KAPITALISMUS, 187.

bb) Early European Development of the Doctrine

The Doctrine of Discovery set the legal foundation of this era. It has been developed as a means to justify the conquest of the American continent and has since remained "an active part of American Law."[420] Attributed to DE VICTORIA and GROTIUS,[421] the two instrumental scholars in the development of international law,[422] the doctrine of discovery is one of the first international law principles. Another early international law scholar instrumental in the development of the doctrine was the Swiss national DE VATTEL.[423] In his work "Le Droit des Gens"[424] DE VATTEL advocates colonization with moderation:

> Aucune Nation ne peut légitimement s'approprier une étenduë de pays trop disproportionnée, et réduire ainsi les autres peuples à manquer de demeure et de subsistence. (No nation can exclusively appropriate to themselves more land than they have occasion for, or more than they are able to settle and cultivate.)[425]

DE VATTEL also mentions an exchange of opinion between the Roman emperor Nero and a Germanic tribal leader which resembles the famous speech of Chief Seattle,[426] both expressing their confusion about their conqueror's concept of property.

As will be seen, the reasonable rules of DE VATTEL did not measure up to the European discoverer's lust for land which had reached an unprecedented dynamic. The sense of superiority over the "uncivilized" population and finally the fierce competition with other conquering empires fueled the spirit of conquest at any cost.[427]

The doctrine of discovery was in line with the European conviction to be authorized "to discover countries then unknown to Christian people, and to take possession of them in the name of the King [...]."[428] The doctrine had developed

---

420 Miller, *The Doctrine of Discovery in American Indian Law*, 42 IDAHO L.J. 2 (2005).

421 FRANCISCO DE VICTORIA, OP (1492–1546), Hugo Grotius (1583–1645).

422 Miller, *id.* at 8 ff.

423 EMER(ICH) DE (VON) VATTEL (1714–1767).

424 The Law of Nations.

425 VATTEL, DROIT DES GENS 39: COHEN'S HANDBOOK OF FEDERAL INDIAN LAW 291 (1945 ed.) with further references; WILLIAMS, ROBERT A., THE AMERICAN INDIAN IN WESTERN LEGAL THOUGHT 244; Suagee, *The Supreme Court's "Whack-a-Mole" Game Theory in Federal Indian Law, a Theory that has no Place in Environmental Law*, 7 GREAT PLAINS NAT. RESOURCES J. 90, 117 (1990).

426 *See infra* Sect. 5a) of this chapter; WILSON, COLLECTED WORKS 390 (referring to JULIUS CAESAR'S account of certain Germanic tribes' communal property concept); HEINSOHN & STEIGER, EIGENTUM, ZINS UND GELD 89 ff. (4th ed. 2006).

427 Even before these three scholars, Pope Innocent IV (born SINIBALDO FIESCHI (1195–1254), Pope from 1243–1254 with his religious but also canon law defense of the Crusades is seen as highly influential to the era of conquests; Miller, *The Doctrine of Discovery in American Indian Law*, 42 IDAHO L.J., 7 (2005); WILLIAMS, ROBERT A, *id.* at 49.

428 Twibell, *Rethinking Johnson v. M'Intosh (1823)*, 23 GEO. IMMIGR. L.J., 171 f., (2008). with reference to *Johnson v. M'Intosh*, 21 U.S., 576.

into a rule of engagement for the competing European nations with only limited regard to the native's interest.

The doctrine of discovery had become a rough *first come, first served* rule amongst the conquerors because "the conflicting claims of European powers to unpopulated areas in the new world were to be resolved.[429]" As a rule to be applied in disputes between competing Europeans, the doctrine of discovery did not directly impact the position of the natives, but the indirect impact was great enough to become a predicament for the native's future power to dispose of their property.

The power of the Indians to convey their land to parties other than their discoverers was permanently limited. A tribe was not allowed to convey its land to the French if the land had been discovered by the English and so forth.[430] What was left to the Indians was the *aboriginal title*, a de facto form of property with no clear definition and delimitation.[431] The conquering nation had acquired the *right of preemption*.[432] The *doctrine of discovery* and the *right of preemption* did provide legal support to the colonization of the new world. It helped to set the foundation for the Conquerors' self-confident sense of superiority which has survived to current times.

cc) Adoption of the Doctrine by the United States

Not only the European nations, but also the young United States soon discovered the convenience of the *doctrine of discovery*. Chief Justice JOHN MARSHALL most prominently applied and justified the doctrine of discovery in his opinion expressed in *Johnson & Graham's Lessee v. M'Intosh*).[433] This case is still considered one of the most influential Supreme Court opinions of the entire history of federal Indian law.

The case is about a dispute between private *non*-Indian parties over land ownership. The dispute itself does not get the main attention, but rather the more fundamental question "what real property rights did Europeans acquire, and indigenous people lose, by virtue of the European 'Discovery' of America?"[434]

Putting the young United States in the line of their preceding European conquerors, MARSHALL concludes:

> The United States, then, have unequivocally acceded to that great and broad rule by which its civilized inhabitants now hold this country. They hold, and assert in themselves, the title by which it was acquired. They maintain, as all others have maintained, that discovery gave

---

[429] COHEN'S HANDBOOK OF FEDERAL INDIAN LAW 291, 293 (1945 ed.).

[430] *See infra* chapter "The Beneficial Ownership Concept Applied in Federal Indian Law", Sect. 3c).

[431] *See supra* note 432.

[432] MILLER, *the Doctrine of Discovery* 5.

[433] 21 U.S. 543 (1823).

[434] Robertson, *The Judicial Conquest of Native America 30.*

> an exclusive right to extinguish the Indian title of occupancy, either by purchase or by conquest; and gave also a right to such a degree of sovereignty, as the circumstances of the people would allow them to exercise.[435]

The exclusive right to extinguish Indian title of occupancy either by purchase or by conquest also implied (*e contrario*), the right to establish Indian title respectively to assign and allot property and property rights to Indian title. These crucial rights and their relation to the beneficial ownership concept will be further scrutinized in chapter "The Beneficial Ownership Concept Applied in Federal Indian Law". Once the land was discovered, land property of the natives was to be respected only at the discretion of the conquerors. Chief Justice MARSHALL[436] describes the impact of the doctrine of discovery on the Indian property as follows:

> [...] their [the Indian's] rights to complete sovereignty, as independent nations, were necessarily diminished, and their power to dispose of the soil at their own will, to whomsoever they please, was denied by the original fundamental principle, that discovery gave exclusive title to those who made it.[437]

Those who made it did not include private individuals but only competing sovereigns with the consequence that the Indian's power to sell their own land was not only restricted by the discovering sovereign, but also by that sovereign's rules regarding sales to individuals.

dd) Conclusion

At this stage, the conclusion can be made that, for the purpose of this thesis, with *Johnson v. M'Intosh* the Supreme Court, by adopting the doctrine of discovery, vested the U.S. government with the power to conquer and thereafter dispose of Indian property at its own discretion. The aboriginal title was not recognized as legally relevant. Aboriginal title was merely a tolerated *status quo ante*.[438] In that sense, the fact that Indians had *de facto* owned the land before the Europeans arrived was *de jure* considered irrelevant. As a next step, a better understanding of the legal status of the parties involved is necessary.

---

[435] *Johnson*, 21 U.S. at 587.

[436] JOHN MARSHALL (1755–1835).

[437] *Johnson*, 21 U.S. at 574.

[438] *See infra* chapter "The Beneficial Ownership Concept Applied in Federal Indian Law", Sect. 3.

d) The Doctrine of Dependent Sovereign: Cherokee Nation v. Georgia

In *Cherokee Nation v. Georgia*, the Supreme Court set the foundation for the interpretation of Indian status which still echoes today. The decision has a decisive impact not only on the general status of independence of Indian tribes but also on their ownership status. The original definition of the status of the Indians can be found in the case *Cherokee Nation v. Georgia*, another decision of the Marshall Court which was issued a good decade after *Johnson v. M'Intosh*,.[439] The relevant facts of the case are summarized in the following.

aa) The Trigger

In 1830, the State legislature of Georgia had issued a series of acts[440] which, according to the Cherokee complainants, were violating several U.S. laws, treaties,[441] court decisions,[442] and even the U.S Constitution.[443] The political intention behind these acts was to strip the Cherokees of their independent legal status. Before *Cherokee Nation v. Georgia*, the Cherokees (as all Indian tribes), were regarded as foreign nations within the territory of the U.S. with their own sovereign government, laws, judiciary powers, and - territory. The Cherokees were a particularly assimilated tribe in these regards having adopted their own constitution in 1827, declaring independences and autonomy from Georgia and the U.S.,

---

[439] 1831.

[440] To name the most important ones:

> "An act to declare void all contracts hereafter made with the Cherokee Indians, so far as the Indians are concerned";
>
> "An act to prevent the exercise of assumed and arbitrary power by all persons under pretext of authority from the Cherokee Indians and their laws, and to prevent white persons from residing within that part of the chartered limits";
>
> "An act to authorize the Governor to take possession of the gold, silver, and other mines lying and being in that section of the chartered limits of Georgia commonly called the Cherokee country, and those upon all other unappropriated lands of the state, and for punishing any person or persons who may hereafter be found trespassing upon the mines", these acts were passed in late December 1830", 30 U.S. 13f.

[441] *Cherokee*, 30 U.S. at 4 (listing namely the Treaty of Hopewell, 7 Stat. 21 (1785), and the Treaty of Holston, 7 Stat. 39 (1791)).

[442] Namely Fletcher v. Peck, 10 U.S. 87.

[443] The term nation in the context of federal Indian law has a variety of connotations. Sometimes used in a technical, international law sense but then also as a synonym to tribe or, as in Worcester v. Georgia, 30 U.S. 559 (1832), "a people distinct from others." The circumstances generally render clear though what kind of definition is meant, United States v. Chavez, 290 U.S. 357,364 (1933); Burke, *The Cherokee Cases*, 21 STAN. L. REV. 522 (1969).

and claiming sole and exclusive property on the soil of their territory where the Cherokees, in the meantime, had abandoned hunting for farming.[444] The refusal to continue to recognize the sovereign status of the Indians was meant to implement the Indian Removal Act[445] which Congress had passed earlier in 1830, an act which set the basis for the removal of the Indians to territories in the west of the Mississippi River. ANDREW JACKSON, the "new President and old Indian fighter"[446] supported this act and so the Cherokees lead by their Chief, JOHN ROSS,[447] applied for an injunction at the federal Supreme Court. It was denied.

bb) The Moral Hazard

At the beginning of *Cherokee Nation v. Georgia*, Chief Justice MARSHALL admits:

> If courts were permitted to indulge their sympathies, a case better calculated to excite them can scarcely be imagined. A people [...] found by our ancestors in the quiet and uncontrolled possession of an ample domain, gradually sinking beneath our superior policy [...], have [only] yielded their lands by successive treaties formerly, each of which contains a solemn guarantee of the residue, until they retain no more of their formerly extensive territory that is deemed necessary to their comfortable subsistence. To preserve this remnant, the present application is made.[448]

Justice JOHNSON addressed the moral aspect in his concurring opinion laconically:

> With the morality of the case I have no concern; I am called upon to consider it as a legal question.[449]

The judges may have rightfully declined to opine on the moral aspects of the case. The Supreme Court was running the risk of being morally criticized for caving from the pressure of the President who wanted expedient and efficient removal of

---

[444] Burke, *The Cherokee Cases*, 21 STAN. L. REV. 503.

[445] "An Act to provide for an exchange of lands with the Indians residing in any of the states or territories, and for their removal west of the river Mississippi: Be it enacted by the Senate and House of Representatives of the United States of America, in Congress assembled, *Section 1*: That [sic] it shall and may be lawful for the President of the United States to cause so much of any territory belonging to the United States west of the river Mississippi, not included in any state of organized territory, and to which the Indian title has been extinguished, as he may judge necessary, to be divided into a suitable number of districts, for the reception of such tribes or nations of Indians as may choose to exchange the lands where they now reside, and remove there; and to cause each of said districts to be so described by natural and artificial marks, as to be easily distinguished from every other", 21st Congress, Sess. I. Ch. 148., approved, May 28, 1830.

[446] Burke, *id.* see also Prucha, *Andrew Jackson's Indian Policy*, 56 J. AM. Hist., 539 (1969) (giving a seemingly fair assessment of Jackson's true motives behind the Indian Removal Policy).

[447] Burke, *id. at* 511.

[448] *Cherokee*, 30. U.S. at 15.

[449] *Id.* at 20; for a thorough account of the moral and political aspects see Burke, *The Cherokee Cases*, 21 STAN. L. REV. 500 ff. (1969).

the eastern Indians westwards. The pressure to cultivate and exploit precious lands which were occupied by the Indians had to be vacated for developers and entrepreneurs willing to increase the countries' prosperity. There was also the much older Cherokee nation, secured by treaties with the U.S. government and now asking for nothing more than the same acknowledgment and recognition that many smaller European countries enjoyed "who had long been surrounded by and under the protection of a stronger power."[450] This starting position is very important in order to understand how the court finally decided and what conclusions can be drawn thereof for this thesis.

cc) Excursion: Sovereignty and Property

In order to answer the question regarding the relevance of sovereignty of an Indian tribe in the context of this thesis, some historical aspects of property law must be recalled at this point.[451] Traditional English common law sees the monarch as the sole owner of the land. Therefore, the monarch has the power to grant property in form of a title to his subjects.[452] "The king stood as the ultimate residual claimant."[453] This conception still echoed to the times of colonization. Chief Justice MARSHALL himself mentioned it in his lengthy introduction in *Worcester v. Georgia* when he wrote about the conditions to acquire property through a contract of sale concluded with the natives:

> This was the [settlers'] exclusive right of purchasing such lands as the natives were willing to sell. The Crown could not be understood to grant what the Crown did not affect to claim; nor was it so understood.

Therefore, "the Crown" did not claim title to Indian lands. In MARSHALL's opinion, the aboriginal title was with the natives and had been conveyed to them voluntarily by treaty.[454] Logically, without a sale there was no conveyance and the Indians could freely dispose of their property with the limitation of the discovery doctrine as described above. If the Indians were to be moved away from their own land, their status as an autonomous sovereign had to be sacrificed. Once subjugated under the new Georgian laws, the Cherokees could be disowned, without compensation because they could not call on the Takings Clause of the 5th Amendment[455]

---

[450] Burke, *id.* at 522.

[451] WILSON, COLLECTED WORKS 387 ff.

[452] 21 U.S. 593 (1823); For the notorious 1757 Yorke/Camden opinion (*a commentary on the property rights of the East India Company versus the King's dominion in newly acquired land in India, forged by American land speculators with the purpose to limit the King's granting power*), see SOSIN, WHITEHALL AND THE WILDERNESS, THE MIDDLE WEST IN BRITISH COLONIAL POLICY 229 f. WILLIAMS, ROBERT A., THE AMERICAN INDIAN IN WESTERN LEGAL THOUGHT 275 ff.

[453] Parisi, *Entropy in Property*, 50 AM. J. COMP. L., 599 (2002).

[454] *Worcester*, 31 U.S. 545.

[455] U.S. Const. amend. V.

nor the Privileges or Immunities Clause of the 14th Amendment of the U.S. Constitution.[456] Once more, the legal status of the Cherokees and, in fact, of all Indians, had a fundamental impact on their property rights. To be recognized as a sovereign nation was a *conditio sine qua non* for the Cherokees' continuous title claim within Georgian territory. The observations that follow are made with this in mind.

dd) Categorization of the Indians

Are the Indians foreign nations, states of the Union, or are they just tolerated inhabitants of Georgia ordered to abide to the laws of that state?

The Supreme Court denied the status of the Cherokees as a foreign nation, amongst other reasons, because the wording of Article I Section 8 of the U.S. Constitution "contradistinguishes" Indian Tribes from foreign nations by listing the two categories separately ("Congress shall have power [...] to regulate commerce with foreign nations, and among the several States, and with the Indian Tribes").[457] Neither did the Supreme Court recognize the Cherokees as member states of the Union. Chief Justice MARSHALL decided for another status tailored to the Indian people by denominating the Cherokees as domestic dependent nations:

> They occupy a territory to which we assert a title independent of their will, which must take effect in point of passion when their possession ceases. Meanwhile they are in a state of pupilage. Their relation to the United States resembles that of ward to his guardian.[458]

It has been suggested that MARSHALL decided to create a new kind of status for tactical reasons. As previously mentioned, the pressure on the Supreme Court to refrain from bringing the implementation of President JACKSON's Removal Policy to a halt was enormous. At the same time, the judges were aware of the political outrage they could cause by approving a policy that would be in breach with the Indian treaties. The Supreme Court decided to create the special status of dependent sovereign for the Cherokees. Decisions of that political caliber could not be decided without regard to the public opinion. Besides, to resist the political pressure and stick to the law would be nothing else but a political statement of its own. The court tried to maneuver out of that tricky situation by addressing jurisdictional concerns. Justice JOHNSON stated:

---

[456] U.S. Const. amend. XIV, § 1; the Indians did not become U.S. citizens until 1924, when the Indian Citizenship Act, 8 U.S.C.A. § 1401(b) (1924), was introduced. Compensation under the Takings Clause is still denied by the Supreme court unless the Indian Title is recognized by treaty or statute, Tee-Hit-Ton Indians v. United States, 348 U.S. 272 (1955); see *infra* chapter "The Beneficial Ownership Concept Applied in Federal Indian Law", Sect. 3a).

[457] *Cherokee*, 30 U.S. at 18.

[458] *Id* at 17; For the meaning of that status, see COHEN'S HANDBOOK OF FEDERAL INDIAN LAW 169 ff. (1945 ed.); for the political trust responsibility emerging from this interpretation see *infra* chapter "The Beneficial Ownership Concept Applied in Federal Indian Law", Sect. 4b).

> Either the Cherokees are a foreign state or they are not. If they are not, then they cannot come here, and if they are, then how can we extend our jurisdiction in their country?[459]

By deciding to grant the Cherokees a special status, the court was able to decline jurisdiction over the case. As mere wards of the United States, there was no *locus standi*, no recognition as a party of the dispute. At the same time, the Court could gain time to further develop its opinion at a later stage in a more suitable case.

> The mere question of right might perhaps be decided by this court in a proper case with proper parties. [. . .] If it be true that the Cherokee Nation have rights, this is not the tribunal in which those rights are to be asserted.[460]

Whether this tactical maneuver was the political motivation behind *Cherokee Nation v. Georgia*, is less relevant here than the legal motivation behind the case. By giving the Indian status a special definition, the Supreme Court ensured that it would reserve its right to elaborate on that definition in future cases. This way the Court kept the definition of Indian property in its hands. By defining the United States as the guardians of the Indians, the Supreme Court was able to call on the responsibility of the President to consider the well-being of the Indians into consideration. In sum, by defining the Indians as wards of the federal (not state) government, the Supreme Court was able to preserve its own sovereignty and simultaneously putting more responsibility on the President. What may be perceived in our day as a paternalistic attitude of the Supreme Court was, as will be discovered, a futile effort to help the Cherokees in their difficult legal position, an effort which would not prevent the removal of 10,000s of Indians of the Five Civilized Tribes[461] (Cherokee, Chickasaw, Choctaw, Muscogee-Creek, and Seminole Indians) in the early 1830s to a Territory west of the Mississippi. This removal is commonly referred to as the Trail of Tears.[462]

ee) Consequences on Indian Property

What are the decision's implications on the Cherokee's property that was situated within the territory of the State of Georgia? To answer this question, it is crucial to understand the difference between mere occupation and full title. Justice Johnson explains that differentiation as follows:

> Their [the Cherokees'] condition is something like that of the Israelites when inhabiting the deserts. Though without land that they can call theirs in the sense of property, their right of personal self-government has never been taken from them and such a form of government may exist though the land occupied be in fact that of another[463]

[459] *Cherokee*, 30. U.S. at 29.

[460] *Id.* at 20.

[461] *See generally* Cohen's Handbook of Federal Indian Law § 1.03. [4] (2005 ed.).

[462] Twibell, *Rethinking Johnson v. M'Intosh (1823)*, 23 Geo. Immigr. L.J., 154, (2008); Waldman, Atlas Of The North American Indian 223 (3rd ed. 2009).

[463] *Cherokee*, 30. U.S. at 27.

COHEN gives another example:

> The area reserved in the Washington Zoo for the exclusive use and occupancy of a herd of buffalo does not, by the fact of such reservation, cease to be the public property of the United States.[464]

These comparisons suggest that, from a property law perspective, the Indians do not have title in a sense of absolute dominion over the land they reside in but instead are only permitted a certain use and occupancy. This perception advocates a reassembly of property rights pertaining to Indian land ownership in a way that ensures title of the bundle to the U.S. guardian while the Indians are left with the sticks that are necessary for their purposes; not more, but not less.[465] Justice JOHNSON argues along that line by using Indian hunting rights for an example:

> It is clear that it was intended to give them [the Cherokees] no other rights over the territory than what were needed by a race of hunters, and it is not easy to see how their advancement beyond that state of society could ever have been promoted, or, perhaps, permitted, consistently with the unquestioned rights of the States, or United States, over the territory within their limits.[466]

For Justice JOHNSON, the assignment of a fixed territory could even be detrimental to the nomadic Indians, quite different than the early European settlers who needed preemptive rights on land with clearly defined borders in order to cultivate their newly acquired land undisturbed by other competitors[467]:

> The hunter state bore within itself the promise of vacating the territory because, when game ceased, the hunter would go elsewhere to seek it. But a more fixed state of society [and its property] would amount to a permanent destruction of the hope, and, of consequence, of beneficial character, of preemptive right.

Of course, special attention is to be drawn to the term *beneficial*. The term is used to describe the quality of mobile hunting grounds. Mobile land assignments are beneficial to a tribe of hunting nomads as they have an existential economic value to the Indians. There is no point in owning a specific piece of land once the buffalos graze on the neighboring fields. To benefit from their trade, the hunters must go where the buffalos roam.

Going back to Justice JOHNSON's first quote where he mentions the potential *advancement* of the Indian society from a nomadic to an agriculturist stage. He contends that it was never the intention that such advancement would change anything on the property status of the Cherokees even though their need for clearly defined property would be as important to Indian farmers as the mobile hunting

---

[464] COHEN'S HANDBOOK OF FEDERAL INDIAN LAW 288 (1945 ed.); see Singer, *Erasing Indian Country* 229.

[465] For the bundle and sticks metaphor see Parisi, *Entropy in Property*, 50 AM. J. COMP. L. 603 (2002).

[466] *Cherokee*, 30 U.S. at 23.

[467] *See supra* chapter "The Beneficial Ownership Concept Applied in Federal Indian Law", Sect. 3c).

grounds are important for the Indian hunters. This contradiction to his quote immediately above can only be explained economically: gold was found on Cherokee territory. The Supreme Court mentioned this fact indirectly by quoting the very legislation of the state of Georgia that the Cherokees asked to be abolished. In their opinion, none of the judges further dwelled on that point. It is not entirely clear if the reasons were too obvious back then, but it would have been interesting to see what thoughts the judges had on the beneficial use of these commodities compared to the beneficial use of the buffalos or the farm land.

To summarize, the case represents a fundamental understanding of the property condition of the Indians as tolerated inhabitants with no permanent title on a specific piece of U.S. territory. The United States Congress reserves the right to extinguish or assign land to the Indians as it deems fit to its own interest.[468] Despite this, the claim of the United States to freely dispose of its territory without having to recognize certain zones within its territory as permanently untouchable Indian land could be contradictory to its interests, particularly in the case of minerals which the Indians did not have the interest or technology to mine.[469]

Cherokee Nation v. Georgia was not necessarily a judgment worthy of King SOLOMON[470] that could satisfy the position of President JACKSON and the State of Georgia on the one hand and the Cherokee nation supported group of "great lawyers" and politicians[471] on the other hand. The creation of a special status of the Cherokee nation as a dependent sovereign ward under guardianship of the U.S. government can rather be seen as a decision preparing a conceptual field for the case *Worcester v. Georgia*[472] that had to be decided in the following year (1832), a case which would become the third case of the so-called *Marshall Trilogy*.[473]

---

[468] *See infra* chapter "The Beneficial Ownership Concept Applied in Federal Indian Law", Sect. 3d).

[469] Twibell, *Rethinking Johnson v. M'Intosh (1823)*, 23 GEO. IMMIGR. L.J., 172 (2008).

[470] 1 Kings 3, 16.

[471] William Wirt, John Sergeant, Supreme Court Justice Story, Theodore Frelinghuysen, Davy Crockett, Daniel Webster, to name only a few; Burke, *The Cherokee Cases* 21 STAN. L. REV. 511 (1969).

[472] 31 U.S. 515 (1832).

[473] For the continuous use of the term *dependent* when speaking of Indian status see Alaska v. Native Village of Venetie Tribal Government, 522 U.S. 520 (1998).

e) Doctrine of Independence from the States: Worcester v. Georgia

aa) A Monumental Decision

Worcester certainly belongs to one of MARSHALL's most famous but also most controversial decisions.[474] The Marshall Court, by holding that individual states have no criminal jurisdiction over Indian Country, marks another defining moment in federal Indian law and, along with that, the self-determination of the United States. Despite being concerned with criminal law, the Supreme Court renders clear at the very beginning that there is much more at stake in this decision. The case thus opened with a respective solemn introduction:

> This case, in every point of view in which it can be placed, is of the deepest interest.[475]

And it is. The decision is not only the third of the *Marshall Trilogy*; it is one of the most comprehensive accounts of federal Indian law. *Worcester* is in many ways the defining overview of all the different forms of legal interaction between the United States and its native inhabitants. The decision stands at the end of a long lasting and heated debate on the fate of the Indians. One of Justice MARSHALL's brethren, Justice STORY,[476] wrote: "The Court has done its duty. Let the nation now do theirs."[477] Legend says that President JACKSON had a rather different comment ready: "John Marshall has made his decision, now let him enforce it." Historians nowadays doubt whether these were the original words of President JACKSON. Be that as it may, the decision was never enforced, but its spirit and many of its arguments survived.[478]

bb) Non-Indians in Indian Country

The facts of the case are quickly told: The state of Georgia had sentenced Samuel A. Worcester, Elizur Butler, and others,[479] missionaries who resided with the Cherokees "engaged in preaching the gospel to the Cherokee Indians, and in

---

474 Located at the end of the lower great wall on the ground floor of the Supreme Court building, visitors find a statute of Chief Justice JOHN MARSHALL, sculptured in 1883 by WILLIAM WETMORE STORY, the son of Supreme Court Justice JOSEPH STORY who sat on the bench with the Chief Justice when Worcester v. Georgia was decided. The special location of the statue is a reminder of the great achievements of the longest serving Chief Justice. MARSHALL served as Chief Justice from 1801–1835.

475 *Worcester*, 31 U.S. 515, 515.

476 JOSEPH STORY (1779–1845).

477 STORY, LIFE AND LETTERS OF JOSEPH STORY 83; Burke, *The Cherokee Cases*, 21 STAN L. REV. 527 (1969) with further reference.

478 A random LexisNexis search for federal court cases quoting *Worcester* delivered 424 hits, Johnson v. M'Intosh 92 hits, and Cherokee Nation v. Georgia 365 hits.

479 Worcester and Butler were the most prominent prisoners, others were James Trott, Samuel Mays, Surry Eaton, Austin Copeland, and Edward D. Losure, 31 U.S. 528.

translating the sacred scriptures into their language with the permission and approval of the said Cherokee Nation,"[480] to four years of prison for violation of one of the 1830 Acts that were already mentioned in *Cherokee Nation v. Georgia*. This particular act was intended to prevent white persons from residing within Cherokee limits without a license or permit from the governor of the State of Georgia. The case was appealed to the Supreme Court with the argument that the State of Georgia had no right to interfere with the laws of the Cherokee nation.[481]

cc) When Dicta Dictate

This time, other than in *Cherokee Nation v. Georgia*, the Indians were not a party to the dispute therefore; there was no question about the jurisdiction of the Supreme Court. This enabled the Court to decide on the constitutionality of the Georgian legislation. The court came to the conclusion that the act on which the imprisonment of *Worcester* et al. was based upon is unconstitutional and void.[482] But, as is in the other two cases of the *Marshall Trilogy*, the result of the decision does not give a full picture of what Worcester was all about. The Supreme Court took the opportunity to give a detailed account on the history of the relationship between the federal government, the States of the Union, and the Indians. Within the 28 page decision, the decision does not address the actual issue until the very last pages.[483]

dd) "For the Benefit and Comfort of the Indians"

In this account, the Court went back to the beginning of the occupation of North America by the European nations. The Court recognized that, before the Europeans came, the inhabitants of the new continent were organized as independent nations with their own laws and institutions. According to the Court, the independent status of the original inhabitants remained untouched, even by the Crown of England, long before the United States were founded.[484] It called the idea that the "feeble settlements on the sea coast" upon landing acquired full political power over the natives and claim dominion over their land "absurd", an idea that "never entered the mind of any man."[485] Case in point, when John Smith founded the Jamestown

---

[480] *Worcester*, 31 U.S. at 538.

[481] A detailed account of the facts surrounding the political circumstances can be found at Burke, *The Cherokee Cases*, 21 STAN L. REV. 519 ff. (1969).

[482] *Worcester*,31 U.S. at 540.

[483] *Worcester*, 31 U.S. at 560; Burke, *id.* at 523.

[484] Burke, *The Cherokee Cases*, 21 STAN L. REV. 548 (1969).

[485] *Id.* at 544.

colony in 1607, he and his 150 colonists encountered a confederation of 9,000 Indians reigned by chief POWATHAN.[486]

The Court also thoroughly analyzed several treaties that were concluded between the United States and the Cherokees, prominently the peace Treaties of Hopewell of 1785[487] and Holston of 1791.[488] Both contained articles that specifically declared the Cherokees to be under the exclusive protection of the United States and no other sovereign.[489] Article 9 of the Hopewell treaty defines the responsibility of the United States towards the Indians:

> For the benefit and comfort of the Indians, and the prevention of injuries or oppressions on the part of citizens and Indians, the United States, in Congress assembled, shall have the sole and exclusive right of regulating the trade with the Indians, and managing their affairs as they deem proper.[490]

The Court emphasized the importance of the expression *for the benefit and comfort of the Indians, and the prevention of injuries or oppressions* which was to define the spirit in which Congress was to exercise its power to manage Indian affairs. The Court did not elaborate or further define the benefit and comfort of the Indians, but at least provided some negative examples of what it considered clearly *not* to be for the benefit and comfort of the Indians, namely to divest themselves of the right of self-government on subjects not connected with trade. However, that spirit was replaced in the younger Holston Treaty. Article 14 gave a more concrete definition of what was considered best for the benefit and comfort of the Indians:

> That the Cherokee nation may be led to a greater degree of civilization, and to become herdsman and cultivators, instead of remaining in a state of hunters, the United States will from time to time furnish gratuitously the said nation with useful implements of husbandry, [...][491]

This article is very representative of one of the two political approaches of the U.S. government. The idea of integration and assimilation of the Native Americans has been a recurring strategy in Indian policy,[492] a policy with sometimes dire consequences for Indian land ownership.[493] Even though this policy is not part of

---

[486] WILLIAMS, ROBERT A., THE AMERICAN INDIAN IN WESTERN LEGAL THOUGHT 204 ff. (1990); WALDMAN, ATLAS OF THE NORTH AMERICAN INDIAN 291 (3rd ed. 2009); an interesting account of the difficult negotiations with POWATHAN see O'Melimn, *The Imperial Origins of Federal Indian Law*, 31 ARIZ. L. REV. 1254 (1999).

[487] 17 Stat. 18 (1785).

[488] 7 Stat. 39 (1791).

[489] *Worcester*, 31 U.S. at 553; Hopewell Treaty, Article 2; Holston Treaty, Article 3.

[490] 7 Stat. 39 § 9 (1791).

[491] *Id.*

[492] *See generally* COHEN'S HANDBOOK OF FEDERAL INDIAN LAW § 1 (2005 ed.).

[493] *See* in particular the times of the General Allotment Act (Dawes Act), 24 Stat. 388 (1887), which, based on the idea that assimilation of the Indians would be fostered if each of them was given property to individually allotted plots of land. See *infra* chapter "The Beneficial Ownership Concept Applied in Federal Indian Law", Sect. 2b).

the current policy of *self-determination*, the underlying notion that it is up to the U.S. government to decide on the fate of the Native Americans has prevailed to our days. With the U.S. giving itself this responsibility, it is always carried out applying U.S. law.

The great significance of *Worcester* is not only due to the fact that it greatly increased the federal government's power and responsibility to manage Indian affairs. *Worcester* is also important for its leading thoughts on the property situation of the Indians. Many deliberations of the following kind can be found in the decision:

> It is difficult to comprehend the proposition that the inhabitants of either quarter of the globe could have rightful original claims of dominion over the inhabitants of the other, or over the lands they occupied, or that the discovery of either by the other should give the discoverer rights in the country discovered which annulled the preexisting rights of its ancient possessors.[494]

According to this statement, preexisting rights of the natives cannot be extinguished by discoverers by the mere fact that they set foot on the new land. The doctrine of discovery does not address the extinction or creation of property; it merely addresses disputes arising between individual discoverers. The resolution of such a dispute has no immediate bearing on the property rights of the aboriginal holder of the title. Whether the Indian property may become extinct depends on their will:

> It [the doctrine of discovery] regulated the right given by discovery among the European discoverers, but could not affect the rights of those already in possession, either as aboriginal occupants [!] or as occupants by virtue of a discovery made before the memory of man. It gave the exclusive right to purchase, but did not found that right on a denial of the right of the possessor to sell.[495]

Such sale of property was based on Article I Section 8 of the U.S. Constitution and on the Non-intercourse Act[496]:

> The treaties and laws of the United States contemplate the Indian territory as completely separated from that of the States, and provide that all intercourse with them shall be carried on exclusively by the government of the Union.[497]

The doctrine of discovery does not touch upon the voluntary sale of land, it only prescribes with whom the contract of sale can be concluded. This clearly more moderate interpretation on the doctrine of discovery did not prevail over the interpretation in *Johnson v. M'Intosh*.

---

[494] *Worcester*, 31 U.S. at 543.

[495] *Id.* at 31.U.S. 544.

[496] A series of six statutes enacted between 1790 and 1834. The original statute can be found in Sess. 2, ch. 33, 1 Stat. 137.

[497] *Worcester*, 31. U.S. at 557.

7. Conclusion

As established, historical, cultural, lingual, and legal differences between Native Americans and Europeans have fundamentally shaped federal Indian law. A basic idea of these differences can be presented in the following table:

	Indians	European colonists
Culture	Hunter/gatherer, agriculture as perceived by Europeans	"Civilized"
Law	Unwritten tribal rules	Written (treaties, precedents, acts)
Language	Hundreds of tribal languages	One language per nation, English dominant
Property concept	Defined by European-Americans	Defined by the different laws of the European nations (namely English law)

This introduction of three of the key doctrines established in the MARSHALL Trilogy revealed before any other aspect an uneven distribution of power between the parties involved. This is not an unusual phenomenon in beneficial ownership situations. In *Laughlin v. Mitchell*,[498] for instance, an old patriarch, convinced he know what is best for her, declared his daughter's ownership to his estates to be merely beneficial.

Of course, an explanation of the inner workings of an entire field of law can never be reduced to just one aspect. Further aspects and concepts of federal Indian law need to be addressed in order to determine the role of the beneficial ownership in federal Indian law. This chapter will provide a foundation that is sufficiently solid and regularly referenced to, for the analysis that will follow in the next chapter.

[498] Laughlin v. Mitchell, 121 U.S. 416 (1887); see *supra* chapter "Beneficial Ownership Used in U.S. Supreme Court Decisions", Sect. 11.

The Beneficial Ownership Concept Applied in Federal Indian Law

Beneficial ownership in federal Indian law manifests itself in concrete, physical relations to land and resources.[499] A brief theoretical analysis of these physical relations shall prepare the field for a discussion of the legal context in which beneficial ownership incidents (may) appear.[500] This discussion shall evolve around the following four prominent property concepts in federal Indian law:

- **Communal property** as the traditional concept of Indian ownership
- **Individual property** as the increasingly significant anti-thesis to communal property
- **Aboriginal title** as the original property concept in federal Indian law
- **Trust** as a property but also a political concept.

The principles, doctrines, and leading cases supporting and defining these four concepts may at times intersect or overlap. Not all the cases and materials contained in the following analysis will explicitly mention beneficial ownership, but all of them will in their own fashion point to factual, legal or political circumstances which are essential for the understanding of the concept. Cases regarding the definition of Aboriginal title may not explicitly mention the beneficial ownership concept, but the underlying mechanisms are based on a notion that clearly differentiates between beneficial and legal entitlement.

[499] *See supra* chapter "Fundamental Aspects of Federal Indian Law", Sect. 2.

[500] Not included in the discussion are, for obvious reasons, cases where the term *beneficial owner* is simply used as a synonym for the term (trust) *beneficiary*.

M. Reinhard-DeRoo, *Beneficial Ownership*, DOI 10.1007/978-3-319-01686-3_7,

1. Physical Relations

In federal Indian law as well as in other fields of law, beneficial ownership is often mentioned merely *en passant* without further comment.[501] The main reason for this laconic use of the term is that beneficial ownership is a concept primarily based on facts. What the Supreme Court stated in *United States ex rel. Hualpai Indians v. Santa Fe Pacific Railroad* with regard to the similarly fact-driven concept of occupancy also applies to beneficial ownership[502]: "Occupancy [...] is a question of fact to be determined as any other question of fact."[503] Of course, this statement appears somewhat trivial because all cases involve questions of fact. What distinguishes concepts like beneficial ownership or occupancy from "usual" legal concepts is their overwhelming focus on factual circumstances. Beneficial ownership is established on almost *nothing but* facts. In that sense, beneficial ownership indicates who spends the money rather than who earned it; and occupancy answers the question who resides on a piece of land rather than who owns it. The relationship between the beneficial owner and an object is thus very concrete and physical. HOHFELD made the following remarks on such physical relationships:

> A man may indeed sustain close physical and beneficial [!] *physical* relations to a given *physical thing*: he may *physically* exclude others from any similar control or enjoyment. But, obviously, such purely *physical* relations could as well exist quite apart from, or occasionally in spite of, the law of organized society: physical relations are wholly distinct from jural relations.[504]

Speaking of physical relations *occasionally in spite of, the law of organized society* corresponds with POUND's concept of non-law discussed above.[505] Physical relations in that sense are non-legal relations. Such physical relations manifest themselves in a variety of scenarios. In many ways, the concept of beneficial ownership is nothing more than the denomination of such actions and

---

[501] *See* Winters v. United States, 207 U.S. 564, 576 f. (1908); Lyng v. Northwest Indian Cemetry, 485, U.S. 439, 453, 458 (1988); United States v. Shoshone Tribe of Indians, 304 U.S. 111, 116 f. (1938); United States v. Algoma Lumber Co., 305 U.S. 415, 420 f. (1993); White Mountain Apache Tribe v. Bracker, 448 U.S. 136 n. 12 (1981) (quoting Algoma); *Montana v. United States*, 450 U.S. 544, 545, 551 (1981); New York Times Co. v. Tasini, 533 U.S. 483, 508 (2001); Cleveland vs. United States, 532 U.S. 12, 16 (2000); United States v. Dorwin Aam, 887 F.2d 190 (9th Cir.1989).

[502] For the *right* of occupancy see *infra* Sect. 3b) of this chapter.

[503] 314 U.S.339, 345 (1941).

[504] Hohfeld, *Fundamental Legal Conceptions*, 26 YALE L.J. 721 (1917).

[505] *See supra* chapter "Fundamental Aspects of Federal Indian Law"; physical relations as described here must be distinguished from the "physical power" element criticized by LANGDELL, *supra* n. 150. Physical relations concern objects while physical power concerns the relationship between people and institutions.

circumstances which are "wholly distinct from jural relations". UMBECK reflects on this in his vivid coconut tree example.[506]

Suppose there is a coconut tree and only one man is able to climb that tree and pick the coconuts. The tree climbing skills of that person does not constitute any rights on the coconuts. In turn, the competitors of the tree climber logically do not end up without rights to pick the coconuts because of their lesser climbing skills. The tree climber has a mere physical but not a legal relation to the coconuts while his competitors have neither. Once he picked the coconuts, the tree climber becomes the beneficial owner.

The coconut tree example could be further elaborated to describe the relationship between beneficial and legal ownership. If the tree climber belonged to an organized society which established a rule that whoever is skilled enough to climb a tree shall be the rightful owner of the coconut. The tree climber would in this case become the *legal* owner of the coconuts he picked. What must be noted here is that this acquired legal ownership does not extinguish beneficial ownership. Beneficial ownership simply becomes an attribute of the acquired legal ownership.[507] In sum, beneficial ownership is a non-legal incident that manifests itself in the physical relation to a resource. Only with the support of legal entitlement can such relevance be achieved.

The early history of property law in the United States is regularly confronted with archetypical situations as described in the coconut example. Before their first encounter, the Europeans and the Native Americans were organized societies with their own laws. Each society's physical relation to land and resources was given its own idiosyncratic legal relevance. When the redistribution of land and resources began, the different societies had to come to terms as to the applicable rules. In that early conflict of laws the stronger civilization would prevail. This happened, however, in a very slow, complex, often painful process. Whenever common law did not allow clear definition or categorization of entitlement, the beneficial ownership concept could at least help describe the factual, physical relations to the resource in dispute. But regardless of this useful aspect, the beneficial ownership concept would not be applied systematically. The reason for this is rather obvious. Systematic application is done with rules and rules are a part of the law. Beneficial ownership, however, is not a legal concept but rather a concept defined by facts. In federal Indian law, these facts relate to land and resources (minerals, timber, fish, game etc.).

---

[506] Umbeck, *Might Makes Rights*, 19 ECON. INQUIRY, 39 (1981); Cole & Grossmann, *The Meaning of Property 'Rights': Law v. Economics?* (April 19, 2000). Available at SSRN: http://ssrn.com/abstract=219408 or http://dx.doi.org/10.2139/ssrn.219408; see generally HEINSOHN & STEIGER, EIGENTUM, ZINS UND GELD 89 ff. (4th ed. 2006) (discussing reasons for the confusion between property and possession).

[507] The choice of the term *attribute* is to be distinguished from the term *accessory*. The former is merely descriptive while the latter implies a (subordinate) legal relation.

2. Communal and Individual Ownership

The differentiation between communal and individual property is one of the great characteristics of the cultural divergence between European and Native American culture. The origin of federal Indian law was influenced by Bentham's *pursuit of happiness*,[508] by emancipation from the English Crown, and by a puritan goal to please God with the fruits of hard labor. John Locke, the seventeenth century philosopher and one of the intellectual godfathers of the English colonizers of the New World said[509]:

> God gave the world to men in common; but since he gave it them for their benefit, and the greatest conveniences of life they were capable to draw from it, it cannot be supposed he meant it should always remain in common and uncultivated.[510]

The juxtaposition of *in common* and *uncultivated* at the end of the quote suggests that individual and cultivated land was considered the more civilized way of ownership. Under the influence of recently increasing concerns about the environment, this perception has lost some of its significance. Civilization is no longer considered as a political goal equally important as the preservation of nature. An increasing sensitivity for environmental protection has fostered a slight value shift away from private to communal property. Preservation of nature has become more desirable than profit oriented exploitation of resources. When Carrie Dann, a famous Indian activist speaks of the preservation of Mother Nature for future generations, she speaks the same language like presidents and Nobel Prize winners.[511] In that sense, the Lockean motto to privatize and cultivate is nowadays challenged by the motto to publicize and regulate.

These cultural differences also translate into different legal conceptions of property. An analysis of the origin and key precedents surrounding communal and individual property in federal Indian law shall be made. Special attention will be paid to incidents which either explicitly mention beneficial ownership or facilitate a beneficial ownership related discussion.

---

508 BENTHAM's philosophy inspired the founding father's *Action of the Second Continental Congress of July 4th, 1776*, better known as the *Declaration of Independence*.

509 WILLIAMS, ROBERT A., THE AMERICAN INDIAN IN WESTERN LEGAL THOUGHT 246 ff.; BARZUN, FROM DAWN TO DECADENCE 364; see generally *supra* chapter "Beneficial Ownership as a Concept", Sect. 1 with further references.

510 LOCKE, SECOND TREATISE OF GOVERNMENT, Section 34.

511 Tsosie, *Property, Power, and American 'Justice', the Story of United States v. Dann* 328.

a) Communal Tribal Ownership

The first Spanish discoverers perceived the Indians as a people with no concept of individual property.[512] This perception survived and became an integral part of federal Indian law. COHEN's handbook thus simply states:

> Tribal property is a form of ownership in common and tribal interests are held in common for the benefit of all living members of the tribe.[513]

In the context of this thesis, this collective benefit aspect points to an important consequence of communal ownership.[514] If the tribe profits as a collective, then individual beneficial owners remain unidentified. While other fields of law prevent this dilution of ownership with strict identification rules, this does not seem necessary in federal Indian law.[515] The tribe and not individual Indians are the counterparty of treaties or the addressees of federal legislation.

aa) Definition of Indian Tribe

Generally, the Indian tribe is the collective (beneficial) owner. Many efforts to define what an Indian Tribe is have been made in federal Indian law. The case *Montoya v. United States* defines a tribe as

> a body of the same or similar race, united in a community under one leadership of government, and inhabiting a particular though sometimes ill-defined territory.[516]

The *sometimes ill-defined territory* hints to the difference between settled Indian tribes like the Pueblo Indians and nomadic tribes. A series of cases discusses the difference between Pueblo and nomadic tribes.[517] Legislation which followed these cases, namely the Indian Reorganization Act defined *Indian tribe* as follows:

---

[512] WILLIAMS, ROBERT A., THE AMERICAN INDIAN IN WESTERN LEGAL THOUGHT 102 f., 211.

[513] COHEN'S HANDBOOK OF FEDERAL INDIAN LAW § 15.02 (2005 ed.).

[514] Indians are not to be considered as *tenants in common* because they are not entitled to "federal rights of partition, conveyance, or succession at death", COHEN'S HANDBOOK OF FEDERAL INDIAN LAW § 16.01[1] (2005 ed.).

[515] *See* e.g. Securities and Exchange Act, 16(b) U.S.C. § 78a et seq. (1934); Credit Suisse Securities v. Simmonds, 132 U.S. 1414, N 1,2 (2012) (corporations may sue beneficial owners as corporate insiders); Handy & Harman v. Burnet, 284 U.S. 136 (1931); Chicago Milwaukee & St. Paul Railway Co. v. Des Moines Union Railway Co., 254 U.S. 198 (1920); Gollust v. Mendell, 501 U.S. 115 n.1 (1991) (referring to the statutory definition of beneficial ownership).

[516] Montoya v. United States 180 U.S. 261, 266 (1901).

[517] United States v. Joseph, 94 U.S. 614, 617 (1876) (holding that Pueblo Indians are more "civilized" than nomadic tribes); United States v. Candelaria, 271 U.S. 432, 441 f. (1926) (holding that, despite *Joseph*, Pueblo Indians were to be treated like "regular" Indians for the purposes of trade and intercourse); United States v. Sandoval, 231 U.S. 28, 48 f. (1913) (confirming the *Joseph* holding); Pueblo of Santa Rosa v. Fall, 273 U.S. 315, 320 (1927) (holding that the restrictions on

> The term "tribe" wherever used in this Act shall be construed to refer to any Indian tribe, organized band, pueblo, or the Indians residing on one reservation.[518]

In 1994 Congress enacted legislation determining the administrative tribe recognition process and giving the Secretary of the Interior the task to create a list of all Indian tribes recognized by the federal government.[519] Such a list may simplify the administration but does not answer more difficult delineation questions like the differentiation between certain groups, often referred to as *bands*, belonging to the same tribe.

bb) Groups and Bands of Indians

In some cases, groups or bands of Indians within a tribe may pursue different interests than the tribe itself. This can lead to a more differentiated recognition of claims and entitlements within the same tribe. *The Cherokee Trust Funds* is a case about the claim of a group of Indians, referred to as the Eastern Band of Cherokees. At issue was the claim for a portion of trust funds which had been set aside for the Cherokee nation by the U.S. government.[520] The funds were based on several treaties with the purpose to provide financial support for the Cherokee nation's removal west of the Mississippi.[521] The Eastern Band of Cherokees did not move westward but remained in North Carolina where they were never recognized as a tribe. The Supreme Court denied the Eastern Cherokee band's claim for a proportionate share in the trust funds by stating that the members of the band forfeited their rights by giving up membership:

> Those funds and that property were dedicated by the Constitution of the Cherokees, and were intended by the treaties with the United States, for the benefit of the united nation, and not in any respect for those who had separated from it, and become aliens to their nation.[522]

The legal basis (Cherokee Constitution and treaties) and the lost member status thus denied the Eastern Cherokees the benefits of the trust funds.

In *Wolfchild v. United States*,[523] a Federal Circuit Court had to decide on the beneficial ownership[524] on land and appropriations of descendants of a group of

---

the conveyance of land also apply to Pueblo Indians and not only to "nomadic" tribes); for the differentiation between Pueblo and "wild" Indians see Torres, *Who is an Indian?* 133.

518 Indian Reorganization Act, 25 U.S.C. § 479 (1934); see generally (1946) Cohen's Handbook of Federal Indian Law § 3.02[6][e] n.105 (2005 ed.) (discussing the definition based on the Indian Claims Commission Act, 25 U.S.C. § 70-70v-3 (1946).

519 Federally Recognized Indian Tribe List Act, 25 U.S.C. § 479a (1994).

520 117 U.S. 288 (1886).

521 *See also* the discussion of Cherokee Nation v. Georgia, 30 U.S. 15 (1831), *supra* chapter "Fundamental Aspects of Federal Indian Law", Sect. 6d).

522 *Cherokee Trust Funds*, 117 U.S. at 311 f.

523 559 F. 3rd 1228 (Fed. Cir.2009).

524 The term *beneficial ownership* is used here as a synonym to the trust beneficiaries' ownership.

Sioux Indians called the "loyal Mdewakantons". The "loyal Mdewakantons" did not participate in the 1862 uprising of the Sioux in Minnesota and instead supported and even protected white settlers.[525] The descendants of the "loyal Mdewakantons" could not successfully establish their claim.[526] But what is noteworthy here is the willingness of the court to distinguish different groups within the same tribe. The success of the claim is less significant here than the fact that the court's willingness to distinguish between "loyal Mdewakantons" and Mdewakantons. Communal property therefore not only rests with an entire tribe but also with groups within the same tribe.

What distinguishes *Cherokee Trust Funds* from *Wolfchild* is the Court's denial to recognize the tribal status of the Eastern Cherokees. The recognition of the "loyal Mdewakantons" was not at issue in *Wolfchild.* As a consequence, the Eastern Cherokee's claim was unsuccessful for lack of standing while the "loyal Mdewakantons'" claim was at least heard.

Whether the loyalty of the Mdewakantons and the recalcitrance of the Eastern Cherokees had an influence on the different outcomes of the cases may be hard to deny. But whatever the underlying motivation of the courts may have been: What can be said in conclusion is that communal ownership can also be claimed by factions of Indian tribes. And this certainly adds to the already existing complexity of Indian claims settlement.[527]

cc) Collective Enjoyment of Benefits

The distribution of benefits within the tribe is a matter of tribal law.[528] This is particularly true in the case where the beneficial ownership manifests itself in the enjoyment of resources which are necessary for the tribe to survive. The government is not interested which individual Indian catches a fish and which individual member of the tribe ends up eating it. What concerns the government is whether the fish was caught in Indian Country.[529]

Fishing is one of the more prominent examples of collective enjoyment. Fishing was an important topic in the famous *Montana v. United States* case.[530] It has even

---

[525] For the 1862 uprising see Waldman, Atlas Of The North American Indian 192.

[526] The claims were declined for lack of trust relationship of the federal government; see *infra* Sect. 4a) of this chapter (discussing the federal Indian law specific trust relationship).

[527] *See infra* United States v. Dann, 470 U.S. 39 (1985); see also Sect. 2b) of this chapter.

[528] The tribes' right to organize internal tribal affairs is based on the Indian Reorganization Act, 25 U.S.C.A. §§ 476 f. (1934).

[529] The term *Indian Country* is reserved for jurisdictional questions (see 18 U.S.C.A. § 1151 (1948) in federal Indian law. The most prominent leading cases surrounding jurisdictional questions and interference of the federal government in internal Indian affairs are United States v. Kagama, 118 U.S. 375 (1886) (for criminal jurisdiction) and Alaska v. Native Village of Venetie, 522 U.S. 520, 527 (1998) (for civil jurisdiction); for jurisdiction on allotments held in trust by the federal government see: Pomerance, *Federal Indian Law*, Ann. Surv. Am. L. 361 (1982).

[530] 450 U.S. 544 (1981).

been suggested that fishing was *all* this case was about because the river at stake was frequently visited by passionate fly-fishing judges (including Supreme Court Justice Byron R. White).[531] What is at issue in the given context, however, is the Indian's freedom from interference of non-Indians fishing on non-Indian territory which is situated within Indian Country.

The Supreme Court explicitly mentions *beneficial ownership* with regard to the legal relation of the Crow tribe to the river. The Court held that the United States had not "conveyed beneficial ownership of the riverbed to the Crow Tribe."[532] Instead, the river or, more specifically, the "land under navigable water" had been held in reserve by the United States in fee until Montana had joined the Union and thereby reached equal footing with the other states.[533]

The Supreme Court held in *Montana* that, apart from the missing beneficial ownership, the interest of Indians to regulate non-Indians is only permissible (1) in commercial dealings with non-Indians and (2) if non-Indian "conduct threatens or has some direct effect on the political integrity, the economic security, or the health or welfare of the tribe."[534] The Supreme Court saw no threat to the economic security caused by recreational fishing. This sport would, in the eyes of the Court, not "imperil the subsistence or welfare of the Tribe."[535]

Two conclusions regarding beneficial ownership can be drawn from *Montana*: First, beneficial ownership is conveyable and second, beneficial ownership can be defended if based on commercial dealings or in cases which threaten Indian existence.[536]

---

[531] LaVelle, *Beating a path of Retreat from Treaty Rights and Tribal Sovereignty*: *The Story of* Montana v. United States 569 f.

[532] *Montana*, 450 U.S. at 550.

[533] *Id.* at 551; Pomerance, *Federal Indian Law*, ANN. SURV. AM. L. 365 (1982); Idaho v. United States, 533 U.S. 262, 272 (2001) (Distinguishing from Montana by considering the equal footing doctrine as a mere default rule; United States v. Holt State Bank, 270 U.S. 49 f. (1985).

[534] Citing, amongst other cases Montana Catholic Missions v. Missoula County, 200 U. S. 118, 128 f.; Leading cases regarding criminal jurisdiction are Oliphant v. Suquamish Tribe of Indians, 435 U.S. 191 (1978) (denying criminal jurisdiction of Indians over non-Indians) and United States v. Wheeler, 435 U.S. 313 (1979) (limiting inherent sovereignty of tribes to protect tribal self-government and control internal relations); Pomerance, *Federal Indian Law*, ANN. SURV. AM. L. 349 f. (1982); for further development of the divestiture of Indian sovereignty as a consequence see Long, *The New Frontier of Federal Indian Law*, BUFF. PUB. INT. L.J. 13 ff., 19 (2004–2005); Suagee, *The Supreme Court's "Whack-a-Mole" Game Theory in Federal Indian Law*, 7 GREAT PLAINS NAT. RESOURCES J. 90, 108 (1990).

[535] *Montana*, 450 U.S. 564 (neglecting the testimony of the tribes official historian who stated that fish was an important food for the Crow Indians in times of scarcity); but see Idaho v. United States, 533 U.S. 262, 274 (2001) (acknowledging a tribes' dependence on fishing); LaVelle, *Beating a Path of Retreat from Treaty Rights and Tribal Sovereignty* 551.

[536] Pomerance, *id.* at 350, 365 ff.

b) Individual Indian Ownership

Individual Indian property is a relatively new concept. Before the late eighteen-hundreds the federal government mainly concerned itself with beneficial or legal ownership of the Indian tribes and not with its individual members. The tribes were granted vast autonomy in that regard. In 1887, a drastic Indian policy change came about. This policy was nourished by the idea that the Indian condition could be substantially improved by introducing individual Indian ownership.

aa) Allotment

"Before 1887, most Indian land was held tribally, with beneficial title in the tribe [. . .]."[537] After 1887, statute-based individual Indian title was introduced with the General Allotment Act.[538] The political idea behind the Allotment Act was "inspired by the highest motives."[539] The enjoyment and use of individual parcels of land, it was believed, would increase the Indian's self-esteem and foster what the Indian Bureau referred to as: "sacred egotism"[540] in each individual Native American.[541] The Act provided the legal basis for this new land redistribution policy.

Simply put, an allotment is a plot of land, a mini reservation designated to an individual Native American. In the late 1900s, thousands of allotments[542] were approved by the U.S. government.[543] But as high as the motives may have been, the reality turned out to be different. In 1880, a minority report was issued by the House Indian Affairs committee with a prophetic comment:

> [. . .] it does not make a farmer out of an Indian to give him a quarter section of land [. . .]. If this were done in the name of greed it would be bad enough; but to do it in the name of humanity is infinitely worse.[544]

---

[537] Williams, David, *Legitimation and Statutory Interpretation: Conquest, Consent, and Community in Federal Indian Law*, 80 Va. L. Rev. 430 (1994).

[538] 24 Stat. 388 (1887).

[539] Cohen's Handbook of Federal Indian Law 208 (1945 ed.).

[540] Cohen, *The Erosion of Indian Rights, 1950 to 1953, A Case Study in Bureaucracy*, 62 Yale L.J. 357 (1953).

[541] O'Melimn, *The Imperial Origins of Federal Indian Law*, 31 Ariz. L. Rev. 1224, 1268 (1999) (Showing that the idea to introduce private property in order to improve the overall economic and social situation of a people had already been applied to catholic Ireland in England of the late 1600); Williams, Robert A., The American Indian In Western Legal Thought 136 ff. (discussing the colonization efforts of the English Crown in catholic Ireland which highly influenced the legal discourse of the colonization of the New World).

[542] *Cohen's Handbook on Federal Indian Law*, 211 (1945 ed.).

[543] Allotments already existed in the early 1900s. But these allotments were less a matter of federal policy than treaty negotiations with the Indians; Young, *Indian Removal and Land Allotment: The Civilized Tribes and Jacksonian Justice*, 64 Am. Hist. Rev. 40 ff.; *Cohen Handbook on Federal Indian Law, id.* at 206; see also *United States v. Shoshone Tribe of Indians*, 304 U.S. 111.

[544] Quoted from Debo, Angie, A History Of The Indians Of The United States 300.

Many allotments were sold as soon as they were allocated and the proceeds of the sales were used for seemingly more pressing short-term needs than the development of the land for generations to come.[545] Many Indians did not have the funds necessary for the upkeep of their new property. Inheritance issues would also complicate the situation.[546] All these circumstances lead to a "checkerboard layout" of land ownership within many reservations.[547] The sale of so-called *surplus lands*, i.e. reservation land that was not allotted by the government, resulted in huge Indian land loss.[548] When comparing these devastating results with the originally well-meaning intentions behind the Allotment Policy, one cannot avoid remembering Karl Popper:

> [...] the attempt to make heaven on earth invariably produces hell. [...] It is our duty to help those who need help; but it cannot be our duty to make others happy.[549]

The allotment system, though officially abolished by the 1934 Indian Reorganization Act, still has an impact today.[550] A particularly important impact of the system is its underlying trust concept with the government as temporary trustee and the individual Indians as beneficiaries.[551] Recently, in 2009, one of the largest class-action settlements, *Cobell*,[552] was settled between the U.S. government and over 100,000 Native Americans, claiming that the U.S. government was in breach of trust for poor accounting and failing correct distribution of proceeds and funding of allotments.[553]

---

545 Tiger v. Western Investment Co., 221 U.S. 286 (1911) (Discussing the legal implications and particularly time limits on the trustee role of the federal government).

546 One particular problem was and still is the so-called *fractionation*. As the property was handed down from generation to generation, more and more heirs were entitled to a fraction of the originally allotted 160 Acres of land with the effect that in the meantime, individual shares on the property are smaller than the size of a postage stamp and the value far below one cent.

547 Weisz, *Constitutional Law – Federal Indian Law*, 80 N.D. L. REV. 222 (2004); Lee, *Rediscovering the Constitutional Lineage of Federal Indian Law*, 27 N.M. L. REV. 317 (1997).

548 By the end of the allotment era in 1934 Indian land holdings had been reduced from 138 million acres to 48 million acres, WEISZ, *id.* at 221 with further references.

549 POPPER, THE OPEN SOCIETY AND ITS ENEMIES, Vol. 2 Chapter 24 with reference to Vol. 1, Chapter 9.

550 LEE, *Constitutional Lineage*, *id.* at n. 549, 319 f. (1997).

551 Williams, David, *Legitimation and Statutory Interpretation*, 80 VA. L. REV. 416 (1994); Black Hills Institute of Geological Research v. South Dakota School of Mines and Technology, 12 F. 3rd 737 N 11 (8th Circ. 1993) (holding that the sale of the largest skeleton of a *tyrannosaurus rex* ever found that was discovered in South Dakota on allotted land needed approval from the federal government); CLINTON et al. eds., AMERICAN INDIAN LAW: NATIVE NATIONS AND THE FEDERAL SYSTEM 1110, 1127 (4th ed. 2005).

552 On December 7th, 2009 a class action settlement was reached. When President BARACK OBAMA endorsed the settlement by signing legislation approving government funding of the settlement in the amount of USD 3.4 billion, 14 years of litigation came to a close. Details including all the important court documents can be found on the official website at www.indiantrust.com.

553 *See infra* Sect. 4a) of this chapter.

The change from communal tribal to individual Indian ownership by implementing the Allotment Policy would also bring about new beneficial ownership incidents.

bb) Choate v. Trapp

Choate v. Trapp is "perhaps the only Supreme Court decision explicitly invalidating, on constitutional grounds, a congressional statute concerning Indians."[554] In the *Choate v. Trapp*[555] case, the Court was faced with the question whether eight thousand Choctaw and Chickasaw Indian allottees had lost their exemption from state taxation based on the 1898 Curtis Act.[556] Congress had passed new legislation in 1908[557] which essentially gave individual Indians unrestricted fee title over their allotments vesting them with "regular" property ownership but also subjecting them to state tax. The Court did not support this new legislation and held that once the individual Indians had been given unrestricted ownership based on a statute, and applying the canons of construction to the treaty based on such statute, made clear that non-taxability of allotted land was part of the federal governments' consideration and, it would be in disregard of constitutional due process rules to rescind the tax-exempt status of the Indians.[558] The Court stated that:

> While Congress, under its plenary power over Indian tribes, can amend or repeal an agreement by a later statute, it cannot destroy actually existing individual rights of property acquired under a former statute or agreement.[559]

Along with their "regular" land owner status, the Indians had also become vested with a property right which Congress was prohibited to interfere with.[560] The Supreme Court thus limits in the present case the *plenary power* doctrine applied in *Lone Wolf v. Hitchcock*.[561] Once granted full fee ownership status, individual Indian ownership ceases to be Indian and becomes "regular" with equal constitutional protection as any private property.

The tax issue at the bottom of *Choate v. Trapp* is also relevant from a beneficial ownership perspective. According to LEFF, tax duties are also associated with

---

[554] Lee, *Constitutional Lineage*, 27 N.M. L. REV. 310 (1997).

[555] 224 U.S. 665 (1912).

[556] Sec. 9, 11, 14 of the Act for the Protection of the People of Indian Territory, and for Other Purposes, 30 Stat. 495 (1898), which added the five Civilized Tribes (Choctaw, Chickasaw, Muscogee, Cherokee, and Seminole) to the allotment program.

[557] 35 Stat. 312 (1908).

[558] *Choate*, 224 U.S. at 672.

[559] *Id.* at 665.

[560] *Id.* at U.S. 666.

[561] 187 U.S. 553, 565 (1903) (holding that plenary authority has always been held by Congress over Indian tribes and is not subject to control of the Supreme Court).

beneficial ownership although the term *beneficial* "ordinarily implies "for the good of."[562]

Choate v. Trapp has recently been criticized for its *Lochner*[563] era *laissez-faire* undertone.[564] It is argued that the Court clearly followed the then ruling ideal of a society of individuals competing in a free economy. By vesting the *individual* Indians with regular citizen property rights, the Court certainly lifted MARSHALL's "wardship" yoke but at the same time expressed its disapproval of ownership by "communistic" tribes.[565] What must be respected in any event is the Court's intention to protect Indian ownership from the breach of promises of the government made in the allotment era.

cc) Jones v. Meehan

The *Jones v. Meehan* case is concerned with the situation where an individual Indian is granted land ownership by a treaty.[566] At the center of the case is a dispute over the lease of such land. The land had been inherited by the son of a Chippewah Indian Chief named Moose Dung. Chief Moose Dung had successfully negotiated with the United States for a particular piece of land to be set aside for him personally. A fundamental question of the case concerned the nature of the ownership that Moose Dung acquired by the treaty. The Supreme Court held that:

> A good title to parts of the lands of an Indian tribe may be granted to individuals by a treaty between the United States and the tribe, [. . .].[567]

By *good title* the Supreme Court means full legal ownership ("complete title in fee simple"[568]). The case was decided over 10 years after congress had implemented the General Allotment Act. The Court's interpretation of the treaty pays tribute to the government's intention to encourage particularly the Chiefs to become role models by adopting the white man's "habits and pursuits of civilized life".[569] Such pursuit required private property. Mere beneficial ownership would not suffice to achieve this goal.[570] This aspect aligns *Jones v. Meehan* with the Allotment Policy and Choate v. Trapp.

---

[562] Leff, *The Leff Dictionary of Law*, 94 YALE L.J., 2149 (1985).

[563] Lochner v. New York, 198 U.S. 45 (1905); see *supra* chapter "The Term Beneficial Ownership", Sect. 1.

[564] Lee, *Constitutional Lineage*, 27 N.M. L. REV. 310 ff. (1997).

[565] *Id.*

[566] 175 U.S. 1 (1899).

[567] *Meehan*, 175 U.S. at 1; LEE, *Constitutional Lineage*, 27 N.M. L. REV. 300 f. (1997) (providing a detailed analysis of the case).

[568] *Meehan*, 175 U.S. at 21.

[569] *Id.* at 3.

[570] For the role of limited recognition of Indian title see *infra* Sect. 3a) of this chapter.

dd) United States v. Dann[571]

United States v. Dann is not concerned with Allotment era issues of individual Indian ownership. Although the case is almost 100 years younger than the Allotment era cases discussed above, *United States v. Dann* deals with aboriginal title—a concept of Indian ownership that is even older. The Danns claimed that their individual aboriginal title had remained unaffected by a claims settlement between the United States and the Western Shoshone.[572] The settlement had been decreed by the Indian Claims Commission (ICC), an institution founded by Congress in 1946,[573] with the highly ambitious purpose to finally settle all Indian claims.[574] One reason why the ICC was dissolved again in 1978 was that the commission did not satisfactorily address the claims of individual and group Indian claims.[575] The Supreme Court reduced the extremely complex case[576] to the question whether a settlement payment made by the United States in 1972[577] to the Western Shoshone tribe would constitute a final judgment and discharge the United States. The Court mentions the possibility that individual Aboriginal title may exist under certain circumstances referring to *Cramer v. United States*.[578] While *Cramer* itself is not as explicitly acknowledging individual aboriginal title, the Court refers to this case in *United States v. Santa Fe Pacific Railroad*:

> Though the *Cramer* case involved the problem of individual Indian occupancy, this Court stated that such occupancy was not to be treated differently from the "original nomadic tribal occupancy."[579]

---

[571] 470 U.S. 39 (1985).

[572] The claim settlement was decreed by the Indian Claims Commission, an institution. For the claim for individual title as a measure of litigation tactics because individual title would "impart a better quality of title" see Tsosie, *Property, Power, and American 'Justice'* 338; the Indian Claims Commission was also held to compensate for the taking of previously unrecognized aboriginal title, Otoe & Missouria Tribe of Indians v. United States, 131 F. Supp. 265 (Ct. Cl. 1955).

[573] Indian Claims Commission Act 25 U.S.C. §§ 70-70v (1946); Indians were barred from suing the government in the Court of Claims by an 1863 provision in the Court of Claims Act (12 Stat. 765, 767). The reason for that provision may be surprising to readers unfamiliar with Native American History: Some large southern Indian tribes (Cherokee, Creeks, Choctaw, and Chickasaw, Seminoles) had owned slaves and fought on the side of the Confederacy in the Civil War, Orlando, *Aboriginal Title Claims in the Indian Claims Commission*, 13 B.C. ENVTL. AFF. L. REV. 251 (1986) with further references.

[574] Orlando, *Aboriginal Title Claims*, at 248 f. (summarizing the history of the Indian Claims Commission).

[575] *Id.* at 250.

[576] Tsosie, *Property, Power, and American 'Justice'* 326.

[577] The settlement amount was USD 26 million, approximately USD 1 per acre, not taking into account the gold and uranium which had not been extracted.

[578] 261 U. S. 219, 227 (1923); "However, the Courts reasoning in *Cramer*, that individual Indians have a legally enforceable right to occupancy in addition to tribal aboriginal title, has not been applied in subsequent decisions." Orlando, *Aboriginal Title Claims*, at 248 f.

[579] 314 U.S. 345 f. (1941).

The nature of the *original* (= aboriginal) title will be discussed in detail in the section immediately below. What should already be noted here is that the Court does not differentiate between homestead farming and nomadic occupancy. The Danns had been successful horse and cattle farmers for generations.[580] The dispute with the federal government arose in connection with an expired grazing permit on public lands adjacent to the Dann's property. The main defense against the suit from the government for trespassing was the family's continuous physical occupancy and use of the land which, they contended, was still protected by a treaty of 1863 and remained unaffected by subsequent settlements reached between the government and Shoshone representatives which they did not acknowledge. The individual, physical approach of the Danns' defense can be interpreted as a fight for the legal relevance of their beneficial ownership in public grazing lands.

3. Aboriginal Title

Many land disputes in the early history of the young United States between powerful speculators, the federal government, and the individual states involved treaties and sales contracts with Indian tribes. Courts and legislature were burdened with the difficult task to define tribal ownership. Traditional common law would not always provide satisfactory answers to questions regarding ownership of land that had been captured by conquest. A new doctrinal foundation which fitted the new situation was created by the Supreme Court with the MARSHALL Trilogy.[581] This foundation provided a legal source for, amongst many other concepts, the concept of aboriginal title.

a) Origin, Significance, and Definition

The doctrine of aboriginal title appears first in *Johnson v. M'Intosh*.[582] A detailed introduction to this case can be found above.[583] The doctrine is in fact already mentioned in the older *Fletcher v. Peck* case,[584] the first Indian case to reach the Supreme Court.[585] *Fletcher* refers to Indian title as a "mere privilege".[586] In *Fletcher*,

580 Tsosie, *Property, Power, and American 'Justice'* at 328.

581 COHEN'S HANDBOOK OF FEDERAL INDIAN LAW § 15.06[3] (2005 ed.); see *supra* chapter "Fundamental Aspects of Federal Indian Law", Sect. 6b).

582 21 U.S. 543 (1823).

583 *See supra* chapter "Fundamental Aspects of Federal Indian Law", Sect. 6c).

584 10 U.S. 87 (1810).

585 Montana v. United States 450 U. S. 565 (1985).

586 *Fletcher*, 10 U.S. at 122.

the Supreme Court held that federal law and treaties protected Indian occupancy and that the extinction of Indian title was in the exclusive domain of the federal government. As this holding implies, the case was less concerned with the Indian status and title than with the relationship between the individual states and the federal Government.

What can be restated here based on earlier findings is that aboriginal title is a "quiet and uncontrolled"[587] possession *sui generis*, which addresses the destiny of Native American ownership before the European conquerors arrived in the New World "to take possession, notwithstanding the occupancy of the Indians."[588]

> The legal centerpiece of the doctrine is that the conquered people maintain merely the right to occupy their own land once the conquering nations have "discovered" it.[589]

Despite being criticized as an "elusive"[590] concept, filled with inadequacies[591] and deriving from the "old chestnut"[592] of *Johnson v. M'Intosh*, the doctrine of aboriginal title is certainly a key concept of federal Indian property law. The concept is also based on the doctrine of discovery which limits the Indians' freedom "to dispose of the soil at their own will, to whomsoever they please."[593] Since the early 1830s, the concept of aboriginal title has been consistently applied by the Supreme Court.[594] COHEN summarizes the essence of the doctrine of aboriginal title as follows:

> While the different nations of Europe respected the right of the natives, as occupants, they asserted the ultimate dominion in themselves; and claimed and exercised, as a consequence of this ultimate dominion, a power to grant the soil, while yet in possession of the natives. These grants have been understood by all, to convey the title to the grantees, subject only to right of occupancy.[595]

There is no uniform legal definition of aboriginal title that goes beyond what has been established thus far. As WATSON points out:

> The Supreme Court, lower courts, jurists, scholars, and others have compared Indian title to the following property rights: tenancy at sufferance, tenancy at will, license, usufructuary right, leasehold interest, term for years, life estate, fee simple subject to an executor

---

587 Cherokee Nation v. Georgia, 30 U.S. 15 (1831).

588 TWIBELL, 234 Geo. Immig. L.J., 172, (2008). Shoshone Indians v. United States, 304 U.S. 111, 117 (1938).

589 Orlando, *Aboriginal Title Claims*, 13 B.C. ENVTL. AFF. L. REV. 240, 244 (1986).

590 Watson, *The Doctrine of Discovery and the Elusive Definition of Indian Title*, 15 LEWIS & CLARK L. REV. 995–1024 (2012).

591 ORLANDO, *Aboriginal Title Claims*, *supra* n. 591 at 243.

592 Lee, *Constitutional Lineage*, 27 N.M. L. REV. 274–357 (1997).

593 Johnson v. M'Intosh, 21 U.S. 574 (1823).

594 A first underdeveloped version of the doctrine appeared in Fletcher v. Peck, 10 U.S. 87 (1810) and the most recent version that could be found was in City of Sherill v. Oneida Indian Nation of New York, 544 U.S. 197, 203 n.1 (2005).

595 United States v. Kagama, 118 U.S. 375, 381 (1886); see also COHEN'S HANDBOOK OF FEDERAL INDIAN LAW 292 (1945 ed.).

> limitation, fee simple subject to a partial restraint on alienation, fee simple to the right of preemption, full beneficial ownership [!], and absolute proprietorship (fee simple absolute).[596]

It is certainly not a coincidence that beneficial ownership also appears on a list of such legal definition helter-skelter. As shown in the chapter with a digest of Supreme Court decisions in Chapter V, the term *beneficial ownership* is often used when precise legal definition is not available to capture a factual situation with sufficient legal accuracy. This can also be observed in federal Indian law. But despite this lack of uniform legal approach to the aboriginal title concept, some characteristics can be identified. These include the right of occupancy, limited transferability of title, and the U.S. government's right to extinguish aboriginal title with compensation at will. These characteristics need to be further discussed in the following after a short introduction of two important delineations.

First, aboriginal title must not be confused with the more recent concept of *recognized title*.[597] Recognized title refers to title that has been officially recognized by Congress by treaty or statute. The main difference between aboriginal title and recognized title is that the latter does not require proof of use or occupation. The letter of the statute or treaty suffices. Another important difference between recognized title and aboriginal title is that the former is eligible for compensation under the Fifth Amendment takings clause.[598] This will be discussed in more detail further below.[599]

Second, there is a rather generic concept of aboriginal title in recent human rights debate.[600] This kind of aboriginal title is described as a form of property that indigenous people have been deprived of by their governments.[601] A very instructive example of this development is the previously mentioned *United States v. Dann*[602] case where a claim to individual aboriginal title in which was unsuccessful in U.S. courts was successfully submitted to an international human rights organization (OAS, UN).[603]

---

[596] Watson, *The Doctrine of Discovery and the Elusive Definition of Indian Title*, 15 Lewis & Clark L. Rev. 995–1024 (2012); the article does, however, not provide further information on the representatives of the individual comparisons.

[597] *See* Shoshone Tribe of Indians v. United States, 304 U.S. 111 (1938).

[598] Cherokee Nation v. Southern Kansas Railway Co., 135 U.S. 641, 657 (1890).

[599] *See infra* Sect. 3e) of this chapter.

[600] Williams, David, *Legitimation and Statutory Interpretation*, 80 Va. L. Rev. 491 f. (1994).

[601] Watson, *The Doctrine of Discovery and the Elusive Definition of Indian Title*, 15 Lewis & Clark L. Rev. 995–1024 (2012), 15 Lewis & Clark L. Rev. 995–1024 (2012).

[602] 470 U.S. 39 (1984).

[603] Tsosie, *Property, Power, and American 'Justice'* 326, 344.

b) Right of Occupancy

The Indian's right of occupancy is a specific form of enjoyment of beneficial ownership in land and as such, evidently, a core element of aboriginal title. The term *right of occupancy* has originally even been used instead of the term *aboriginal title*.[604] In *Beecher v. Wetherby*, the Supreme Court states that "the right which the Indians held was only that of occupancy. The fee was in the United States, subject to that right."[605] In other words, the Indians could continue to reside on *their* land and their "right to retain possession was to be respected as long as they remained at peace with the government"[606] and as long as the government did not have other plans. The Indians thus occupied their land at "the sufferance of the European sovereign".[607] Under these conditions, the Indians had a "right" to remain undisturbed. This appears to be a rather straight-forward arrangement with the federal government. But this arrangement only addresses the relationship between the Indians and the government. It does not address the relationship with third parties such as settlers or intruders who were often a much more imminent disturbance. And this relationship is the true litmus test of the right of occupancy.

As a matter of principle, Chief Justice Marshall held in *Mitchel v. United States* that the Indian "right of occupancy is considered as sacred as the fee simple of the whites".[608] This holding is often quoted in court decisions addressing problems with third parties.[609] More concretely, the protection of aboriginal title from third party disturbance has been at issue in the already discussed *United States v. Shoshone Tribe of Indians* case.[610] In this case, the Supreme Court protected the tribe's beneficial ownership in timber and minerals, but only because such protection was recognized by treaty.[611]

In *Tee-Hit-Ton Indians v. United States*, the Supreme Court stated that:

> [Aboriginal title] is not a property right but amounts to a right of occupancy which the sovereign grants and protects against the intrusion of third parties.[612]

On second review, the wording appears rather descriptive than coercive. To grant implies power and not duty. At best, a grantor is motivated by a moral sense of

[604] Canby, American Indian Law In A Nutshell 413 (5th ed. 2009).

[605] 95 U.S. 517, 525 (1877) with further references.

[606] Cramer v. United States, 261 U.S. 219, 227; Cohen's Handbook of Federal Indian Law § 15.04 [2] (2005 ed.).

[607] Frickey, *Domesticating Federal Indian Law*, 81 Minn. L. Rev. 54 (1996).

[608] 34 U.S. 711, 746 (1835).

[609] Cramer v. United States, 261 U. S. 219, 227 (1923); Beecher v. Wetherby, 95 U. S. 517, 526 (1877); United States (Hualpai Indians) v. Santa Fe Pacific Railroad, 412 U.S. 339, 345 (1941); *United States v. Algoma Lumber Co. et al.*, 305 U.S. 415 (1939).

[610] 304 U.S. 111 (1938); see *supra* chapter "Beneficial Ownership Used in U.S. Supreme Court Decisions", Sect. 4.

[611] *See supra* Sect. 3a) of this chapter.

[612] 348 U.S. 272, 279 (1955).

responsibility, which may well apply particularly in federal Indian law. Neither does the statement of the Supreme Court imply a clear duty of the sovereign to protect the right of occupancy. Only in cases where a statute or treaty explicitly imposes a duty on the sovereign to grant and protect, aboriginal title may prevail. And finally, even if such duty could be construed, such duty may protect Indians from third party interference but not from the government itself.[613]

Ever since *Worcester v. United States*, the Supreme Court has continuously protected the property interests of the Native Americans from third party intrusion.[614] But the Court has never gone so far as to vest the United States with a *duty* to protect Indian title and consequently the right of occupancy for obvious reasons. Such a duty would have deprived the United States of its power to dispose of "its own" territory at its own discretion. This lack of duty has a significant impact on the nature of the Indians right of occupancy. There is no right without a correlative duty.[615] In that strict sense the choice of the term *right* is unfortunate. The express willingness of the United States to protect aboriginal title from third party intrusion construed a no-right of the intruders but not a right of the Indians. Even more, a duty of the United States to protect Indian title would be contrary to its power to extinguish Indian title without owing just compensation.[616]

The right of occupancy can thus be described as a revocable privilege or, as SINGER names it, a "revocable permission" of the Indians to beneficially own land.[617] This privilege prohibits third parties from intruding. HOHFELD would speak of a respective no-right being imposed on third parties. The United States has the power to grant and protect but also to revoke the right of occupancy.

c) Limited Transferability

The Native American's limited "power to dispose of the soil at their own will, to whomsoever they please"[618] is another hallmark of aboriginal title. The limitation on title transfer is also referred to as the federal government's *right of preemption* and as such related to the discovery doctrine.[619] As has been already explained above[620] behind the right of preemption was initially the idea to prevent the Indians

---

[613] *See infra* Sect. 3a) of this chapter.

[614] Worcester v. Georgia, 31 U.S. 515 (1832), where protection from state interference was at stake, see *supra* Sect. 3b) of this chapter.

[615] *See supra* chapter "Beneficial Ownership as a Concept".

[616] *See e.g.* Brown et al. v. Legal Foundation of Washington et al., 538 U.S. 216, 218, 229 (2003) (explicitly mentioning the taking of beneficial use).

[617] Singer, *Erasing Indian Country: The Story of Tee-Hit-Ton Indians v. United States*, 241.

[618] Johnson v. M'Intosh, 21 U.S. 543, 574 (1823); underline added.

[619] *See supra* chapter "Fundamental Aspects of Federal Indian Law", Sect. 6c).

[620] *See id.*

from selling land to any other European nations than the one who first discovered it.[621] But even once the distribution of the land amongst the European conquerors had developed clearer contours, the right of preemption concept survived.

Rules or decisions limiting the transfer of aboriginal title played an eminent role already in the times before the American Revolution. King George III. issued the notorious Royal Proclamation of 1763 which prohibited direct land purchases from Indians without proper license from the Crown.[622] The purpose of the Proclamation was to consolidate the territory conquered from the French after a long and costly war effort. The Crown was also worried because of the "rising temper of the tribes" manifested by the successful uprising of Chief PONTIAC under the Rasputinian influence of the Delaware prophet NEOLIN.[623] Restrictions on purchases of Indian lands infuriated speculators who sided with the Indians:

> Suddenly, even the most hardened land-market capitalist assumed the mantle of zealous advocate of the Indians' natural-law right to engage in unregulated real-estate transaction.[624]

This change of sides of early colonists would only last until the colonies were free from the "Norman Yoke" of the English Crown.[625] From this point on, disputes with the English Crown were replaced with quarrels between individual and groups of states and the new government which, with limited success, insisted on the monopoly to regulate commerce with the Indians.[626] Regarding the role of the Indians, "the only issue on which all European-descended parties agreed [...] was that Indians did not have the natural-law right to sell their land to whomever they pleased."[627] The mantle of zealous advocate had served its purpose and the concept of limited transferability of Indian title had once more survived.

The restrictions on the transfer of Aboriginal title have not substantially changed since these early days. The United Sates Code still contains the language of the Trade and Intercourse Acts which were first issued in the 1790s[628]:

> No purchase, grant, lease, or other conveyance of lands, or of any title or claim thereto, from any Indian nation or tribe of Indians, shall be of any validity in law or equity, unless the same be made by treaty or convention entered into pursuant to the Constitution.[629]

---

621 COHEN'S HANDBOOK OF FEDERAL INDIAN LAW § 15.03 (2005 ed.).

622 *Id.* at § 15.06[1] (2005 ed.]; see also Mitchel v. United States, 34 U.S. 711, 746 (1835).

623 WILLIAMS, ROBERT A., THE AMERICAN INDIAN IN WESTERN LEGAL THOUGHT 238 ff.; SOSIN, WHITEHALL AND THE WILDERNESS 226.

624 WILLIAMS, *id.* at 272 ff.

625 One of the more famous promoters of the Norman Yoke symbolism was THOMAS JEFFERSON; WILLIAMS, *id* at 271.

626 Fletcher v. Peck, 10 U.S. 87 (1810); U.S. Const. art. I, § 8; see also the Act of July 22, 1790, 1 Stat. 13 (regulating the sale of Indian land and trade and intercourse with the Indians).

627 WILLIAMS, *supra* n. 627 at 309.

628 BERGER, *Sheep, Sovereignty and the Supreme Court* 367.

629 Indian Trade and Intercourse Act 25 U.S.C. § 177 (1790).

In recent times, violations of the federal preemption right clauses in the Trade and Intercourse Acts of the 1790s have served several tribes as an important basis for the so-called *Eastern Land Claims*.[630] The tribes claimed that states purchased land without proper authorization of the federal government. It may well be called an irony of history that regulations which originally deprived the Indians of their right to dispose of their land turn out to the great financial benefit of the Indians. In any event, from a beneficial ownership perspective, cases like the *Eastern Land Claims* can be compared with the previously discussed *Central Pacific Railroad v. United States* and *Bothwell vs. Bingham County* cases.[631] All these cases discuss incomplete legal ownership. While in *Bingham* and *Central Pacific R.R.* legal ownership is not yet complete, legal ownership in the *Eastern Land Claims* about to be incomplete. These *ad interim*, or previously referred to as a-float status invite the utilization of the beneficial ownership concept.[632]

d) Extinction of Indian Title

Extinction of Indian title had already taken place when America was still under the rule of the English Crown.[633] In these days, the extinction needed approval of the English Crown. After the United States had reached independence, the approval had to be granted by the federal government. Though not mentioned explicitly, the right to extinguish Indian title had already found a basis in the Trade and Intercourse Acts of the late eighteenth century.[634] The Supreme Court supported the right to extinguish Indian title in *Johnson v. M'Intosh*,[635] and, according to *United States ex rel. Hualpai Indians v. Santa Fe Pacific Railroad*,

> [the right] has never been doubted. And whether it be done by treaty, by the sword, by purchase, by the exercise of complete dominion adverse to the right of occupancy, or otherwise, its justness is not open to inquiry in the courts.[636]

---

[630] Prominent Eastern Claims Cases are Oneida Indian Nation v. County of Oneida, 414 U.S. 661 (1974); County of Oneida v. Indian Nation, 470 U.S. 226 (1985); Oneida Nation of Indians v. City of Sherrill, 337 F. 3rd 139 (2nd Cir.2003); Joint Tribal Council of Passamaquoddy Tribe v. Morton, 528 F.2d 370 (1st Cir.1975); Pomerance, *Federal Indian Law*, ANN. SURV. AM. L. 369 (1982).

[631] *See supra* chapter "Beneficial Ownership Used in U.S. Supreme Court Decisions", Sect. 7c).

[632] Leff, *The Leff Dictionary of Law*, 94 YALE L.J. 2152 (1985), speaks of an "interest of one who has a potential but certain right, e.g. one who is kept from total ownership only by some trivial technicality not within anyone's power to prevent fulfillment."

[633] A vivid example is the extinction of Cherokee title in connection with the failed creation of the state of Vandalia; SOSIN, WHITEHALL AND THE WILDERNESS 181 ff.; WILLIAMS, THE AMERICAN INDIAN IN WESTERN LEGAL THOUGHT 261.

[634] 25 U.S.C. § 177 (1790), see generally Weisz, *Constitutional Law – Federal Indian Law*, 80 N.D. L. REV. 217 f., 230 f. (2004) (discussing the current impact of the essentially unchanged Trade and Intercourse Act on land purchased by Indians).

[635] 21 U. S. 586 (1823).

[636] 314 U.S. 339, 347 (1941).

The holding that the right to extinguish Indian title *is not open to inquiry in the courts* renders clear: the Supreme Court considers the extinction of aboriginal title to be a concern of the legislative and thus of politics. *Lone Wolf v. Hitchcock* demonstrates the Court's uncompromising fidelity to this rule.[637] In 1867, over 30 years before the case was decided, the federal government had concluded the treaty of Medicine Lodge[638] with members of several south-western Indian tribes. The treaty contained a massive reduction of the reservation territory of the tribes. Article 2 of the treaty provided for the remaining land to be "set aside for the absolute and undisturbed use and occupation of the tribes [...] [and no unauthorized person or official was] permitted to pass over, settle upon, or reside in the territory described."[639]

At the core of the *Lone Wolf* dispute was Article 12 of the Medicine Lodge treaty which provided that any further reduction of the reservation needed the agreement of at least three fourths of all the male Indians.[640] Decades later, when government officials applying dubious methods tried to force the tribes into allotment of their reservation, lengthy litigations ending in the Supreme Court began. The tribes claimed that the majority of three fourths necessary to abrogate the Medicine Lodge treaty had never been met and the tribes were victims of deceit and fraud. The tribes consequently asked the Supreme Court to bring the allotment efforts to a halt. However, the Supreme Court would not do so. Instead, the Court supported the *plenary power* of Congress to abrogate treaties at its own discretion.[641]

It must be noted here that, since the signing of the treaty of Medicine Lodge, congress had changed its Indian policy substantially. In 1871, Congress had passed legislation which ended the era of treaty making with the Indians.[642] Although treaties concluded before 1871 were not impaired by this new legislation, the unfavorable attitude towards treaties was *en vogue*. Furthermore, the Allotment Policy still enjoyed strong political support. Consequently, the Supreme Court decided that these political aspects had to be respected by the Court and were

---

[637] 187 U.S. 553 (1903).

[638] 15 Stat. 581 (1867).

[639] *See id.*

[640] Frickey, *Domesticating Federal Indian Law*, 81 MINN. L. REV. 33 (1996) (questioning the constitutionality of the plenary power doctrine based on the fundamental constitutional principle [...] that Congress ordinarily possesses only that authority delegated to it in the Constitution).

[641] Frickey, *id.* at 31, 34 ff., compares *Lone Wolf* with the *Chinese Exclusion* case, 130 U.S. 581 (1889) (the Court permitted the abrogation of an international treaty with China which permitted Chinese citizens who had visited their home country to re-enter the U.S.) and reaches the conclusion that the two cases "demonstrate the essentially unlimited power of Congress over immigration and Indian affairs."

[642] 25 U.S.C. § 71; Orlando, *Aboriginal Title Claims in the Indian Claims Commission*, 13 B. C. ENVTL. AFF. L. REV. 250 (1986); Torres, *Who is an Indian?* 128 (questioning the constitutionality of this deprivation of the Executive branches' treaty making power).

"not subject to be controlled by the judicial department of the government."[643] With its refusal to interfere with Congress' political treatment of Indian affairs, the Supreme Court gave Congress a *carte blanche* to extinguish Indian title at will and to continue with the implementation of the Allotment Policy.

The congressional intent to extinguish Indian title must at least be expressed in a clear matter. This is the one requirement that the Supreme Court established.[644] In *Burlington Northern Railroad Company v. Blackfeet Tribe of Indians* the Supreme Court holds that:

> [...] the United States technically "owns" reservation lands, [...], the Tribes retain "beneficial ownership." [The beneficial ownership of the tribe] may be diminished only by clear expression of congressional intent.[645]

In other words, as long as Congress clearly expresses its will to extinguish, the Supreme Court will not interfere. The Supreme Court uses the term *beneficial ownership* unambiguously to describe the lesser form of ownership. Technical, i.e. legal ownership trumps beneficial ownership.

The extinction can be seen as an equivalent of ceasing a grant. As already shown in *Montana v. Missoula*,[646] it is typical for a privilege that a granting party can cease "granting" at any time with no legal consequences. The requirement that the grant has to be ceased expressly is merely a formal requirement that does not substantially impair the power of the grantor. From the grantees perspective, Damocles' sword still hangs from the ceiling.

---

[643] 187 U.S. 553, 567; the doctrine of *plenary power* is based on the Constitution (U. S. Const., art. I, § 8, cl. 3) and discussed by the *Supreme Court* in earlier cases. In United States v. Rogers, 45 U.S. 567 (1846), the Court stated that: "The United States has adopted the principle originally established by European nations - namely that the aboriginal tribes of Indians in North America are not regarded as the owners of the territories which they respectively occupied. Their country was divided and parceled out as if it had been vacant and unoccupied land. If the propriety of exercising this power were now an open question, it would be one for the lawmaking and political department of the government, and not the judicial." The Court further elaborated on the doctrine in United States v. Kagama, 118 U.S. 375 (1886);, and ten years later the Court continued with "further entrenching" the doctrine of plenary power in *Lone Wolf*, Frickey, *Domesticating Federal Indian Law*, 81 MINN. L. REV. 31, 32 (1996); see also United States v. Sandoval, 231 U.S. 28 ff.; Harring, *The Distorted History that Gave Rise to the "So Called" Plenary Power Doctrine*: *The Story of United States v. Kagama* 149, 180 ff.; Suagee, *The Supreme Court's "Whack-a-Mole" Game Theory in Federal Indian Law*, 7 GREAT PLAINS NAT. RESOURCES J. 90, 111 ff., n.46 (1990).

[644] 314 U.S. 339, 353 f. (1941); as far as the discretion of the Court to review congressional intent see Chevron U.S.A., Inc. v. NRDC, 467 U.S. 837, 838 (1984); Ex parte Crow Dog, 109 U.S. 556, 568 f. (1883) (constituting lack of *clear* congressional intent to apply criminal law in Indian reservations, which lead to the acquittal of the Brulé Sioux Indian *Crow Dog*, the presumed killer of Chief *Spotted Tail*); United States v. Pelican, 232 U.S. 442 (1914) (holding that criminal jurisdiction on allotments was not limited to liquor prohibition rules); see generally Skibine, *The Chevron Doctrine in Federal Indian Law*, 11 ST. THOMAS L. REV. 15–54 (1998) (providing comprehensive background information on the doctrine).

[645] 924 F.2d 899 n.14 (9th Cir.1990) also referring to United States. v. Santa Fe, 314 U.S. 346 (1941) and to Cramer v. United States, 227, 261 U.S. 442 (1923).

[646] *Supra* chapter "Beneficial Ownership Used in U.S. Supreme Court Decisions", Sect. 7c).

e) Compensation

aa) United States v. Alcea Band of Tillamooks

Once Indian title has been extinguished, the question of compensation arises. In *United States v. Alcea Band of Tillamooks* (*Tillamooks I*),[647] the Supreme Court stated that, despite the power of Congress to extinguish aboriginal title without compensation, "the Indians have more than a merely moral claim for compensation."[648] The *Tillamooks I* court also declined the differentiation between aboriginal and recognized Indian title insisting on the sacred right of occupancy.[649] Only the dissenting opinion supported the differentiation. Justice Reed, the author of the dissent stated:

> Indians who continued to occupy their aboriginal homes, without definite recognition of their right to do so are like paleface squatters on public lands without compensable rights if they are evicted.[650]

The dissenters come to this rather formalistic comparison by solely referring to the doctrine of discovery.[651] The mere fact that squatters and Indians both occupy land without a regular legal title does not allow the same legal treatment. This would be in complete disregard of the complex political and legal relationship that the United States shares with its native inhabitants which has created a doctrine of dependent sovereign, the trustee responsibility, and the guardianship role of the United States. Surprisingly enough, the dissenters' idea to separate between recognized and aboriginal title survived for longer. It was applied later in the unsurprisingly controversial leading case that followed *Tillamook*, which will be discussed immediately below.[652]

bb) Tee-Hit-Ton Indians v. United States

In *Tee-Hit-Ton Indians v. United States*,[653] the Supreme Court held that compensation based on the Fifth Amendment of the U.S. Constitution would only apply to cases where Indian title was recognized by Congress by treaty or statute.[654] The

---

[647] 329 U.S. 40 (1946).

[648] *Id.* at 47 referring in n.18 to an embezzlement case which allowed suit by an Indian tribe despite lack of jurisdiction.

[649] *Id.* at U. S. 52, n. 30.

[650] *Id.* at 58.

[651] Lee, *Constitutional Lineage*, 27 N.M. L. REV. 344 (1997).

[652] There are two *Tillamook* cases. The one discussed here is also referred to as *Tillamook I*, *supra* n. 649, while *Tillamook II* (United States v. Alcea Band of Tillamooks, 341 U.S. 48 (1951) (holding that no interest payments were owed by the government because there was no constitutional taking).

[653] 348 U.S. 272 (1955).

[654] United States v. Creek Nation, 295 U.S. 103 (1935); United States v. Sioux Nation of Indians, 448 U.S. 371 (1980).

Court refers to "the rule derived from *Johnson v. M'Intosh*, that the taking by the United States of unrecognized Indian title is not compensable under the Fifth Amendment."[655] The Court does not give a precise page number but merely quotes the initial page of *Johnson v. M'Intosh.* A closer review of *Johnson v. M'Intosh* reveals that this decision does not mention the 5th Amendment, and *compensation* of Indians is only mentioned in a *dictum* stating that the "old world potentates" considered the Indians sufficiently compensated for their loss of "unlimited independence" with the blessings of civilization and Christianity.[656] Furthermore, the *dictum* is made in a part of the decision which discusses the European origins of the doctrine of discovery. The Court based its opinion on this doctrine with utter disregard to the unique situation of the Indian tribe.

The unique situation of the Tee-Hit-Tons is rather obvious and quickly described. Tee-Hit-Tons are an Alaskan tribe and Alaska had neither been discovered nor conquered. Alaska had been sold to the United States by Russia in 1867. However, the Supreme Court did not consider this circumstance as relevant in *Tee-Hit-Ton*, holding that

> the use of their lands was like the use of the nomadic tribes of the States Indians, and there was no evidence that the Russian handling of the Indian land problem was different from ours.[657]

What is particularly interesting in the context of this thesis is the weight that the Supreme Court gave the factual *use* of the land. According to the Court, "strong evidence" suggested that the way in which the Tee-Hit-Tons enjoyed their beneficial ownership in the lands was comparable to the way regular nomadic tribes use their land. The strong evidence consisted mainly of a testimony of one single expert witness. Remarkably the parts of the expert's testimony which the Supreme Court considered relevant were only a descriptive factual summary of the tribe's nomadic way of life under the Russians. It included several stories about direct dealings with the Russians, for example, a story about an Indian Chief *permitting the Russians* to build a house on Indian territory. There is no discussion of the historical relationship between the Russians and the Indians, no mentioning of treaties, statutes, conflicts, and (missing) colonial ambitions. In sum, the *de facto* use of the land was the deciding criterion to classify the Tee-Hit-Ton title as aboriginal title. With regard to aboriginal title, Justice Reed, the author of the *Tee-Hit-Ton* opinion candidly stated:

> Every American schoolboy knows that the savage tribes of this continent were deprived of their ancestral ranges by force and that, even when the Indians ceded millions of acres by treaty in return for blankets, food, and trinkets, it was not a sale, but the conquerors' will that deprived them of their land.[658]

---

[655] *Tee-Hit-Ton*, 348 U.S. at 285.

[656] 21 U.S. 543, 573 (1823).

[657] *Tee-Hit-Ton*, 348 U.S. at 272.

[658] *See supra* n. 659 *id.*

It appeared irrelevant to the Court that the Tee-Hit-Ton Indians had never experienced what every American schoolboy knows.[659] The Tee-Hit-Tons *de facto* use of the land seemed to be the decisive argument to fall in the category of old fashioned regular nomadic tribes with mere (extinguishable) aboriginal title.

cc) Compensation Value

Even if congress in its discretion decides to compensate, the problem of *just* compensation for taking of Indian lands remains.[660] The economic value of land may be estimated but the cultural value that a specific piece of land represents for Indians may not. Especially in case of aboriginal land which has been occupied from time immemorial, financial compensation may even be seen as an insult by some Indian cultures.[661] A prominent example for the missing equivalence of land v. money can be found in *United States v. Sioux Nation*.[662] After decades of litigation over the taking of the Black Hills reservation, the Supreme Court awarded the Sioux Nation with an amount exceeding USD 1 billion (including compound interest). To this day, the money is deposited with the United States treasury because the tribes still hope to return to the land where their ancestors had defeated General Custer in the battle of Little Big Horn.[663]

In conclusion, the fact that taking of aboriginal title is not compensated under the 5th Amendment takings clause suggests that the government has the power to take aboriginal property without having to pay for the consequences. Fortunately, this harsh result only applies to a small group of cases like *Tee-Hit-Ton*, because the vast majority of Indian title is now considered as trust land, a concept which will be discussed immediately below.

4. Indian Trust Concepts

Indian trust has two forms of appearance in federal Indian law: one form is similar to the traditional common law trust and the other is the politically influenced trust responsibility based on MARSHALL's doctrine of dependent sovereign.

---

[659] For the inaccuracy of school maps illustrating the historical landownership of the United States see Singer, *Erasing Indian Country*, 250 ff.

[660] For just compensation in general see Brown v. Legal Foundation of Washington, 538 U.S. 216, 218 (2003); for the relationship between the public purpose requirement and the just compensation requirement see Frickey, *Domesticating Federal Indian Law*, 81 MINN. L. REV. 81 (1996).

[661] For inadequate pricing see also Singer, *id.* at 247.

[662] 448 U.S. 371, 424 (1980).

[663] Frickey, *id.* at 82; WALDMAN, ATLAS OF THE NORTH AMERICAN INDIAN 193 (3rd ed. 2009).

a) *Trust Title*

Towards the end to the nineteenth century, a different conception of Indian title came about. Several political, demographical, economic, and social reasons explain this change. Immigration to the United States had continued and new immigrants needed new land. The Removal Policy had not solved but only delayed this problem. The eastern Indian tribes had been moved to the west of the Mississippi by force only to be followed by a new generation of settlers and adventurers shortly thereafter. The West with its bounty of natural resources (gold being just the most symbolic), had become the new Promised Land within the New World. Gruesome stories about ferocious previously undiscovered warrior tribes like the Apaches, Comanche, and Kiowa whose fierce attacks threatened progress and new settlements were abundant and once more fed the old notion that nomadic Indians were incapable of making proper use of the land. Shocking reports about the living conditions of reservation Indians had reached Washington who, influenced and inspired by the east coast intelligenzia, was driven by Christian, humanitarian, and early capitalist ambition to improve coexistence with the natives. A change in focus of the relationship with the Indians from tribe to individual Indian was the solution *en vogue*. Congress was, however, not ready to release the individual Indians into complete freedom of property. The MARSHALL Court concept of aboriginal title was eventually followed by a special type of Indian trust concept created by Congress.

> Over many decades, the federal government's interest in tribal land was gradually reconceived as a trustee's fee title, and the tribal interest as beneficial ownership under trust.[664]

The trust concept was introduced for the first time in the 1887 Allotment Act. The Act stated that:

> The United States does and will hold the land thus allotted, for the period of twenty-five years, in trust for the sole use and benefit of the Indian to whom such allotment shall have been made [. . .].[665]

The 1934 Indian Reorganization Act extended this trust period indefinitely.[666] The permanent trust status of Indian land with the federal government as trustee and the Native Americans as beneficiaries set the basis for a renewal of federal Indian law. A maybe unexpected strong promoter of this renewal was President NIXON.[667]

The courts started to more explicitly describe the nature and content of the trust relationship between the federal government and the Indians. The courts differentiate between the

---

[664] For compensation based on statutes see United States v. Alcea Band of Tillamooks (*Tillamooks I*), 329 U. S. 40; COHEN'S HANDBOOK OF FEDERAL INDIAN LAW § 15.04 [3][a] (2005 ed.).

[665] 25 U.S. § 348 (1887).

[666] Indian Reorganization Act, 25 U.S.C. § 479 (1934).

[667] Juliano, *A Step Backward in the Government's Representation of Tribes: The Story of Nevada v. United States*, 304.

- "*general trust relationship* between the United States and the Indian people", and
- "*context-specific trust relationships* of varying depth and responsibilities."[668]

The general trust relationship will be discussed further below.[669] Many aspects of the context-specific trust are comparable to ordinary trusts. For instance, there are no specific words or phrases necessary to determine a trust relationship.[670]

The context most trust decisions can be found in is the administration of natural resources. "Indian tribes are the beneficial owners of the natural resources located on and under their lands."[671] The content of the United States' responsibility as trustee is defined in the two *Mitchell* cases.[672] The two cases are representative of the Supreme Court's cautious pace in defining and expanding on the trustee responsibility of the federal government. In *Mitchell I* the Supreme Court held that the General Allotment Act did not foresee any specific management duties of the federal trustee. The Court stated that the congressional intent behind the Indian trust concept merely was to protect the Indians from state taxation.[673] The Court thus declined a fiduciary duty of the federal government, the breach of which could be sued in court.[674] In *Mitchell II*, the Supreme Court on remand differentiated from this holding and further developed this "bare trust" concept by holding that, based on *other* statutes than the General Allotment Act, specific duties may well be construed. *In casu* the Court saw specific fiduciary duties set forth in federal legislation regarding the sale of timber on trust land.[675] The court stated that

> In contrast to the bare trust created by the General Allotment Act, the statutes and regulations now before us clearly give the Federal Government full responsibility to manage Indian resources and land for the benefit of the Indians.[676]

In sum, the *Mitchell* cases marked the beginning of a continuous refinement of the definition of the fiduciary responsibility.[677] In *Seminole Nation v. United States*,

---

[668] Jicarilla Apache Tribe v. Supron Energy Corporation 782 F. 2d 1555 (10th Cir.1984).

[669] *See infra* Sect. 4 of this chapter.

[670] *Jicarilla, supra* n. 670 *id.*; Whiskers v. United States, 600 F.2d 1338 (10th Cir.1979); Colton v. Colton, 127 U.S. 310 (1888); Unif. Trust Code § 400–401 (2005); HUDSON, EQUITY AND TRUSTS 14; Skibine, *The Chevron Doctrine in Federal Indian Law*, 11 ST. THOMAS L. REV. 31 (1998).

[671] COHEN'S HANDBOOK OF FEDERAL INDIAN LAW § 17.01 (2005 ed.).

[672] United States v. Mitchel 1 (Mitchell I), 445 U.S. 535, (1980); United States v. Mitchel (Mitchell II), 463 U.S. 206 (1983).

[673] *Mitchell I*, 445 U.S. at 547.

[674] *Id.* at 543 f.

[675] *Mitchell II*, 463 U.S. at 209; For the sale of timber on lands held under trust see 25 U.S.C.A. § 406 f., 466.

[676] *Mitchell II*, 463 U.S. at 224.

[677] Jicarilla Apache Tribe v. Supron Energy Corporation 782 F. 2d 1555 (10th Cir.1984). (trust duty to ensure the accounting of oil and gas royalties for the Indian beneficiaries); for the effect e.g. on federal environmental statutes see Skibine, *The Chevron Doctrine in Federal Indian Law*, 11 ST. THOMAS L. REV. 34 f. (1998).

the Court burdened the government with "the most exacting fiduciary standards" when administering Indian treaty based trust fund assets.[678] At the same time, the Court never explicitly set the trust relationship between the government and the Indians on equal standards with the "fastidious standards of a private fiduciary."[679] The increasing usage of regular trust concepts law to federal Indian law has somewhat obfuscated the clear conceptual and terminological distinction between beneficial ownership and trust beneficiary.[680]

In *Minnesota v. United States*,[681] the trustee status of the United States had significant jurisdictional impact. The Supreme Court held that the United States as trust holder for Indian allottees is an indispensable party in a litigation over a right of way of lands. *Minnesota* was applied in the Circuit Court decision *Fredericks v. Mandel* which with the same *indispensability* argument, denied jurisdiction of a tribal court (Fredericks and his counterparty, the Mossets, were Indians).[682] *Fredericks* mentions beneficial ownership most prominently in the first sentence of the decision:

> Pete Fredericks is a rancher and the beneficial owner of approximately 4,600 acres of restricted trust allotments in the Fort Berthold Indian Reservation.[683]

As the case often is, there follows no further explanation to the term *beneficial ownership* but the context renders clear that *beneficial ownership* is used here as a synonym to *beneficiary*. It is not unusual in federal Indian law that even the Supreme Court uses the term *beneficial owner* instead of the more accurate term *beneficiary*.

The trust concept never entirely replaced the concept of aboriginal title. Leading federal Indian law cases like *United States v. Dann*[684] or *Tee-hit-ton Indians v. United States*[685] involve aboriginal title. Although the concept is only regarded in cases which go back to the time before the Indian trust concept was introduced.

---

[678] 316 U.S. 286, 297 (1942).

[679] Nevada v. United States, 463 U.S. 110, 128; *Jicarilla*, 782 F. 2d 1555 (10th Cir.1984) (holding that trustee must apply whichever accounting method that yields the greatest royalties); Juliano, *A Step Backward in the Government's Representation of Tribes* 320.

[680] E.g. Burlington Northern Railroad Co. v. Blackfeet Tribe of Blackfeet Indians Reservation, 934 F. 2d 899 (9th Cir. 1991).

[681] 305 U.S. 382, 386 (1939).

[682] 650 F 2d 144, 146 (8th Cir.1981); Pomerance, *Federal Indian Law*, ANN. SURV. AM. L. 361 (1982).

[683] *Fredericks*, see *supra* n 684 *id.*

[684] United States v. Dann, 470 U.S. 39 (1985) (discussing *individual* aboriginal title).

[685] 348 U.S. 272 (1955).

b) General Trust Responsibility

The trust doctrine uses the term *trust* in a less legal but more political sense. The doctrine refers to the United States' special responsibility towards its native inhabitants. COHEN's handbook speaks of the *trust or special relationship* with Indian tribes thereby combining a reserved term with a very general term.[686] In the context of the general trust responsibility sometimes even typical trust law terms such as *trustee* and *beneficiary* are used.[687] This can be misleading because the trust doctrine has not been developed from trust law.

The general trust responsibility was developed from the doctrine of dependent sovereign and the doctrine of independence from the states discussed earlier.[688] As has been shown above, both doctrines were created from *dicta* in the two so-called *Cherokee Cases*.[689] In *Cherokee Nation v. Georgia*, the Supreme Court referred to the Indians as "wards" of the United States "in a state of pupilage."[690] This state was described by the Court in *United States v. Kagama* in a fashion that HARRING calls "among the most infamous language quoted in federal Indian law history"[691]:

> The power of the General Government over these remnants of race once powerful, now weak and diminished in numbers, is necessary for their protection, [. . .].[692]

As established above, by declaring the Indians as dependent sovereigns under the protection of the United States, the Supreme Court responded to the increasing pressure of the Executive to remove the Indian tribes from their original habitat in the east to the west of the United States in the early nineteen-hundreds.[693] The appeal of Chief Justice MARSHALL to the trust responsibility of the federal government in *Cherokee v. Georgia*, may have not been heard in the Removal Era, but, in the aftermath, became "one of the cornerstones" of federal Indian law.[694]

---

[686] COHEN'S HANDBOOK OF FEDERAL INDIAN LAW § 5.04 [4][a] (2005 ed.).

[687] E.g. in her recount of United States v. Dann, 470 U.S. 39 (1985), TSOSIE refers to a statement of one of the defendants, Carrie Dann, that [the United States] is the "trustee" of the Western Shoshone people, but what kind of "trustee" allows the destruction of the life ways of the people it is supposed to protect?" Although trust law also prohibits the destruction of the trust property, it is clear that Carrie's statement clearly refers to a political or, if you will, moral responsibility of the United States; Tsosie, *Property, Power, and American Justice* 354.

[688] *See supra* chapter "Fundamental Aspects of Federal Indian Law", Sect. 6e).

[689] Cherokee Nation v. Georgia, 30 U.S. 1 (1831); Worcester v. Georgia, 31 U.S. 515 (1832); Anonymus, *Rethinking the Trust Doctrine in Federal Indian Law*, 98 HARV. Law REV. 423 (1984).

[690] 30 U.S. 18 (1831); see also Tiger v. Investment Co., 221 U.S. 286 (1911).

[691] Haring, *The Distorted History* 180.

[692] 118 U.S. 375, 384 (1886); see also Beecher v. Wetherby, 95 U.S. 517, 525 (1877) (appealing to the responsibility of the United States "as a Christian people in their treatment of an ignorant and dependent race.").

[693] *See supra* chapter "Fundamental Aspects of Federal Indian Law", Sect. 7.

[694] COHEN'S HANDBOOK OF FEDERAL INDIAN LAW § 5.04[3] (2005 ed.); ANONYMOUS, 98 HARV. L. REV. 424 f. (1984) (assuming that the conception of the trust obligations were created by *Marshall's*

VOLTAIRE's famous quote "With power comes great responsibility" works both ways: With responsibility comes great power. And in federal Indian law, the latter version seems to have prevailed more often than the former. U.S. Court of Appeals Judge WILLIAM CANBY stated: "The trust responsibility in time had become far more a sword for the government than a shield for the tribe."[695] The good intentions of the MARSHALL Court aside, declaring the Indians as wards, pupils, or even children of the United States is also an act of incapacitation.[696] To declare a part of the population *dependent* in a country which is founded on a document entitled Declaration of *In*dependence seems contradictory. In view of all this, the trust doctrine stands in contrast to the modern ideals of Native American self-determination and autonomy of Native Americans.[697]

This analysis of the general trust responsibility recalls *Laughlin v. Mitchell* where an old Southern patriarch unwilling to vest his daughter with legal ownership of his estate simply states: "I think it best for you."[698] In this regard, the *Laughlin* case is quite comparable with a situation in which the federal government is unwilling to grant Indians fee title by stating that the Indians are wards and thus do not know as well as the government what is best for them. As a political rather than legal basis, the trust doctrine is a perfect realm for concepts like beneficial ownership. In combination with the trust doctrine, beneficial ownership provides maximum flexibility in the exercise of power over property. At least there is one counterbalance: The trust doctrine only becomes an effective means to challenge legislative action *in combination with* statutory or constitutional provisions.[699]

c) Combination in Bryan v. Itasca County

Apart from *California v. Cabazon Band of Indians*,[700] *Bryan v. Itasca County*[701] is "the bedrock [decision] on which the [Indian] gaming industry began."[702] The case

"own moral judgment about the role that a powerful nation should play toward a weaker one with which it had close relations.").

[695] CANBY, AMERICAN INDIAN LAW IN A NUTSHELL 39 (5th ed. 2009).

[696] Lee, *Constitutional Lineage*, 27 N.M. L. REV. 353 (1997).

[697] ANONYMOUS, 98 HARV. L. REV. 430 ff. (1984) with further references.

[698] *See supra* chapter "Beneficial Ownership Used in U.S. Supreme Court Decisions", Sect. 11.

[699] COHEN'S HANDBOOK OF FEDERAL INDIAN LAW § 5.04[4][b] (2005 ed.).

[700] 480 U.S. 202 (1987) (holding that certain gambling activities monitored federal agencies encourage self-determination and self-sufficiency of Indian tribes and are not to be interfered by state law restrictions).

[701] 426 U.S. 373 (1976).

[702] Washburn, *How a $147 County Tax Notice Helped Bring Tribes More than $200 Billion in Gaming Revenue*, 421; see *also* California v. Cabazon Band of Mission Indians, 480 U.S. 202, 209 (1987); for gaming regulation see 102 Stat. 2467 (1988).

is of particular interest here because it combines the concept of Indian trust with the general trust responsibility.

The Indian trust aspect concerns the question whether the mobile home of a Chippewa Indian is considered real estate or private property.[703] The differentiation is important because the county could only tax private property (not permanently attached to the ground) but not property that was held in trust by the federal government (permanently attached to the ground). The Supreme Court did not discuss this differentiation which had already been decided in the lower courts without controversy. It simply speaks of *non-trust property*.[704]

The political trust responsibility appears in the holding regarding the scope of Public Law 280.[705] This holding made the case famous. Public Law 280 was enacted in the termination era with the aim to vest certain states[706] with criminal and civil jurisdiction over Indian country.[707] The political purpose behind Public Law 280 was to deal "with the problem of lawlessness on certain Indian reservations, and the absence of adequate tribal institutions for law enforcement."[708] The idea of Public Law 280 was not to replace this lack of *tribal* institutions with state and county institutions.[709] The Court refused an interpretation that would have the consequence that "governments and reservation Indians were subordinated to the full panoply of civil regulatory powers, including taxation, of state and local governments."[710]

What may be the most interesting trust responsibility aspect of *Bryan*, was a memorandum discussing whether certiorari should be granted. The memo stated that, far beyond the narrow tax issue, this case presented an opportunity to the Court to be more solicitous of Indian interest than the lower courts.[711] Since the trust responsibility is not a legal doctrine it deserves to be mentioned even if applied only at the outskirts of a court decision. As a non-legal element the general trust

---

703 *See Black Hills Institute of Geological Research v. South Dakota School of Mines and Technology*, 12 F. 3rd 737 N 11 (8th Circ. 1993) (Change of trust ownership status to mobile property of an excavated Dinosaur skeleton).

704 *Bryan, id.*

705 67 Stat. 588 (1953).

706 Alaska (added in 1958), California, Minnesota, Nebraska, Oregon, Wisconsin; Krakoff, *Mark the Plumber v. Tribal Empire, or Non-Indian Anxiety v. Tribal Sovereignty? The Story of Oliphant v. Suquamish Indian Tribe*, 274 (referring to the Public Law 280 that also deprived these states of criminal jurisdiction); for the reasons leading to Public Law 280 see Berger, *Sheep, Sovereignty and the Supreme Court* 364.

707 *See generally* Cohen's Handbook of Federal Indian Law § 1.06 (2005 ed.) (providing background information on the Termination Policy era (1943–1961)).

708 *Bryan*, 426 U.S. at 379.

709 Washburn, *How a $147 County Tax Notice Helped Bring Tribes More than $200 Billion in Gaming Revenue* 440.

710 *Bryan*, 426 U.S. 388 (1976).

711 Washburn, *id.* at 441.

responsibility may belong in the same category but not in the same sub-category as beneficial ownership since beneficial ownership is not a political concept.

5. Conclusion

In federal Indian law, the beneficial ownership concept is not applied systematically. The concept is often mentioned *en passant* without further elaboration. Nevertheless, beneficial ownership is at the heart of cases concerned with the use of resources or the occupancy of land. Beneficial ownership describes a non-legal, physical relation to an object. The federal institutions may or may not attribute legal relevance to beneficial ownership. In this chapter, several idiosyncratic federal Indian law doctrines and concepts have been reviewed. The results of this review can be summarized as follows:

- Beneficial ownership appears in situations where tribal or individual ownership rights are discussed. In such situations, beneficial ownership serves as a legally neutral starting position.
- The identification of the beneficial owner as the person or entity who *de facto* controls a resource is not an important issue in federal Indian law.
- The courts protect Indian beneficial ownership from third party but not from government interference.
- Beneficial ownership is often mentioned in connection with the traditional federal Indian law concept of aboriginal title. Aboriginal title cannot be freely transferred and is not protected by the takings clause of the Constitution. In this regard, beneficial ownership can be described as a naked factual title.
- The U.S. Congress has unlimited discretion to extinguish aboriginal title. This confirms the privilege nature of beneficial ownership.
- The change of Indian policy has not only an often drastic impact on Indian legal but also on Indian beneficial ownership.
- The current legal relationship between the federal government and the Indians is defined as a special trust relationship. In this relationship, the Indians are considered as beneficiaries and often referred to as beneficial owners.
- Apart from the legal trust relationship, federal Indian law also recognizes a political trust responsibility of the federal government. This responsibility is frequently exercised with a paternalistic undertone.

The above points allow the conclusion that plain beneficial ownership has never gained legal recognition *per se*. The United States always, for better or worse, retained control over Native American beneficial ownership in resources or land.

Epilogue

The introduction in chapter "The Term Beneficial Ownership" explains the motivation behind this thesis: The refusal to accept the popular but desperate elephant metaphor and the expression *I know it when I see it* as the best explanation for beneficial ownership that the world of legal professionals and constitutional experts has to offer. The early discovery that beneficial ownership could not easily be qualified as a simple legal phenomenon requires additional analytical elements. These elements are: perception, functionality, history, experience, language, and certain legal theories. Only one of these elements, Law & Economics, proves to be unhelpful. The chapter closes with a review of the etymology of beneficial ownership and the translation of the term into German, French, and Italian. This reveals that the meaning of the term *beneficial ownership* gets lost in translation.

Chapter "Beneficial Ownership as a Concept" of the thesis approaches beneficial ownership from a conceptual point of view. It is one of the most fascinating discoveries of the thesis that the beneficial ownership fits perfectly into HOHFELD's system of *Fundamental Conceptions of Legal Reasoning*. In HOHFELD's terms, beneficial ownership can be clearly categorized as a mere privilege or liberty rather than as a right.

Chapter "Common Law, Equity, and Beneficial Ownership" shows that beneficial ownership is neither a common law (legal) nor an equity (anti-legal) concept. Beneficial ownership is a mere factual (non-legal) concept.

Chapter "Beneficial Ownership Used in U.S. Supreme Court Decisions" demonstrates the ubiquitous and multi-faceted application of the beneficial ownership concept U.S. law. An analysis of a selection of Supreme Court decisions that mention the concept reveals certain typical elements of the concept. The most important of these elements are the factual nature, the privilege status, control issues, discrimination from beneficiary, and a certain paternalistic undertone in cases which involve parties with unequal power.

Chapter "Fundamental Aspects of Federal Indian Law" deals with federal Indian law, a field of law which has been found to be the most prolific and visual for the purposes of this thesis. An overview of the historical, cultural, and political context of this field of law is followed by an introduction of three of the most important

M. Reinhard-DeRoo, *Beneficial Ownership*, DOI 10.1007/978-3-319-01686-3_8,

Supreme Court decisions and their underlying doctrines. The monumental redistribution combined with a clash of civilizations with fundamentally different property concepts is a perfect playground for concepts like beneficial ownership.

The closing chapter "The Beneficial Ownership Concept Applied in Federal Indian Law" discusses the concrete role that beneficial ownership plays in idiosyncratic federal Indian law ownership constellations such as tribal and individual ownership, aboriginal title, and Indian trust. The concept comes to play in these constellations to capture at least factual certainty in moments of legal uncertainty. The legal uncertainty is caused by changing perceptions and interpretations of Indian status and ownership.

It was never the ambition of this paper to create a concrete definition of beneficial ownership. As we have mentioned in the introduction of this thesis, the days when ghosts were dispelled by simply finding out their names are long gone. If these pages have enabled the reader to catch a glimpse of that universal concept called beneficial ownership, I consider the effort a success.

Bibliography

Anonymus, *Rethinking the Trust Doctrine in Federal Indian Law*, 98 HARVARD LAW REVIEW, 422-440 (1984).

Arrowsmith, William, *Speech of Chief Seattle*, 8 ARION [Boston University], 461-464 (1969).

BARZUN, JACQUES, FROM DAWN TO DECADENCE, New York, NY (2000).

Belleau, Marie-Claire & Johnson, Rebecca, *I Beg to Differ: Interdisciplinary Questions about Law, Language and Dissent* in: ATKINSON, LOGAN & MAJURY, DIANA eds., LAW, MYSTERY, AND THE HUMANITIES: COLLECTED ESSAYS, 171-192, Toronto (2008).

BECCARIA, CESARE, DEI DELITTI E DELLE PENE, Milano (1973).

Bederman, David J., *Beneficial Ownership of International Claims*, 38 INTERNATIONAL AND COMPARATIVE LAW QUARTERLY, 935-946 (1989).

BENTHAM, JEREMY, THE WORKS, Edinburgh (1838).

Berger, Bethany R., *Sheep Sovereignty, and the Supreme Court: The Story of Williams v. Lee, in* INDIAN LAW STORIES 359-388 (GOLDBERG, CAROLE & WASHBURN, KEVIN K. & FRICKEY, PHILIP P. eds., New York, NY (2011).

BLACKSTONE, WILLIAM, COMMENTARY ON THE LAWS OF ENGLAND, available at: http://avalon.law.yale.edu/18th_century/blackstone_intro.asp#2.

Blurton, David M., *Canons of Construction, Stare Decisis, and Dependent Indian Communities: A Test of Judicial Integrity*, 16 ALASKA LAW REVIEW, 37-60 (1999).

Bowers, Amy & Carpenter, Kristen A, *Challenging the Narrative of Conquest: The Story of Lyng v. Northwest Indian Cemetery, in* INDIAN LAW STORIES 489-534 (GOLDBERG, CAROLE & WASHBURN, KEVIN K. & FRICKEY, PHILIP P. eds., New York, NY (2011).

Burke, Josef C., *The Cherokee Cases: A Study in Law, Politics, and Morality*, 21 STANFORD LAW REVIEW, 500-531 (1969).

Calabresi Guido & Melamed A. Douglas, *Property Rules, Liability Rules, and Inalienability: One view of the Cathedral*, 85 HARVARD LAW REVIEW, 1089-1128 (1972).

CANBY, WILLIAM B., AMERICAN INDIAN LAW IN A NUTSHELL, St. Paul, MN (5th ed. 2009).

CARDOZO, BENJAMIN N., THE NATURE OF THE JUDICIAL PROCESS, New Haven, CT (1921).

Claeys, Eric R., *Jefferson meets Coase, Land-use Torts, Law and Economics, and Property Rights*, 85 NOTRE DAME LAW REVIEW, 102-164 (2010).

Cohen, Felix S., *Transcendental Nonsense and the Functional Approach*, 35 COLUMBIA LAW REVIEW, 809-849 (1935).

idem, *The Erosion of Indian Rights, 1950 to 1953, A Case Study in Bureaucracy*, 62 YALE LAW JOURNAL, 348 (1953).

COHEN'S HANDBOOK OF FEDERAL INDIAN LAW, (NEWTON, NELL JESSUP ED.), Albuquerque, NM (2005 ed.).

COHEN'S HANDBOOK OF FEDERAL INDIAN LAW, Washington D.C. (1945 ed.).

M. Reinhard-DeRoo, *Beneficial Ownership*, DOI 10.1007/978-3-319-01686-3,

Cole Daniel & Grossmann, Peter Z., *The Meaning of Property 'Rights': Law v. Economics?* (April 19, 2000). Available at SSRN: http://ssrn.com/abstract=219408 or http://dx.doi.org/10.2139/ssrn.219408.

Corwin, Edward S., *The "Higher Law" Background of American Constitutional Law*, 42 HARVARD LAW REVIEW, 149-185 (1928).

Cunningham, Lawrence E., *Traditional Versus Economic Analysis: Evidence from Cardozo and Posner Torts Opinions*, 62 FLORIDA LAW REVIEW, 1-56 (2010).

Clark, Jerry L., *"Thus spoke Chief Seattle": The Story of an undocumented Speech*, 18 National Archive, 1-6 (1985).

CLINTON, ROBERT N., GOLDBERG, CAROLE E. & TSOSIE, REBECCA eds., AMERICAN INDIAN LAW: NATIVE NATIONS AND THE FEDERAL SYSTEM (4th ed. 2005).

D'Amato, Anthony, *Legal Uncertainty*, 71 CALIFORNIA LAW REVIEW, 1-35 (1983).

DEBO, ANGIE, A HISTORY OF THE INDIANS OF THE UNITED STATES, Oklahoma City, OK (1970).

ENZENSBERGER, HANS MAGNUS, DIE ELIXIERE DER WISSENSCHAFT, Frankfurt a.M. (2002).

Fortier, Mark, *Equity and Ideas: Coke, Ellesmere, and James I*, 51 RENAISSANCE QUARTERLY, 1255-1281, (1998).

Frickey, Philip P., *Domesticating Federal Indian Law*, 81 MINNESOTA LAW REVIEW 31 (1996).

FURTWANGLER, ALBERT, ANSWERING CHIEF SEATTLE, Seattle, WA (1997).

Gaudiosi Monica M., *The Influence of the Islamic Law of Waqf on the Development of the Trust in England: The Case of Merton College*, 136 UNIVERSITY OF PENNSYLVANIA LAW REVIEW, 1231-1261 (1988).

GEIGER, CLAUDIA, DER WIRTSCHAFTLICH BERECHTIGTE IM SINNE DER VEREINBARUNG ÜBER DIE STANDESREGELN ZUR SORGFALTSPFLICHT DER BANKEN (VSB), Bern (2006).

GEORGAKOPOULOS, NICHOLAS L., PRINCIPLES AND METHODS OF LAW AND ECONOMICS, New York, NY (2005).

GOETHE, JOHANN W., FAUST, DER TRAGÖDIE ERSTER TEIL, München (2007).

Goldberg, Carole, *What's Race Got to Do With It? The Story of Morton v. Mancari, in* INDIAN LAW STORIES 389-420 (GOLDBERG, CAROLE & WASHBURN, KEVIN K. & FRICKEY, PHILIP P. eds., New York, NY (2011).

Grechenig, Kristoffel R. & Gelter, Martin, *The Transatlantic Divergence in Legal Thought: American Law and Economics v. German Doctrinalism*, 31 HASTINGS INTERNATIONAL AND COMPARATIVE LAW REVIEW, 295-360 (2008).

Green, Michael S., *Dworkin's Fallacy, Or What the Philosophy of Language Can't Teach Us About the Law*, 89 VIRGINIA LAW REVIEW, 1897-1952 (2003).

GROSSWALD CURRAN, VIVIAN, *Comparative Law and Language*, in: ZIMMERMANN, REINHARD & REIMANN, MATHIAS ed., THE OXFORD HANDBOOK OF COMPARATIVE LAW, Oxford (2006).

Halpin, Andrew, *Fundamental Legal Conceptions Reconsidered*, 16 CANADIAN JOURNAL OF LAW AND JURISPRUDENCE, 41-54 (2003).

Hand, Learned, *Due Process and the Eight-Hour Day*, 21 HARVARD LAW REVIEW, 495-509 (1908).

Harring, Sidney L., *The Distorted History that Gave Rise to the "So Called" Plenary Power Doctrine: The Story of United States v. Kagama, in* INDIAN LAW STORIES 149-188 (GOLDBERG, CAROLE & WASHBURN, KEVIN K. & FRICKEY, PHILIP P. eds., New York, NY (2011).

Hart, H.L.A., *American Jurisprudence through English eyes: The Nightmare and the Noble Dream*, 5 GEORGIA. Law. REVIEW. 975 (1958).

HEINSOHN, GUNNAR & STEIGER, OTTO, EIGENTUM, ZINS UND GELD, Marburg (4th ed. 2006).

Hohfeld, Wesley N., *Fundamental Legal Conceptions as Applied in Judicial Reasoning*, 26 YALE LAW JOURNAL, 710-770 (1917).

idem, *The Relations between Equity and Law*, 11 MICHIGAN LAW REVIEW, 537-571 (1913).

idem, *Some Fundamental Legal Conceptions as Applied in Judicial Reasoning*, 23 YALE LAW JOURNAL, 16-59 (1913).

HOLMES, OLIVER WENDELL, THE COMMON LAW, Boston, MA (1881).

idem, *The Path of the Law*, 10 HARVARD LAW REVIEW, 457-469 (1879).

HUDSON, ALISTAIR, EQUITY AND TRUSTS, London (2001).

JHERING, RUDOLF VON, *Im juristischen Begriffshimmel in* DER ZWECK IM RECHT, Leipzig (1893).
Juliano, Anne Carrie, *A Step Backward in the Government's Representation of Tribes: The Story of Nevada v. United States in* INDIAN LAW STORIES 297-324 (GOLDBERG, CAROLE & WASHBURN, KEVIN K. & FRICKEY, PHILIP P. eds., New York, NY (2011).
KANT, IMMANUEL, PROLEGOMENA, available at: http://gutenberg.spiegel.de/buch/3511/1.
KASER, MAX, RÖMISCHE RECHTSGESCHICHTE, Göttingen (15th ed. 1986).
Kent, Michael B., *From 'Preferred Position' to 'Poor Relation': History, Wilkie v. Robbins, and the Status of Property Rights Under the Takings Clause,* 39 NEW MEXICO LAW REVIEW, 89-121 (2009).
KLEIST, HEINRICH von, DER ZWEIKAMPF / DIE HEILIGE CÄCILIE / SÄMTLICHE ANEKDOTEN / ÜBER DAS MARIONETTENTHEATER / UND ANDERE PROSA, Stuttgart (1998).
Krakoff, Sarah,, *Mark the Plumber v. Tribal Empire, or Non-Indian Anxiety v. Tribal Sovereignty?: The Story of Oliphant v. Suquamish Tribe, in* INDIAN LAW STORIES 261-296 (GOLDBERG, CAROLE & WASHBURN, KEVIN K. & FRICKEY, PHILIP P. eds., New York, NY (2011).
Lee, Yuangchung, *Rediscovering the Constitutional Lineage of Federal Indian Law,* 27 NEW MEXICO LAW REVIEW, 273-357 (1997).
LaVelle, JOHN P., *Beating a Path of Retreat from Treaty Rights and Tribal Sovereignty: The Story of Montana v. United States, in* INDIAN LAW STORIES 535-590 (GOLDBERG, CAROLE & WASHBURN, KEVIN K. & FRICKEY, PHILIP P. eds., New York, NY (2011).
Leff Arthur A., *The Leff Dictionary of Law: A Fragment, 94* YALE LAW REVIEW, 1855-2251 (1984-1985).
idem, Some Realism about Nominalism, 60 VIRGINIA LAW REVIEW, 451-482 (1974).
LIEBS, DETLEF, LATEINISCHE RECHTSREGELN UND RECHTSSPRICHWÖRTER, Munich (4th ed. 1982).
Llewellyn, Karl N., *A Realistic Jurisprudence – The Next Step,* 30 COLUMBIA LAW REVIEW, 431-465 (1930).
Long, E. Andrew, *The New Frontier of Federal Indian Law: The United States Supreme Court's Active Divestiture of Tribal Sovereignty,* 25 BUFFALO PUBLIC INTEREST LAW JOURNAL, 1-50 (2004-2005).
LOCKE, JOHN, SECOND TREATISE OF GOVERNMENT, Indianapolis / Cambridge (1980).
Macauly, Stewart, *The New versus the Old Legal Realism: "Things Ain't the Way They Used to Be"*, 2 WISCONSIN LAW REVIEW, 365-402 (2005).
MATTEI, UGO, BASIC PRINCIPLES OF PROPERTY LAW: A COMPARATIVE LEGAL AND ECONOMIC INTRODUCTION, Westport, CT (2000).
MAUTHNER, FRITZ, WÖRTERBUCH DER PHILOSOPHIE, Zürich (1980).
Meyer, Hermine Herta, *Trusts and Swiss Law,* 1 INTERNATIONAL AND COMPARATIVE LAW QUARTERLY, 378-381 (1954).
Miller, Robert J., *The Doctrine of Discovery in American Indian Law,* 42 IDAHO LAW REVIEW, 1-96 (2005).
NEW OXFORD AMERICAN DICTIONARY, Hamburg (2nd ed.2008).
NIETZSCHE, FRIEDRICH, *Über Wahrheit und Lüge im aussermoralischen Sinn,* in: WERKE IN DREI BÄNDEN, München (1954).
O'Melimn, Liam Seamus, *The Imperial Origins of Federal Indian Law: The Ideology of Colonization in Britain, Ireland, and America,* 31 ARIZONA STATE LAW JOURNAL, 1207-1275 (1999).
Orlando Caroline L., *Aboriginal Title Claims in the Indian Claims Commission: United States v. Dann and Its Due Process Implications,* 13 BOSTON COLLEGE ENVIRONMENTAL AFFAIRS LAW REVIEW, 241-280 (1986).
Ostas, Daniel T., *Postmodern Economic Analysis of Law: Extending the Pragmatic Visions of Richard A. Posner,* 36 AMERICAN BUSINESS LAW JOURNAL, 193-228 (1998).
Parisi, Francesco, *Entropy in Property,* 50 AMERICAN JOURNAL OF COMPARATIVE LAW, 595-632 (2002).
PETER, HANS, ACTIO UND WRIT, EINE VERGLEICHENDE DARSTELLUNG RÖMISCHER UND ENGLISCHER RECHTSBEHELFE, Tübingen (1957).

Pomerance, John R., *Federal Indian Law,* 1982 Annual Survey OF American Law, 347-372 (1982).

Popper, Karl Raimund, The Open Society And Its Enemies, London (2002).

Powell, H. Jefferson, *"Cardozo's Foot": The Chancellor's Conscience and Constructive Trusts,* 56 Law and Contemporary Problems 7-27 (1993).

Posner, Richard A., Economic Analysis Of Law, Boston/Toronto (1973).

Pound, Roscoe, *The Decadence of Equity*, 5 Columbia Law Review, 20-35 (1905).

idem, Law in Books and Law in Action, 44 American Law Review, 15-28 (1910).

idem, Legal Rights, 26 International Journal Of Ethics 92,-116 (1915).

idem, The Maxims of Equity, 34 Harvard Law Review 809-836, (1921).

Prucha, Francis Paul, *Andrew Jackson's Indian Policy: A Reassessment:* 56 Journal of American History, 527-539 (1969).

Radin, Max, *The Chancellor's Foot,* 49 Harvard. Law Review, 44-67 (1935).

Riley, Angela R. *The Apex of Congress' Plenary Power over Indian Affairs: The Story of Lone Wolf v. Hitchcock, in* Indian Law Stories 189-228 (Goldberg, Carole & Washburn, Kevin K. & Frickey, Philip P. eds., New York, NY (2011).

Robertson, Lindsay, *The Judicial Conquest of Native Americans: The Story of Johnson v. M'Intosh, in* Indian Law Stories 29-60 (Goldberg, Carole & Washburn, Kevin K. & Frickey, Philip P. eds., New York, NY (2011).

Sawyer, G. J., *Kennewick Man,* 280 Science, 18-19 (1998).

Scott, Austin Wakeman, *The Nature and Rights of the "Cestui Que Trust",* 17 Columbia Law Review, 269-290 (1917).

Singer, Josef William, *Property and Coercion in Federal Indian Law: The Conflict between Critical and Complacent Pragmatism,* 63 Southern California Law Review 1821 (1989-1990).

idem, Erasing Indian Country, *The Story of Tee-Hit-Ton Indians v. United States, in* Indian Law Stories 229-260 (Goldberg, Carole & Washburn, Kevin K. & Frickey, Philip P. eds., New York, NY (2011).

Skibine, Alex Tallchief, *The Chevron Doctrine in Federal Indian Law and the Agencies' Duty to Interpret Legislation in Favor of Indians: Did the EPA Reconcile the Two in Interpreting the "Tribes as States" Section of the Clean Water Act?* 11 St. Thomas Law Review, 15 (1998).

Sloterdijk, Peter, Im Weltinnenraum des Kapitalismus, Frankfurt am Main (2006).

Sosin, Jack M., Whitehall And The Wilderness, The Middle West In British Colonial Policy 1760-1775, Lincoln, NE (1961)

Stanford Encyclopedia of Philosophy, available at http://plato.stanford.edu.

Stone, Katherine V.W., *John R. Commons and the Origins of Legal Realism; Or, The Other Tragedy of Commons,* UCLA School of Law, Law and Economics Research Paper Series, Research Paper No. 08-19, 1-28 (2009).

Story, William W., Life And Letters Of Joseph Story, Boston, MA (1857).

Suagee, Dean B., *The Supreme Court's "Whack-a-Mole" Game Theory in Federal Indian Law, a Theory that has no Place in Environmental Law,* 7 Great Planes Natural Resources Journal, 90-168 (2002).

Swann, BRIAN & KRUPAT, ARNOLD, Recovering The Word: Essays On Native American Literature, Berkeley/Los Angeles/London (1987).

Tamanaha, BRIAN Z., Law As A Means To An End: Threat To The Rule Of Law, New York, NY (2006).

Tate, Joshua C., *Ownership and Possession in Early Common Law,* 48 American Journal of Legal History, 280-313 (2006).

Toro, Luisa Angel, *"A People Distinct From Others": Race and Identity in Federal Indian Law and the Hispanic Classification in OMB Directive No. 15,* 26 Texas Tech Law Review, 1219-1274 (1995).

Torres, Gerald, *Who Is an Indian? The Story of United States v. Sandoval, in* INDIAN LAW STORIES 109-148 (GOLDBERG, CAROLE & WASHBURN, KEVIN K. & FRICKEY, PHILIPP. eds., New York, NY (2011).

Tsosie, Rebecca, *Property, Power and American "Justice" : The Story of United States v. Dann, in* INDIAN LAW STORIES 325-359 (GOLDBERG, CAROLE & WASHBURN, KEVIN K. & FRICKEY, PHILIP P. eds., New York, NY (2011).

TWAIN, MARK, FOLLOWING THE EQUATOR, Stilwell, KS (2008).

Twibell, T. S., *Rethinking Johnson v. M'Intosh (1823): The Route of the Continued Forced Displacement of American Indians Despite Cobell v. Norton (2001),* 23 GEORGETOWN IMMIGRATION LAW JOURNAL, 129-200 (2008).

Umbeck, John, *Might Makes Rights: A Theory of the Formation and Initial Distribution of Property Rights,* 19 ECONOMIC INQUIRY, 39-59 (1981).

Valencia-Weber, Gloria, *Three Stories in One: The Story of Santa Clara Pueblo v. Martinez, in* INDIAN LAW STORIES 451-488 (GOLDBERG, CAROLE & WASHBURN, KEVIN K. & FRICKEY, PHILIP P. eds., New York, NY (2011).

VATTEL, EMER DE, DROIT DES GENS, London (1758).

WALDMAN, CARL, ATLAS OF THE NORTH AMERICAN INDIAN, New York, NY (3rd ed. 2009)

WALKER, FRANCIS A., THE INDIAN QUESTION, Boston, MA (1874).

WARDLE, LYNN D. & NOLAN, LAURENCE C., FUNDAMENTAL PRINCIPLES OF FAMILY LAW, Buffalo, NY (2nd ed. 2006).

Washburn, Kevin K., *How a $147 Tax Notice Helped Bring Tribes More Than $200 Billion in Indian Gaming Revenue, in* INDIAN LAW STORIES 149-188 (GOLDBERG, CAROLE & WASHBURN, KEVIN K. & FRICKEY, PHILIP P. eds., New York, NY (2011).

Watson, Blake A., *The Doctrine of Discovery and the Elusive Definition of Indian Title,* 15 LEWIS & CLARK LAW REVIEW, 995-1024 (2012).

Weisz, Sheree R., *Constitutional Law – Federal Indian Law: The Erosion of Tribal Sovereignty as the Protection of the Nonintercourse Act Continues to be Redefined More Narrowly,* 80 NORTH DAKOTA LAW REVIEW, 205-238 (2004).

Wetlaufer, Gerald B., *Systems of Belief in Modern American Law: A View from Century's End,* 49 AMERICAN UNIVERSITY LAW REVIEW, 1-52 (1999).

Williams, David, *Legitimation and Statutory Interpretation: Conquest, Consent, and Community in Federal Indian Law,* 80 VIRGINIA LAW REVIEW, 403-500 (1994)

WILLIAMS, ROBERT A. Jr., THE AMERICAN INDIAN IN WESTERN LEGAL THOUGHT, THE DISCOURSES OF CONQUEST, Oxford (1990).

WILSON, JAMES, COLLECTED WORKS, Indianapolis, IN (2007).

Young, Mary E., *Indian Removal and Land Allotment: The Civilized Tribes and Jacksonian Justice,* 64 AMERICAN HISTORICAL REVIEW, (1958).

Zulauf, Urs, *Gläubigerschutz und Vertrauensschutz – zur Sorgfaltspflicht der Bank im öffentlichen Recht der Schweiz,* ZSR 113 II, 357 (1994).

ZWEIGERT, KONRAD & KOETZ, HEIN, AN INTRODUCTION TO COMPARATIVE LAW, Oxford (TONY WEIR trans., 3rd ed. 1998). Tony Weir.

Zweigert, Konrad & Siehr, Kurt, *Jhering's Influence on the Development of Comparative Legal Method,* 19 AMERICAN JOURNAL OF COMPARATIVE LAW, 251-231 (1971).

The manufacturer's authorised representative in the EU is Springer Nature Customer Service Centre GmbH, Europaplatz 3, 69115 Heidelberg, Germany. If you have any concerns regarding our products, please contact ProductSafety@springernature.com

Printed and bound by CPI Group (UK) Ltd, Croydon, CR0 4YY
22/09/2026
02221054-0020